EAT STREET

EAT STREET

THE MANBQUE GUIDE TO MAKING STREET FOOD AT HOME

JOHN CARRUTHERS, JOHN SCHOLL, AND JESSE VALENCIANA

PHOTOGRAPHY BY CLAYTON HAUCK

RUNNING PRESS
PHILADELPHIA · LONDON

Books published by Running Press are available at special discounts for bulk purchases
in the United States by corporations, institutions, and other organizations. For more
information, please contact the Special Markets Department at the Perseus Books Group,
2300 Chestnut Street, Suite 200, Philadelphia, PA 19103, or call (800) 810-4145, ext.
5000, or e-mail special.markets@perseusbooks.com.

ISBN 978-0-7624-5869-1
Library of Congress Control Number: 2015959425

E-book ISBN 978-0-7624-5870-7

9   8   7   6   5   4   3   2   1
Digit on the right indicates the number of this printing

Designed by Joshua McDonnell
Edited by Zachary Leibman
Typography: Avenir & Brandon
Prop Stylist: Liz Klafeta

Running Press Book Publishers
2300 Chestnut Street
Philadelphia, PA 19103-4371

Visit us on the web!
www.offthemenublog.com

INTRODUCTION

Great food requires years of training, respect for established standards, and an exacting focus on local, organic, and artisan cooking philosophies. With every bite, every taste, and every aroma, we need to holistically consider our impact on tradition, the environment, and local foodways. Only by mindfully and deliberately internalizing all sides of the food system through years of preparation can we produce truly meaningful food.

...

At least, that's according to the assholes.

Consume too much food media today and you're likely to be wracked with a combination of insecurity and guilt before you can even pick up your knife. Why should I try and whip up a po' boy when this guy's been doing it flawlessly for two decades and I live two time zones away from the only acceptable local bread? How can I use this beef when I don't know the name of the rancher who raised it (It's Hank. It's always Hank.)? How can I ethically cook if I don't know which traditional Welsh lullabies my lamb chop was sung to sleep with?

It's fantastic that people are paying so much more attention to food and cooking these days—we did get a couple of books out of this whole phenomenon—but you come away with a lot of messages about The Best and The Worst: "Only The Best will do! Why would you get a hot dog anywhere else, you idiot?" "Commercially raised produce? That's literally the worst thing since Hitler!" Food's a world of almost limitless possibility, but all of our 2,000-word articles on "what

does it all MEAN" leave things weirdly codified and stringent. It's why the word "foodie" gets an eye roll from us.

For us, food isn't a referendum on your personal ethos. It's messy. It's loud. Most importantly, it's fun. That's why we love to make it and eat it ourselves. And at the heart of things, food connects you to the best memories of your life: grabbing tavern pizza with the family and shouting over each other; finding the perfect empanada at a packed street festival in the middle of summer; finally saying "fuck it" and trying a dish you can't pronounce at a market stall during study abroad. It's why one whiff of food across a crowded street can bring back a rush of memories you hadn't thought of in years.

The food you eat standing up isn't any better or worse than the food you pay the $200 prix fixe tag for, it's just different. While we're glad that you can buy a previously unthinkable amount of ethically-sourced ingredients, sometimes you've got fifteen people coming over, a family to feed, or you just want to get dinner on the table. So we've put together recipes that draw from the highs and lows of what this great food nation has to offer, from specially bred (and expensive!) wagyu beef to the corn dog, King of Midwestern Garbage Foods.

So go ahead, do your thing. Make a Philly steak with the regular torpedo roll from your local grocery. Press a Cubano with a brick. Make some takoyaki and dunk it in a spicy mayo like the flavor-seeking barbarian you're born to be. We've got a limited amount of meals on this earth, so let's try to enjoy all of them.

We've got a lot of delicious stuff in this book, so let's get started. Call some friends up. Buy a quantity of beer, then reconsider and go back for double that amount. We'd remind you to preheat the oven, but you'll probably forget anyway. That's fine—there's no rush.

Eat this. Drink up. Welcome to Eat Street.

THE GRIDDLE

The wide, hot expanse of the griddle is like the desert in one of those Cormac McCarthy murder novels we enjoy so much. Forged in heat, brutally unforgiving, it exists only to force change and bring something face-to-face with its essence.

Or maybe we're putting too much thought into it. While you're reading this, there's a sullen teenager somewhere manning an electric griddle at a Ralph's supermarket offering tiny bites of regrettable cheese-injected sausage and making nine dollars an hour. But, as a cook, isn't it much more fun to put yourself in the middle of something epic?

The ultimate point is, you can make some delicious stuff on a griddle, even if—no, ESPECIALLY if—it's a two dollar cast iron resident of the Island of Misfit Kitchen Toys at your local thrift store. If the Waffle Hut cook who hasn't slept in forty-six hours and who appears to be tweaking can manage to create delicious food on this blank slate of possibility, so can you.

When buying a griddle, look for:

- Something heavy: You want it to get hot and stay hot. Cast iron may not be the most even-heating material, but you can get a crispy sear on a diner-style burger so delicious it can single-handedly solve the student loan debt crisis.

- Something suited to your kitchen: Are you a kitchenette dweller? Maybe you don't have room for some four-burner beast of a slab. A smaller model could be in the cards. If you don't care much about high-heat searing, then (*gasp*) an electric skillet will give you the heat and quick set up you're after.

- Something you can maintain: There's nothing sadder than gesturing to a piece of kitchen equipment you spent good money on and saying, "I used that once. I wish I hadn't bought it." Nothing sadder. Maybe puppies with cancer. Cute ones. We're getting off track: The point is, ask yourself beforehand things like "do I want to maintain cast iron?", "do I have room for this?", and "will this cook exactly what I want exactly how I want it?" Don't buy something, find it inconvenient, and then send it off as a tax-deductible donation. Griddles feel your rejection. It's like *Toy Story*.

Now you're equipped and ready to cook. Let's do this. Try not to burn yourself.

(You will most likely burn yourself. Have fun anyway.)

THE JAMES DEAN

RECIPE BY MATT KUHNEN

Brunch gets all the glory among diners these days, owing greatly to the "vodka's okay at 10:00 a.m. if there's Vitamin C along for the ride" line of reasoning. We can remember a simpler time when brunch wasn't a part of our vocabulary and you had to have some real "breakfast for dinner" rebelliousness to get your fix outside of regular hours. Sometimes we can't wait for the weekend to enjoy twelve dollar eggs and a Bloody Mary. Enter the breakfast-topped burger—the O.G. way to say "breakfast any time."

MAKES 4 BURGERS

1 large onion, sliced

1 teaspoon olive oil

½ teaspoon kosher salt, divided

½ cup mayonnaise

⅛ cup pure maple syrup

1½ tablespoons brown sugar

2½ tablespoons Sriracha

1 pound ground sirloin

½ pound maple sausage

½ teaspoon black pepper

1 egg

¼ cup Italian seasoned bread crumbs

1 tablespoon bacon fat

4 slices bacon cheddar

4 large buttermilk biscuits

1. In a saucepan, sauté onion in olive oil and a pinch of salt. Cook onion on low heat stirring occasionally, for 35 minutes, or until soft and dark brown. Set aside.

2. Combine mayonnaise, maple syrup, brown sugar, and Sriracha. Whisk thoroughly. Set aside in refrigerator.

3. In a large mixing bowl, add the sirloin, maple sausage, remaining salt, pepper, egg, and breadcrumbs. Mix thoroughly.

4. Divide meat into 4 equal portions, roll into balls, and flatten to make patties.

5. Heat griddle over medium-high heat.

6. Add bacon fat to hot griddle. Add the patties and cook for 3 to 4 minutes per side.

7. Add 1 slice of bacon cheddar to each patty, a splash of water, and cover with metal bowl on the griddle for 60 to 90 seconds, or until cheese is fully melted.

8. Transfer patties to cutting board to rest for a few minutes while you slice the biscuits.

9. Place a spoonful of caramelized onions on the bottom half of the biscuit and place burger on top of onions. Spread a healthy spoonful of the Sriracha-maple mayo on the top biscuit and place on top of burger.

SUGGESTED BEER PAIRING: COFFEE STOUT

AREPAS

RECIPE BY EFRAIN CUEVAS

Visit any Columbian or Venezuelan street food stall and you'll soon sing the praises of the arepa. They are the capital-T Truth, and can be stuffed with any number of delicious things. Go looking for arepas in the right place and you can find literally anything from chicken and cheese to shark. We've included our favorite three ingredients to stuff into them, but you can probably chop up and throw in anything in this book—up to and including hot dogs.

MAKES 12 TO 16 AREPAS

4 cups warm water

1 tablespoon kosher salt

3 tablespoons unsalted butter, softened

1 pound corn flour (also known as harina pan or masarepa)

Vegetalbe oil, for grill

Yucatan Pork (page 185), Black beans (page 222), and/or Sweet Plantains (page 53), to fill

1. In a large mixing bowl, combine the water, salt, and butter. Slowly add the corn flour, mixing quickly to avoid lumps.

2. When a smooth dough forms, cover the bowl with a damp towel and allow to rest for at least 5 minutes.

3. Portion the dough into small balls slightly larger than a golf ball.

4. Flatten each ball into a 1-inch-thick disc, about 4 to 5 inches in diameter.

5. Heat a griddle over medium, grease with vegetable oil, and sear each of the discs for 2 minutes per side. You can do this ahead of time and finish the arepas when you're ready to serve.

6. Return the arepas to the griddle (or grill over a wood fire) for 5 to 8 minutes per side. Remove and let cool for a few minutes, then split with a sharp knife halfway so that the top and bottom stay together, similar to a pita.

7. Fill them with the pork, beans, plantains, or whatever you wish and serve hot.

BEER PAIRING: VIENNA LAGER

ALL-DAY MACMUFFINWICH

Our friends (and yours) rant about the greasy homogeneity of American fast food culture, but deep down, 95 percent of people secretly carry a torch for the simple joy of a drive-thru breakfast. Due to the twin menaces of alcohol and a 10:30 a.m. cutoff, most weekends of our youth went by with nary a sodium-rich meat biscuit. Here's our version, so you can kill the hangover that much closer to home.

MAKES 8 BREAKFAST SANDWICHES

1 tablespoon instant espresso

1 cup mayonnaise

½ teaspoon cayenne pepper

Vegetable oil, for griddle

8½-inch slices Tennessee Breakfast Sausage (see insert)

4 tablespoons butter

8 English muffins, split

8 slices cheddar, Gouda, or (for authenticity's sake) American cheese

1. Using a hand blender or whisking like a madman, blend the espresso powder into the mayo. When it begins to color and flavor the mayo (you'll both see and taste the effect), add the cayenne. Taste for seasoning and set aside.

2. Heat your griddle to medium and give it a thin sheen of vegetable oil. Cook your sausage 2 minutes per side, until well-browned on both sides and cooked through to 165°F. Set aside sausages.

3. Add the butter to the griddle and toast the muffin halves 30 to 45 seconds, until lightly colored.

4. Remove muffins and give each a swipe of the coffee mayo across the top.

5. Return the sausage to the pan in a tight grouping, topping each slice with a slice of cheese. Add a couple of tablespoons of water next to each slice and cover briefly with a bowl or pan. That few seconds of steam will make your cheese hug the sausage like a long-lost brother.

6. Remove the sausages to the prepared muffins, then use them to return your overnight guests to something approaching normal function. You'll be a hero to the people.

BEER PAIRING: HONESTLY, PROBABLY WHATEVER'S LEFT FROM LAST NIGHT. VERY GOOD CHANCE THAT'S A HIGH LIFE OR PBR.

TENNESSEE BREAKFAST SAUSAGE

RECIPE BY TOM BROOKS

If you're a displaced Southerner located far from the spicy breakfast sausage you love, we've created a version that is incredibly close to the delicious clothbound country sausage served throughout the Southeast.

The only real stipulation is that you need to use some high-quality bacon to replicate the cold smoking effect used on the original product. Don't go this far and cheap out on us with crappy bacon. As with any sausage or grinding project, make sure absolutely everything—the grinder, the bowl, the meat—is very cold to ensure good distribution of fat.

MAKES 2½ POUNDS

2 pounds fatty pork, cubed to 1 inch

135 grams kosher salt

4 grams Prague powder #1

8 grams black pepper

½ teaspoon crushed red pepper flake, shaken through a fine mesh strainer

½ cup cold water

½ pound hickory-smoked bacon, chopped and frozen

15 inches- of 2 inch-diameter synthetic casing

1. Coarsely grind the pork. You know, swear at it, drink whiskey at 10:00 a.m. around it, take it to the dog track.

2. Make a slurry with the salt, Prague powder, black pepper, red pepper flake, and cold water.

3. In a stand mixer, add slurry to ground meat and mix with paddle at low speed until sticky.

4. Add the frozen bacon, mix until incorporated.

5. Run the meat mixture through the grinder again.

6. Stuff the casing with the meat. Tie it off and hang in the refrigerator for 1 to 3 days, then slice and serve to hungover students and homesick Southerners.

BEER PAIRING: IPA

BACON BUTTY

It's not the super-rich bacon we grew up with, but the lean, hammy back bacon (also known as rasher bacon) that is a worthy centerpiece to England's favorite hangover cure. A little brown sauce, some butter, and you've got comfort food before you've even showered. That's living.

Rashers? Brown sauce? They really need to workshop some more appetizing ingredient names. This may be why British food gets a bad rap.

MAKES 4 EXCEEDINGLY BRITISH SANDWICHES

2 tablespoons vegetable oil, for griddle

12 slices rasher bacon

4 tablespoons unsalted butter

8 thick slices white bread

UK Brown Sauce (page 276), to serve

1. Oil the griddle and heat to medium-low.

2. Cook the bacon, turning frequently, for 10 minutes, until slightly crisp but not dried out. Remove and set aside under foil.

3. Add the butter to the griddle and toast the bread 45 seconds per side, until well-browned.

4. Divide the bacon between the sandwiches, top with brown sauce, and serve.

BEER PAIRING: ENGLISH BITTER

REDEYE COUNTRY BISCUIT

This is the breakfast the man on the paper towel commercials eats every morning. Let's get you ready to fell some old-growth timber.

MAKES 10 BREAKFAST SANDWICHES.
GROWS HAIR ON YOUR CHEST, EVEN.

2 center-cut slices country ham

1 cup olive oil

5 serrano peppers, chopped

12 ounces coffee stout

1 egg yolk

1 tablespoon water

1 tablespoon fresh lemon juice

2 teaspoons instant espresso powder

1 teaspoon kosher salt

2 tablespoons olive oil

10 warm buttermilk biscuits, split

Fried Shallots (page 274) or canned shoestring onions

1. Heat griddle over medium-low and cook the country ham slices, turning frequently until slightly browned and warmed through. Move it to a cooler part or set aside if it cooks through quickly so it won't toughen.

2. Grease your griddle with olive oil and sauté the serrano peppers 5 minutes, until softened. Pour over the coffee stout 2 ounces at a time, refreshing as the beer evaporates, until you've got soft, beer-rich hot peppers.

3. Make the coffee mayo by whisking the egg yolk, water, lemon juice, espresso powder, and salt. Whisk in the oil gradually until your mayo forms, then set aside.

4. Remove ham from the griddle, trim away the bone and any gristle, and slice into biscuit-sized pieces.

5. Spread the mayo on the tops of the biscuits. Add the ham and peppers, then top with fried onions.

BEER PAIRING: BARREL-AGED IMPERIAL COFFEE STOUT

MOROCCAN LAMB MINI BURGERS WITH HARISSA YOGURT AND FRESH MINT

RECIPE BY ADAM HOLTZAPFEL

This is a great way to introduce people to lamb with a kick from the harissa yogurt and fresh mint.

MAKES 8 SLIDERS

4 tablespoons Greek yogurt

1 tablespoon Harissa (page 286)

Juice of ½ lemon

¾ teaspoon kosher salt, divided

2 teaspoons olive oil

1 tablespoon Ras el Hanout (page 294)

1 pound ground lamb

8 mini buns, split

8 fresh mint leaves

1. Heat griddle to medium.

2. Mix the yogurt, harissa, lemon juice, ¼ teaspoon salt, and olive oil in a bowl.

3. In a shallow dish, combine the remaining salt with the Ras el hanout.

4. Divide the ground lamb into 8 equal 2-ounce portions and flatten to make patties. Dredge the patties in the spice mixture.

6. Cook the patties for approximately 3 minutes per side. Remove, place on buns, and top with the harissa yogurt and a fresh mint leaf.

SUGGESTED BEER PAIRING: WEE HEAVY/ SCOTCH ALE

CHIPOTLE PORK SLIDERS

RECIPE BY ADAM HOLTZAPFEL

MAKES 8 SLIDERS

1 pound ground pork

½ pound bacon, chopped

1 tablespoon chipotle powder

1 teaspoon ground cinnamon

1 teaspoon nutmeg

1 teaspoon cardamom

Yellow mustard

8 Hawaiian rolls, split

Chihuahua cheese, to top

Ancho Chile BBQ Sauce (page 286), to serve

1. Heat griddle to medium.

2. In a large bowl, mix the ground pork and bacon. Divide into 8 equal 2-ounce portions and form into sliders.

3. Mix the chipotle, cinnamon, nutmeg, and cardamom.

4. Add a thin layer of mustard on each side of the slider and dip both sides into the spice mixture.

5. Griddle your burgers for 2 minutes. Flip, top with cheese, and griddle another minute.

6. Serve on Hawaiian roll topped with Ancho Chile BBQ Sauce.

BEER PAIRING: BOCK

THE MANBQUE MELT

The patty melt is our late-night, 4:00 a.m., "I need to find a Greek diner soon or I'll die of a hangover" dish nine times out of ten. If you haven't yet enjoyed a patty melt after an evening of drinking, then congratulations, you've failed our unofficial citizenship test and are clearly a Soviet spy. Better luck in Minsk, Comrade.

For you freedom-loving drunks still reading, we added crunchy bacon and a honey-Sriracha mayo to complement the richness. Unchanged is the traditional rye bread, heaps of onions, and deluge of cheese. Uncle Sam wants you! (To make this sandwich.)

MAKES 4 SANDWICHES

⅓ cup mayonnaise

½ teaspoon lime juice

3 teaspoons Sriracha

3 teaspoons honey

1 pound ground beef

2 onions, cut in half through the root and sliced thin

6 tablespoons salted butter, at room temperature

8 slices marble rye bread

8 slices sharp cheddar

8 strips thick-cut bacon, cooked (page 175)

1. Whisk the mayonnaise, lime juice, Sriracha, and honey together in a bowl and refrigerate.

2. Preheat griddle over medium heat.

3. Gently pack the beef into four patties and season with salt and pepper.

4. Cook the patties 3 to 4 minutes per side and remove to a wire rack.

5. Lower the griddle heat to medium-low and add the sliced onions. Cook the onions in the rendered fat for about 6 minutes. Remove and set aside. Wipe the griddle clean.

6. Butter both sides of the rye bread and toast 1 side on the griddle. The toasted sides will be the interior of the sandwich.

7. Assemble the sandwich by spreading a generous layer of Sriracha mayo on the toasted side of the bread, followed by slice of cheese, ¼ of the onions, 2 slices of bacon, a beef patty, and another slice of cheese. Slap the second piece of bread over the whole thing. If it doesn't explode, you probably did it right.

8. Turn the heat down to low and then toast sandwiches for 3 to 4 minutes per side, until the cheese is melted but before the bread burns. If the cheese is being stubborn, add a tablespoon of water to the griddle and cover the sandwiches for 30 seconds.

BEER PAIRING: AMBER ALE

TAYLOR STREET PORK CHOP SANDWICH

You know what's a great idea? A pork chop sandwich with onions grilled so long on the flat top that they almost fall apart. It's a classic dish at Jim's Original in Chicago. You know what's a hilarious idea? Giving a drunk person (Jim's has quite the late night business) a pork sandwich on a bun with the bone still attached. Yet it happens, and it's beloved locally. No offense to Jim's Original and the rest of the places serving up bone-in chop sandwiches but we made our version sans-bone to make it slightly more user-friendly.

You'll notice there's some brining and waiting before you cook. That's to ensure a really juicy bite of pork no matter how heavily you sear. It's to get the best result. But if you'd rather just eat, then skip it once and test your pork mastery.

MAKES 6 SANDWICHES

½ cup salt

½ cup sugar

4 country-style pork chops, butterflied

2 tablespoons vegetable oil, plus more to rub and sear

2 white onions, chopped

2 tablespoons Dijon mustard

16 ounces brown ale

4 tablespoons kosher salt

1 tablespoon sweet smoked Hungarian paprika

2 teaspoons mustard powder

1 teaspoon dried oregano

½ teaspoon black pepper

½ teaspoon garlic powder

6 white buns

4 tablespoons room temperature butter

Diner Sauce (page 278), to serve

1. Boil a quart of water in a large pot and add the salt and sugar. Stir to dissolve and remove from heat. Stir in a quart of ice to chill. When the mixture has cooled, add the butterflied chops and let brine in the refrigerator for at least 1 hour. Remove, pat dry, and place on a rack in the refrigerator to air-dry for at least 45 minutes before cooking.

2. While the pork brines, heat the vegetable oil on the griddle over medium heat. Cook the onions for 5 minutes, tossing to coat evenly with oil. Add the Dijon and stir to coat onions.

3. Pour over a couple of tablespoons of the beer and let cook until evaporated. Repeat this whole process until you've got some super-caramelized onions or you get bored. Either way, you have to wait for that pork. Push them to a warm but non-central part of the grill. They'll be fine there, and they'll only get better as you go along.

4. Mix the salt, paprika, mustard powder, oregano, black pepper, and garlic powder. Rub the chops with oil and season with the spice mixture.

5. Cook the chops on the griddle for 5 minutes. Flip, cook 3 minutes, and test the temperature. If you've bought some respectable pork (the lack of a big red CLEARANCE sticker is a good clue) then you can remove from the griddle at 140°F for a nice medium-rare, which is a thing with pork. Otherwise, let it go to 160°F before removing and resting.

6. While the chops rest, spread the buns with butter and toast on the griddle for 45 seconds to 1 minute, until browned. Remove and spread with Diner Sauce or, failing that, some good mustard.

7. Place a chop on each bun and top with the grilled onions.

BEER PAIRING: BROWN ALE

HANGER STEAK AND KIMCHI BURRITO

While you can get a mediocre burrito nationwide (Karen from accounting swears by them), San Francisco is still the home of the tremendous burrito-as-street-art version. This is our super-rich take on those unforgettable foil-wrapped meat-and-starch bombs. If you've never had one, just know that it should be roughly the size of a Nativity-scene Baby Jesus and twice as delicious.

MAKES 4 BIG-ASS BURRITOS

2 hanger steaks (about 1½ pounds total)

2 teaspoons vegetable oil, plus 2 tablespoons

4 tablespoons kosher salt

1 tablespoon garlic powder

2 teaspoons black pepper

1 cup white rice

¼ cup fish sauce

1½ cups chicken stock

½ cup plucked cilantro leaves

1 cup kimchi, to top

4 flour burrito wraps

1. Pat the hanger steaks dry, brush with 2 tablespoons vegetable oil, and season with the salt, garlic powder, and black pepper. Set aside in the refrigerator.

2. Bring the rice, fish sauce, and stock to a boil in a large saucepan. Bring to a boil, cover, reduce heat to the lowest setting, and let cook 30 minutes.

3. Remove lid and check rice for doneness. Fluff with a fork and stir in cilantro. Cover and keep warm.

4. Heat griddle to medium-high and sear the hanger steaks for 2 minutes per side. Remove, let rest for 5 minutes, and slice thin, then chop into appropriately burrito-sized pieces.

5. Reduce griddle heat to medium and warm the burrito wraps for 30 to 40 seconds on one side.

6. Spread the rice over the toasted inside of each burrito, then top with a quarter of the sliced meat and a ¼ cup of the kimchi. Wrap tightly.

7. Heat the remaining vegetable oil on the griddle and cook each burrito, seam side down, for 90 seconds. Flip, press down gently, and cook another 60 seconds.

8. Serve immediately, or wrap it in something halfway to look super-cool and authentic. Complain a bunch about how your neighborhood is gentrifying.

BEER PAIRING: JAPANESE RICE LAGER

STEAMED HAMS

It's weird to think of it now, but once upon a time, dudes in hot wool suits were singing the praises of this new lunch counter treat, the Hamburger Sandwich. That's why it's important to eat street—the wild-ass market foods of today could be the classics of tomorrow.

As for the name "Steamed Hams," it's an upstate New York expression. Albany, not Utica. If there's one thing we love more than a juicy griddled burger served with plenty of melted cheese, it's a *Simpsons* reference that no one under or over a certain age gets. We steam a good ham.

MAKES 4 DOUBLE BURGERS

1 pound ground chuck

½ pound ground shortrib

½ pound ground brisket

2 tablespoons vegetable oil, for griddle

Kosher salt

Black pepper

8 slices American cheese

Mayo

Yellow Mustard

8 potato rolls, toasted

2 cups shredded iceberg lettuce

1 white onion, thinly sliced (on a mandoline, if you have it)

Dill pickle slices

8 dill pickle spears

Fries for serving (page 89)

1. If you're grinding the meat yourself, toss the ground meats together after the first go-round and re-grind them together to distribute the fat. If not, gently mix the meats.

2. Form the meat into 4-ounce balls.

3. Preheat griddle to high and oil it.

4. Add 2 beef balls to your smoking-hot griddle, season the top with salt and pepper, and let cook 45 seconds.

5. Flip your burgers and give them one (ONE!) good smack with your spatula. This gives them a delicious craggy surface area, while your initial sear keeps them together. If they fall apart, one of those two things is off.

6. Season the top side of the patties, cook 90 seconds, and flip.

7. Add a slice of cheese to each patty and cook another 30 seconds to melt.

8. Remove from the griddle and place on a rack above a foil-lined sheet pan to rest for 5 minutes while the juices redistribute.

9. To serve, spread mayo and mustard on the tops of each bun, and line the bottoms with lettuce. Add your 2 burger patties, see-through-thin sliced onions, and the pickle slices. Serve with a dill pickle spear and two handfuls of fries.

BEER PAIRING: PALE LAGER (OR DUFF)

THE CUBANO

The greater sandwich marketplace has been infiltrated in recent years by sorry-ass paninis, served by indifferent and untalented chefs, masquerading as the original south Florida classic. If it's served on an artisan brioche, it's not Cuban. If it's got arugula in it, it's not a Cuban. And if it's got pesto, then we seriously question your idea of geography.

Here's a Cuban as classic as it gets. If you can't get real Cuban bread (and admittedly, most of us can't), then sub in some soft but hearty Italian or French rolls. Don't make the mistake of using a baguette—you want a softer chew and a buttery crust.

You can make this with a sandwich press, or you can use a foil-wrapped brick. At forty cents, a brick is the thinking man's sandwich press.

MAKES 4 CUBANOS

1 loaf Cuban bread, cut into four equal pieces (or four Italian rolls, split)

8 tablespoons clarified butter, at room temperature

Yellow mustard (all of it)

½ pound Swiss cheese, sliced

½ pound shaved Cuban Mojo Pork (page 178)

½ pound sweet ham, sliced thin

16 dill pickle slices

1. Heat the griddle to medium. Slather (and we do mean *slather*) the outside of the bread with the butter.

2. Now it's mustard's turn for the slathering. Give the interior of the bread a little more of the yellow stuff than you think is responsible.

3. Assemble the sandwiches like this, from the bottom up:

- Half the Swiss
- Cuban Mojo Pork
- Sweet ham
- Dill pickle slices
- The other half of the Swiss

4. Place a sandwich on the griddle, press down firmly, and then press with the brick. Hold it in place for 60 to 90 seconds, flip, and repeat. The bread should be perfectly browned and mottled. Repeat with remaining sandwiches, adjusting time and temperature as necessary.

5. Cut diagonally and serve with Tostones (page 71).

BEER PAIRING: RUM BARREL-AGED BEER AND A RESPECTFUL NOD TO 90 MILES SOUTH OF THE COUNTRY.

ROOM SERVICE MEDIANOCHE

Do you ever get to a hotel after everything but the crappy room service kitchen is closed? Do you sometimes fall victim to the ham sandwich, lowliest of the half-assed hotel foods? They make the ham sound delicious and the cheese sound handcrafted, and deliver you the same sad meal that's been fucking over travelers since the beginning of the Interstate system. Almost as depressing as the nine dollar bottle of skunky Dutch beer that came with it.

No more. We've combined our love of sweet, eggy bread, salt-bomb cured meats, and honey mustard to create the sandwich that every guest at every lonely outpost craves to their very core.

MAKES 4 SANDWICHES

¼ cup honey

¼ cup mustard powder

8 slices challah bread

¼ pound shaved Manchego cheese

½ pound thin-sliced salami

½ pound sweet ham

¼ pound Swiss cheese

4 tablespoons clarified butter, at room temperature

1. Preheat griddle to medium-low.

2. Mix the honey and the mustard powder and spread on one side of each slice of bread.

3. Assemble the sandwiches with Manchego on the bottom, alternating layers of ham and salami, and Swiss on the top.

4. Slather the outside of the sandwiches with the clarified butter.

5. Press your sandwiches 45 to 60 seconds per side, until the bread begins to brown and the Swiss melts.

6. Remove medianoches and serve whole with chips and a Coke.

BEER PAIRING: KOLSCH

HANGOVER BAGELWICH

It could be the Midwest in us, but we've never been huge fans of the traditional cream cheese/lox/capers that accompany our bagels. We were asked to shoot a morning show segment on breakfast grilling a little while ago, and we settled upon this hearty bastard based on what was left in the refrigerator and what would sustain us through an hour of standing in the rain waiting for the coals to catch.

MAKES 4 SANDWICHES

4 everything bagels, split

Supper Club Beer Cheese (page 301), to top

1 pound thinly sliced pastrami

Pickled Mustard Seeds (page 293), to top

Cooking spray

1. Preheat griddle to medium.

2. Spread both halves of the bagels with cheese. Add ¼-pound sliced pastrami and a tablespoon of the mustard seeds.

3. Lay out four sheets of aluminum foil. Spray with cooking spray, then wrap bagels tightly.

4. Griddle your bagelwiches, pressing down with a brick-weighted sheet pan, for 3 minutes per side.

5. Remove, unwrap, and have that breakfast beer your mom says makes her worry about you.

BEER PAIRING: STOUT AND A SHOT
PRODUCTIVITY: NONE

BREAKFAST TACOS

Any of you who have ever met a Texan know their shtick. The Republic of Texas is the greatest thing and anything you don't like you probably don't understand. It's a "Texas thing," like scorpions and gerrymandering. But while we have fun with our prideful Texan friends, there's one thing they're irritatingly dead-on about: Breakfast tacos are the best.

MAKES 6 TACOS

6 ounces Mexican chorizo, removed from casing

2 tablespoons butter

6 large eggs

2 ounces goat cheese

6 warm corn or flour tortillas

2 tablespoons fresh chives chopped

Habanero hot sauce, to serve

Red onion, chopped, to serve (optional)

Chilula cheese, shreded, to serve (optional)

Cilantro, chopped, to serve (optional)

1. Heat griddle to medium and cook the chorizo until rendered. Remove, set aside, and wipe the griddle clean.

2. Reduce the heat to low and add the butter. Then crack the eggs directly onto the griddle—don't beat them, don't salt them, just let nature and your spatula do their thing.

3. Stir eggs with the spatula as they begin to solidify. Take your time—5, even 10 minutes. Morning show guy mocked us for how much time we took, but those were some damn good eggs. He'll pay for that.

4. When the eggs are beginning to form up but still a bit runny, toss in the cooked chorizo, then kill the heat and stir in the goat cheese.

5. Remove the eggs from the griddle a serving at a time, delivering them to the loving arms of the tortillas. Top with chives and habanero sauce, and onion, cheese, and cilantro if you desire. Serve immediately.

BEER PAIRING: HELLES LAGER

HATCH CHILI BURGERS

Once you cross a certain point in the Rockies, green Hatch chiles show up in EVERYTHING—chili, salads, burgers, or steeping in an infant's bottle of formula. One of our members brought back a suitcase-load of them, and this burger was the result. You can use dried or even canned Hatch chiles if you don't live near a source of fresh ones.

MAKES 8 BURGERS

22 ounces (1⅓ pounds) ground chuck

6 dried Hatch chiles

2 white onions, chopped

3 tablespoons unsalted butter

2 shallots, diced

2 cloves garlic, minced

¼ cup molasses

1 (15-ounce can) fire-roasted diced tomatoes

4 tablespoons cider vinegar

1 tablespoon bourbon

1 teaspoon kosher salt, plus more to season

½ teaspoon black pepper, plus more to season

4 potato rolls, split

1. Form the burger patties into equal 5½-ounce portions.

2. Place the chiles in a heatproof bowl and rehydrate with boiling water, covering for 20 minutes. Reserve the steeping liquid.

3. Caramelize the onions over medium-low heat while the chiles steep, adding water to draw out the sugars.

4. Heat the butter over medium heat. Add the shallots and cook 5 minutes, until soft and translucent. Add the garlic and cook another minute.

5. Add the molasses, tomatoes, vinegar, bourbon, salt, and pepper. Stir to combine.

6. Add 3 sections of the rehydrated chiles and 2 tablespoons of the steeping liquid to the sauce.

7. Bring to a boil, reduce heat to a simmer, and cook 10 minutes. Purée with a food processor or hand blender and strain the sauce through a fine mesh strainer.

8. Season the burgers with salt and pepper and griddle 2 minutes per side. Remove to a wire rack and let rest 4 minutes.

9. Chop the remaining Hatch chiles and toss with the caramelized onions.

10. Serve the burgers on the potato rolls with the chile sauce and the chopped onions and chiles.

BEER PAIRING: MARZEN

OBATZDA BURGER

RECIPE BY DANIEL SISTO

Obatzda is a mixture of Camembert (think Brie), butter, onion, and hot paprika. It's a smooth, funky beer garden cheese dip from Germany with a little heat that's traditionally served with pretzels, rye bread, or radishes.

MAKES 4 BURGERS

8 ounces mature Camembert, at room temperature

3 tablespoons butter, at room temperature, divided

2 tablespoons sweet onion, minced

4 tablespoons weissbier

¼ teaspoon salt, plus more to season

¼ teaspoon pepper, plus more to season

½ teaspoon hot paprika powder

¼ teaspoon caraway seed

2 tablespoons Dijon mustard

1½ pounds ground beef

2 onions, split through the root and sliced thin

4 pretzel buns, split

1. To make the Obatzda, combine the Camembert and 2 tablespoons butter in a blender or food processer and pulse until creamy. Add the minced onion, weissbier, salt, pepper, paprika, and caraway and pulse again until combined. Cover and refrigerate until ready to serve.

2. Sauté the sliced onions in 1 tablespoon of butter over medium heat for 5 to 10 minutes, until golden brown.

3. Remove the onions and increase the heat to medium-high.

4. Form four 6-ounce patties and season with salt and pepper. Cook 4 minutes per side, until medium rare, then remove and let rest for 5 minutes.

5. Spread the Dijon over the bottom half of the buns and top with the onions. Top with the burger patties and 2 tablespoons of the Obatzda.

BEER PAIRING: HEFEWEIZEN

SPAM MUSUBI

Hawaii, despite its status as the forty-ninth US state, is really far away from the rest of America. John C. lived there briefly, and the one thing that's immediately noticeable to new arrivals is the prevalence of Spam, which came over during the meat-strapped times of WWII and which holds a large place in the collective Hawaiian heart. Glance up at a McDonald's menu on the Big Island and your hot cakes and breakfast platters are nowhere to be found, replaced by spam platters, burritos, and sandwiches. MADNESS. But hey, they live in paradise and wear flip flops to work, so they clearly know a few things about life.

This dish, which shows the dovetailing American and Japanese influences so recognizable on the islands, is basically Spam sushi. People will think you're crazy creative (or regular crazy), and you won't necessarily have to tell them that every decent snack shop, golf course, grocery store, and gas station from Waimea to Pāhoa turns out dozens of fresh 'ono (delicious) musubi every day. Prepare to go through more canned luncheon meat than you ever thought possible.

MAKES 2 LARGE MUSUBI OR 8 NIGIRI-STYLE MUSUBI

½ cup water

½ cup rice vinegar

1 teaspoon sugar

1 teaspoon salt

4 cups cooked sushi rice

2 sheets nori, cut into 3-inch-wide strips

4 ½-inches-thick slices of Spam

¼ cup tamari

¼ cup mirin

1. Heat the water, rice vinegar, sugar, and salt in a saucepan, stirring until dissolved. Fold into the rice with a wooden paddle.

2. Lay a musubi mold (or even a Spam can with both ends carefully removed) over a sheet of the nori.

3. Heat griddle to medium and cook the Spam slices 2 minutes per side.

4. Mix the tamari and mirin, pour over the Spam, and cook 30 seconds more per side.

5. Pack ½ cup sushi rice into your musubi mold. Lay in a slice of the Spam, then pack in another ½ cup musubi before pressing down.

6. Carefully remove the mold and fold the nori over the sides of the rice block. Dampen a finger and slide down the nori to seal. Flip over the musubi, seam side down, and repeat.

7. Serve immediately or wrap tightly in plastic wrap. They're good on the go, and they're even good reheated in a gas station microwave. How many other foods can say that?

BEER PAIRING: COCONUT PORTER

THE PHILLY CHEESESTEAK

RECIPE BY JAMES GOTTWALD AND JENNIFER MONTI

This may be the one American classic that people enjoy arguing over more than they like cooking. We teamed up with the chef/owner of one of our favorite Philly places—Monti's Cheesesteaks—to try to change that. The key here is thinly sliced high-quality meat. You can achieve this through a number of strategies:

- Grab a whole 18 to 20 pound ribeye at the meat market and lovingly carry it out of there like you're Richard Gere and this piece of cow is Debra Winger at the end of *An Officer and a Gentleman*. Take it home, trim most of the fat cap, then blast-chill it to an internal temperature between 26 and 28°F. Run it through a slicer at a level thin enough to see through it.

- Find a butcher from that same market to do everything above in your chosen quantity (minus the Gere/Winger show).

- Visit an Asian supermarket and grab the pre-packed super-thin beef slices used for Korean BBQ.

- Some places sell the trimmings from beef tenderloin, usually with the word "filet" on the label. You can lay them between two pieces of plastic wrap or parchment, pound the Satan out of them, and use those.

Do not, under any circumstances, use the frozen stacks of steak sandwich meat with the cute names, bright box, and listed microwave time. The low-quality crap meat within is so fatty and rank that it's really only good for rendering down to make a Yankee Candle that smells realistically of a New Jersey boardwalk.

Finally, the roll: While the whole culture of Philly steaks depends on having a roll from one specific hundred-year-old bakery or another, we realize you probably don't have access to that. So find a sub roll you like and use that. Go for something with a light crust but enough heft to stand up to the juices. If this requires eating cheesesteak after cheesesteak in a bacchanalian orgy of consumption...well, no one ever said food science was easy.

MAKES 8 CHEESESTEAKS

2 pounds white onions (about 2 large onions), peeled, halved, and sliced into thin half-moons

8 tablespoons table salt

1 tablespoon garlic powder

1 tablespoon onion powder

4 pounds thin-sliced ribeye steak

2 pounds sliced provolone or white American cheese

8 8-inch sub rolls, sliced

RECIPE CONTINUES

1. Heat griddle to medium-high heat. The surface should read between 375 to 400°F. Scrape and oil your griddle.

2. Griddle your onions 2 to 3 minutes, turning them with your spatula, until they begin to sizzle. Squirt some water on them, turn, scrape, and repeat the process when the water evaporates. Eventually, you'll have delicious, deeply browned onions. You can do a whole bag of these ahead of time to speed up future cheesesteak sessions.

3. While you're in onion-land, mix the salt, garlic powder, and onion powder and put it into a shaker. This is your secret seasoning. Like all secret seasonings, you can tell someone you're taking the recipe to the grave while you're actually just embarrassed it's so simple.

4. Lay your ribeye slices out across the griddle and just let them sit to sear 2 to 3 minutes. Season generously with your salt/garlic/onion trifecta.

5. Flip ribeye, season again, and begin to mix in the onions as the rest of the meat browns.

6. Now it's time to get all choppy-choppy with your spatula. The difficulty/effectiveness of this will largely depend on the quality of your meat and how thin you were able to get the meat sliced. This is why it's nice to have a butcher with a nice sharp slicer to harass.

7. Spatula your meat into 8 ounce portions that resemble how they're going to lay in the roll. Now, if you're going to yell something Cheez Whiz-related at us, skip this step and check out the sidebar. Drape each with a full 4 ounces of provolone. Squirt a tablespoon or so of water under the meat and cover for 30 seconds, until the cheese has become one with the meat in accordance with *The Prophecy* (starring Christopher Walken).

8. Game time! Take the spatula in your dominant hand and the open roll in your weaker, punier hand. Slide your spatula under the cheesy onion meat and flip it into the sandwich.

BEER PAIRING: AMERICAN BARLEYWINE, OR, FOR THE PURISTS, YOUR FAVORITE REGIONAL AMERICAN ADJUNCT LAGER

BUT WHAT ABOUT MY WIZ?!?

A select and vocal subset of cheesesteak fandom prefers the cheese on their steaks to come foamy and from an Aqua Net can. In the interest of meeting those taste and texture points, we've created the following completely delicious cheddar sauce. It's preferable to cheese whiz, in the same way that a hug from a friend is preferable to getting stabbed in the neck by a rail-yard hobo.

MAKES ABOUT 2 CUPS OF CHEESE SAUCE

8 ounces heavy cream

8 ounces cheddar

1 teaspoon hot sauce

¼ teaspoon black pepper

Heat the heavy cream over low heat. Add the cheddar gradually, whisking, and bring to a gentle simmer. Let reduce, whisking frequently, until it's uniformly thick, cheddary, and all-around kickass. Add the hot sauce and black pepper, whisk vigorously, and ladle over your steaks.

BUT WHAT ABOUT MY WIZ?!?

Oh fine, you big fucking baby. Please remit your request in email form, including mailing address and the reasoning behind your request, to Editor@ManBQue.com. We'll select ten "lucky" readers for a complimentary can of aerosol cheese-stuff, along with a handwritten note detailing our withering contempt.

ENDLESS QUESADILLAS

RECIPE BY DAVE KOOB

Once you've mastered this (easy) recipe, you'll be empowered to make perfect quesadillas for the rest of your life. Teach it to a second person, who teaches it to someone else, and you've begun the process of creating endless quesadillas for the universe. And here you'd thought you've never done anything with your life. Also, it explains our weird *NeverEnding Story* of a title.

The best way to get the cheeses for this recipe is in block form from your deli so that you can grate it. Don't let them slice it. You're the one holding the tiny paper number, so you make the rules.

MAKES 4 QUESADILLAS

1 pound skirt steak

1 tablespoon peanut oil

1½ tablespoons kosher salt

1 teaspoon black pepper

1 pound hot pepper deli cheddar, grated

½ pound garlic cheddar, grated

Bacon grease or vegetable oil, for griddling

4 10-inch flour tortillas (tortillas with the fewest amount of ingredients or local is your best bet here)

1. Brush the steak with the peanut oil and season with the salt and pepper.

2. Griddle the steak over high heat for 90 seconds per side. Alternately, if you're outside, grilling the steak directly on the coals will yield awesome results.

3. Remove the skirt steak, wrap tightly in foil, and let rest for 5 minutes before slicing across the grain into ½-inch strips.

4. Mix your cheeses and bring your griddle back to medium heat.

5. Wipe down the griddle with your bacon grease or oil and a paper towel.

6. Place one tortilla on the griddle and add 6 ounces of the mixed cheeses over the tortilla, leaving a ¼-inch gap around the perimeter.

7. Add a quarter of the sliced skirt steak and let cook open-faced for 3 minutes.

8. Fold the tortilla in half with a spatula and cook each side for an additional minute, until tortilla becomes golden brown.

9. Remove from griddle, slice into quarters, and serve with your favorite condiment.

BEER PAIRING: INDIA PALE ALE

MEXICAN TRUFFLE QUESADILLAS

Mexican truffles. Corn smut. Huitlacoche. Cuitlacoche. Corn mushrooms. Whatever you want to call the fungus that grows on ears of corn, there's one thing that's certain. It's delicious. For many of us, it's a strange food, but in Mexico it's a delicacy. Since it can be difficult to get fresh, we buy our huitlacoche in jars from Mexico We also recommend buying frozen because canned, it's not very good.

MAKES 6 QUESADILLAS

1 tablespoon olive oil

½ Vidalia onion, chopped

1 clove garlic, minced

1 serrano pepper, seeded and chopped

1 12-ounce jar huitlacoche

½ teaspoon salt

½ teaspoon chili powder

½ cup chopped cilantro

2 to 3 cups Chihuahua cheese, shredded

12 tortillas (if you can find blue corn tortillas, get them)

Salsa, to serve

2 avocados, sliced, to serve

Sour cream, to serve

1. Heat the olive oil over medium heat and sauté onions until translucent. Add the garlic, serrano, huitlacoche, salt, and chili powder, and cook for 4 minutes.

2. Preheat griddle to medium high heat.

3. Scoop ¼ cup huitlacoche mixture onto 1 tortilla, then top with cheese, cilantro, and another tortilla.

4. Cook for 3 to 4 minutes per side until tortilla is brown and cheese is melted. Serve with salsa, avocado slices, and sour cream.

BEER PAIRING: BELGIAN TRIPEL

PANS

Pots and pans are the backbone of any kitchen. You probably bought some shitty ones in your twenties when you were stoned and watching late night TV. You may have been given a set of them at your wedding at a cost approaching your mortgage payment.

Since food channels exist now, there are hundreds of companies trying to sell you pots and pans at varying levels of quality. This almost always leads to questions, and here are the most important ones we get.

What are "clad" pans?

Clad pans feature a super-conductive metal sandwiched between two layers of an easy-to-clean metal. Copper is awesomely conductive for instance, but cleaning it is like polishing a hilariously large piece of tarnished jewelry. Clad pans offer the best of both worlds.

Why do recipes tell me not to cook tomatoes in aluminum?

The acid in tomatoes will cause the reactive aluminum to impart a metallic taste. The same goes for any acidic food.

Is stainless steel good?

It's fine—looks spiffy, doesn't tarnish, and doesn't react to acidic foods (perfect for your tomato gravy!). The drawback is that it isn't particularly great at conducting heat.

I don't really need a twelve piece set, do I?

Noooope. We cook most everything in one 12 inch clad skillet or a 5-quart Dutch oven.

What is this tall, skinny pot for?

Asparagus. You'll use it once, then never think of it again until you run across it in a cabinet years down the line and ask the same question.

BUFFALO CAULIFLOWER DIP

While we're mostly glad that home cooks have collectively moved past the post-WWII years (salmon and asparagus Jello, anyone?), there's something to be said for distilling the flavors of an entire dish into an easy sharable dish. We ran across this one at some hipster Charleston (or maybe Nashville?) food fest, because we noticed the long line. They called it some-such-revamped-street-food-deconstruction or other, and it was legitimately delicious. Halfway down the block, we realized this "our take on ..." technique was actually something straight from Mom's sauce-stained binder labeled "Entertaining." It was a fancified version of the classic "We have to have the Hendersons over, they had us over last month" suburban dinner party food. You pay attention long enough, and you'll notice that cooking is really just a snake eating its own tail. Buy enough old cookbooks at Goodwill and eventually you'll see into the future.

MAKES 2 CUPS

¾ cup cayenne hot sauce (Frank's would be traditional)

1 head cauliflower, grated

8 ounces cream cheese

¾ cup sour cream

¼ teaspoon dried parsley

¼ teaspoon garlic powder

¼ teaspoon dried dill

¼ teaspoon onion powder

Pita chips, to serve

Carrots, to serve

Celery, to serve

1. Heat the hot sauce in a pan over medium heat and add the cauliflower. Stir until heated through.

2. Add the cream cheese and heat until combined.

3. Add the sour cream and spices, bring to a simmer, and remove from heat. Serve immediately or store covered in a glass jar. Serve with carrots and celery if you want to be cutesy about it, but people probably want chips because chips are objectively better than vegetables.

BEER PAIRING: MAIBOCK

CAST IRON APPLE CRUMBLE

This stupid dish . . .

Allow us to explain.

So we got called to cater a rum-company-sponsored party at one of those new bar/arcades (we refuse to use the word "barcade") that everyone of a certain generation loves. For some reason, free tattoos were involved in the place's promotion. We thought this was the perfect dessert for the spread we put out. And it was! Perfectly caramelized, crisp oat clusters, and a rich, sweet, buttery backbone.

But it needed something to finish it. Something smooth and cool and that used the free rum we had. And our vanilla-rum whipped cream was excellent. Until we forgot to chill the CO_2 whipped cream canister and it shot half-formed dessert foam onto the black jeans of this dipshit in a vest who was probably too old to be dressing like a 1990's mall punk. He pretended to be mad and proceeded to demand free tattoos or free beer from us. I think we bought him a PBR to shut him up.

And that, kids, is how the perfect dessert can still blow up in your face. We hope you have better luck with it than we did. It's delicious if you beware of vested men seeking free stuff.

MAKES ONE 9 X 9-INCH PAN

1½ pounds golden delicious apples, sliced

½ cup (5 ounces) cane sugar

2 tablespoons (½ ounce) tapioca starch

2½ tablespoons (¾ ounce) cornstarch

2½ teaspoons (½ ounce) salt

½ teaspoon nutmeg, plus ¾ teaspoon

½ teaspoon cinnamon, plus ¾ teaspoon

1 tablespoon lemon juice

2 tablespoons butter, melted

¾ cup light brown sugar

½ cup all-purpose flour

½ cup rolled oats

⅓ cup butter, softened

1. Preheat oven to 375°F.

2. Toss the apples with the sugar, tapioca starch, cornstarch, salt, ½ teaspoon nutmeg, ½ teaspoon cinnamon, lemon juice, and melted butter in a large mixing bowl. Set aside.

3. Mix the brown sugar, flour, rolled oats, and softened butter until evenly coated.

4. Spread the apple mixture evenly into a greased 9 x 9-inch baking pan, and top with the oat mixture and remaining nutmeg and cinnamon.

5. Bake for 30 minutes, until golden brown on top. Serve far, far away from freeloading people who are too old to be wearing skinny black jeans. Stay away from whipped toppings.

BEER PAIRING: BOCK

EUROZONE WAFFLES

You'll need a waffle pan or iron for this, so get married. That's where everyone we know picked up their waffle-related accoutrements.

When you've made this, you can top it with anything from maple syrup to Nashville Hot Chicken (page 86). Magical.

MAKES 8 TO 10 WAFFLES

About 1½ cups (6½ ounces) unbleached all-purpose flour

About ½ cup (2 ounces) cornstarch

1 teaspoon baking powder

½ teaspoon baking soda

½ teaspoon salt

2 cups buttermilk

⅔ cup coconut oil

2 eggs, beaten

3 teaspoon sugar

¾ teaspoon vanilla

Whipped butter, to serve

Grade B maple syrup, to serve

1. Mix the flour, cornstarch, baking powder, baking soda, and salt in a large bowl. Add the buttermilk, coconut oil, eggs, sugar, and vanilla. Beat well, cover, and let sit in a warm area for 20 minutes.

2. Do whatever the untouched instruction manual that came with your waffle iron tells you. Cook them waffles and pile them like a whiskey-mad lumberjack is coming to breakfast.

3. Serve with butter and syrup. If you're bold, try Fried Chicken (page 85) or Nashville Hot Chicken (page 86) and some pickles.

BEER PAIRING: HEFEWEIZEN

THE ULTIMATE MEATBALL SUB

RECIPE BY LUKE GELMAN

Forget thin, oily meats that taste only of the refrigerator. The true apex of the submarine sandwich art form is the glorious meatball sub. It's not so much that this is the true ultimate meatball sub (though it totally is), but that the meatball sub itself is the ultimate sandwich. We salute you, meatball sub, even though you're a sandwich and thus don't respond to external stimuli.

If you want a more old-school version, just make the meatballs and slice some fresh mozzarella and top with our incredibly easy Red Gravy (page 299).

MAKES 4 SUBS

1½ pounds ground bison

1 large egg, beaten

¾ cup Italian bread crumbs

1 medium white onion, minced (about ¾ cup)

6 cloves garlic, crushed and minced

1 teaspoon chipotle powder

1½ tablespoon Worcestershire sauce

⅓ cup flat-leaf parsley, plus ¾ cup, chopped

¼ cup grated Parmesan or Romano

1 teaspoon kosher salt

2 teaspoon fresh cracked black pepper, divided

6 tablespoons butter (plus 2 tablespoons)

1 large shallot, sliced into thin strips

8 cloves of garlic

1 pint of cherry tomatoes

10 shiitake mushrooms, sliced into thin strips

1 tablespoon bullion base

375ml Madiera wine

1 teaspoon salt

1 teaspoon fresh thyme

1 teaspoon fresh rosemary

3 tablespoons Gorgonzola

4 sub rolls, cut halfway through

1. Place the ground bison in a large mixing bowl and press a well in the middle. Pour the beaten egg into the center, then add the bread crumbs, onion, garlic, chipotle, Worcestershire, ⅓ cup parsley, cheese, salt, and pepper.

2. Mix gently with your hands until all ingredients are evenly distributed. Gently roll the meatballs into 16 golf ball-sized meat balls. If you handle them a lot and compress the meat, they'll have a less tender and more sausage-ish bite to them. Your preference. Refrigerate them for 30 minutes while you work on the sauce.

3. Place the butter in a large skillet over medium heat. Add the shallots, cook, stirring, for 2 minutes. Then add the garlic and sauté for another minute. Add the tomatoes, mushrooms, bouillon base, and remaining ¾ cup of parsley. Bring the mixture to a boil, reduce the heat to a simmer, and cook for 15 minutes.

4. Heat a large cast-iron skillet to medium heat. Add the remaining butter and 8 meatballs. Sear them in batches, turning every 60 to 90 seconds, until all the sides have a nice brown crust. When all the meatballs are done, keep them in a warm oven under foil until your sauce is finished.

5. After the sauce has reduced and the tomatoes have begun to break down, pour in the Madiera, return the mixture to a simmer, and let cook for 5 minutes.

6. Add the salt, pepper, thyme, and rosemary and cook another 5 minutes. Add the Gorgonzola and turn the heat down to the lowest setting, stirring constantly until the Gorgonzola melts into the sauce.

7. Open your hinged sub rolls and place 4 meatballs in each. Top with the sauce and enjoy.

BEER PAIRING: PILSNER

SWEET PLANTAINS

RECIPE BY EFRAIN CUEVAS

Most people's first introduction to plantains is as a bodega-purchased chip or a crispy fried side dish. This more often than not leads to the "it looks like a banana but it's not sweet!" comment. Life is hard. Confuse those poor souls even further by serving these delicious, rich sweet plantains. They're good and (not) good for you.

Ripe plantains look like ripe bananas, so if you've been suspecting your grocery of selling Hulk-sized bananas, you're probably in luck. Grab a handful and get to frying.

MAKES 8 SERVINGS

¼ cup unsalted butter

3 ripe plantains, peeled and cut into ½-inch diagonal slices

Kosher salt

1. Melt the butter in a heavy skillet over medium-low heat.

2. Add the plantain slices and shallow-fry for 3 to 4 minutes per side, until well caramelized.

3. Remove to a plate lined with paper towels or brown paper and salt immediately.

BEER PAIRING: INDIA PALE ALE

TATANKOS

RECIPE BY ADAM PALMER

This is the perfect Southwestern use of our Native American Fry Bread (page 99), apart from just opening a jar of honey and eating 5,000 calories worth of them.

MAKES 8 TACOS

2 tablespoons peanut oil

2 pounds ground bison

4 teaspoons chili powder

¼ cup chopped green chilis

1 teaspoon cayenne pepper

½ tablespoon minced garlic

1 teaspoon paprika

1 full can beer (bock or ale)

1½ cups salsa

½ tablespoon sea salt

8 pieces Native American Fry Bread (page 99), to serve

New Mexico Red Chili Sauce (page 298), to serve

New Mexico Green Chile Sauce (page 297), to serve

1. Heat a skillet or cast-iron pan over medium heat and add the oil. Brown the meat, breaking up.

2. Transfer the meat to a large pot and add the chili powder, chiles, cayenne, garlic, paprika, beer, salsa, and sea salt. Bring to a boil, reduce the heat to a simmer, and cook for 40 minutes, stirring occasionally.

3. Serve the meat on the frybread and garnish with the red and green chile sauces.

BEER PAIRING: NUT BROWN ALE

TAKOYAKI

These fried batter spheres from Japan are addictive. Plus, they're a great way to get your daily, recommended intake of octopus and beer.

MAKES 25 PIECES

1 tablespoon chili oil

¼ pound cooked octopus, chopped

¼ cup bonito flakes, plus more to garnish

1 cup all-purpose flour

2 teaspoons baking powder

½ teaspoon salt

2 large eggs

1 teaspoon soy sauce

1⅔ cups dashi

½ cup finely chopped green onion

⅓ cup puffed rice cereal

¼ cup mozzarella

Japanese mayonnaise, to serve

Takoyaki sauce, to serve

Aonori

1. Pour the chili oil over the chopped octopus and mix. Let it sit in the fridge for about 15 minutes.

2. Grind your bonito flakes into a fine powder. Although the bags of bonito flakes may look big and packed, when they're ground they render a surprisingly small amount. Annoying secret!

3. In a large bowl, add all of your dry ingredients and mix together.

4. In a medium bowl, use a whisk to mix your eggs and soy sauce together.

5. Add egg mixture to the dry ingredients, and then slowly add dashi stock while whisking the ingredients together. Pour your ingredients into a large measuring cup or something with a handle and a lip.

6. Heat your takoyaki pan (or an ebelskiver pan, like we did) over medium heat and coat evenly with a high melting point oil. When the oil begins to smoke, pour in enough batter to fill to the line of the pan.

8. Drop the octopus into the batter and sprinkle green onion, puffed rice, and mozzarella into each.

9. Cook for about 1½ minutes. Using the sharp end of a skewer, try to turn the ball 90 degrees. If they're not turning easily, let it cook a bit longer and then try giving it another 90 degree turn. As the balls are being cooked, they will become easier to turn. You want them to have an even shape and a light brown color.

10. Cook for about 10 minutes total, then serve with bonito flakes, takoyaki sauce, Aonori, and a generous squeeze of Japanese mayo.

BEER PAIRING: JAPANESE PILSNER

OFFSEASON ELOTES

RECIPE BY LUKE GELMAN

We love elotes—so much so that our first book featured them (a vegetable!) on the cover. But even in the Midwest, corn isn't available year-round, and we'll be damned if we're trekking outside in February to grill crappy packaged corn in a sad imitation of our summer ritual. So we've created an off-season version that features all the traditional flavors.

MAKES 12 SIDE-DISH SERVINGS

2 tablespoons corn oil

1 pound frozen corn

2 tablespoons butter

2 teaspoons salt

One small jalapeño, minced
  (about 1 tablespoon)

3 tablespoons lime juice

2 tablespoons Mexican crema
  (or, failing that, sour cream)

2 tablespoons Tajín seasoning

3 ounces queso fresco

½ bunch cilantro, chopped

1. Heat a large cast-iron skillet over medium heat. Add the corn oil and spread it around as the pan heats up.

2. Add the corn to the pan. (Did you defrost it first? If not, no big deal. Stir 2 to 3 minutes until it's defrosted.) Add the butter, salt, and minced jalapeño.

3. Cook 2 minutes, then add the crema. Don't try to brown the corn, fry the corn, or do anything but gently heat it and bring the flavors together.

4. Gently fold in the crema or sour cream, remove from heat, and stir in the lime juice.

5. Sprinkle half the Tajín over the top, add the queso, then sprinkle the rest of the Tajín. Garnish with the cilantro and you're good to serve.

BEER PAIRING: MEXICAN LAGER

FURNITURE STORE MEATBALLS AND SWEDEN SAUCE

If you're going to buy a couch that wobbles, you might as well fill up on delicious meatballs while you're at it. But what if you could just do it at home? You don't need furniture. Just sit on the floor or eat over the sink. It's minimalist.

MAKES 24 MEATBALLS

2 cups potatoes, boiled, peeled, and grated

½ pound ground beef

½ pound ground pork

1 egg, beaten

¾ cup whole milk

2 tablespoons onion, grated

1 tablespoon kosher salt, plus more to taste

1½ teaspoon black pepper, plus more to taste

Olive oil, to sauté

⅓ cup heavy cream

⅔ cup chicken stock

2 teaspoons soy sauce

1 tablespoon flour

Lingonberry jam, to serve

1. Mix the potato, beef, pork, egg, milk, onion, salt, and 1 teaspoon pepper.

2. Form into 24 equal balls, line up on a baking sheet, and chill in the refrigerator for 45 minutes.

3. Heat the oil in a large, wide pan over medium low and add the meatballs.

4. Cook, turning frequently, for 12 minutes, until cooked to 165°F.

5. Mix the cream, stock, soy sauce, and remaining pepper in a medium saucepan over medium heat. Bring to a boil, reduce the heat to a simmer, and whisk in the flour. Taste for seasoning, remove from heat, and serve with meatballs and jam.

BEER PAIRING: OATMEAL STOUT

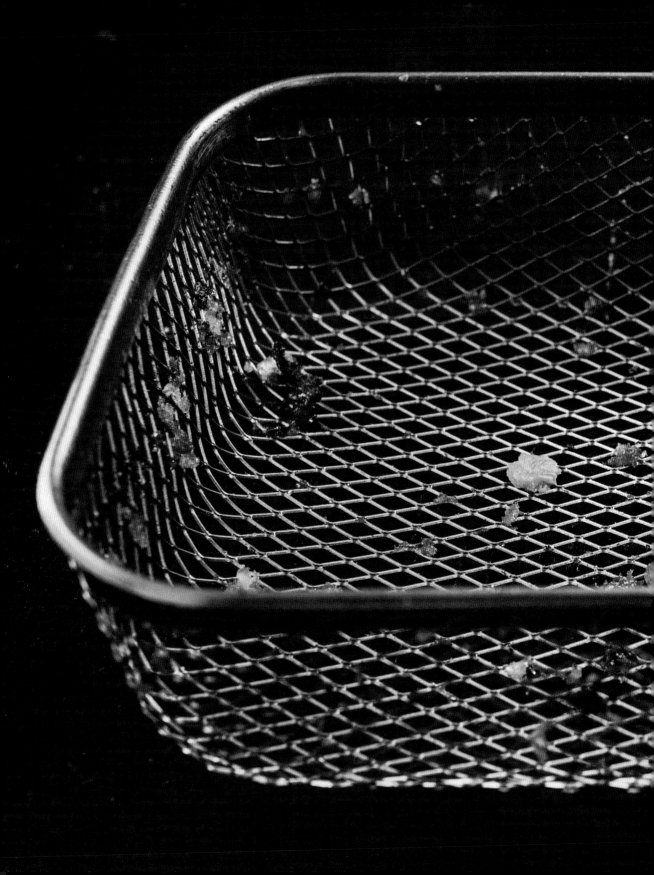

FRYER

FRYER

The deep fryer has long been a symbol of American (say it with a French accent for maximum snooty disdain) excess and our unhealthy modern lifestyles. This would be fair if a) the Colonists and not early humans had invented immersive cooking in animal fat, and b) we ignore the fact that most of us sit sedentary for 8-plus hours a day like sentient office plants. Don't blame America for deep frying, and don't blame the deep fryer for anything. It just wants to make you happy. Imagine doing your job, serving millions of happy customers, only to come home, relax, flip on Netflix, and see 398 recommended documentaries about how you're the devil.

Despite some truly horrifying re-enactments on the old William Shatner show *Rescue 911*, deep frying isn't dangerous at home unless you're careless (leaving the cord hanging) or kind of an idiot (filling it to the brim, throwing in some ice to test the temperature).

If you don't have, or would not like to have a deep fryer, then this is all completely doable with a heavy pot, a reliable oil thermometer or two, and the understanding that you'll have to adjust the burner yourself to keep the temperature on point.

When you're done making delicious food, kill the heat and let everything chill until the oil is cool enough to handle without risk of melting plastic or skin. If you plan to use it again, filter it through fine mesh into a container, seal it, and store it in a cool, dark place.

Thanks to much smarter people than us (namely the Culinary Institute of America, the team at Modernist Cuisine, and SeriousEats.com) already having done the work, we can provide you this reliable chart of how long various oils take to heat. Once oil starts smoking, it begins to turn acrid and produce harmful byproducts. So avoid that.

OIL	SMOKES AT:
Olive	465°F
Virgin Olive	325-375°F
Vegetable	400-450°F
Canola	400°F
Peanut	450°F
Grape seed	390°F
Coconut	350°F
Sesame	350-410°F
Good Ol' Reliable Lard	370°F
Schmaltz	375°F
Duck Fat	375°F
Shortening	360°F
Butter	350°F
Clarified Butter	450°F

ARANCINI

RECIPE BY ED KOWALSKI

In the Italian language, *arancina* means "little orange." These tasty fried treats, which resemble said small citrus fruits, are a great way to use up leftover rice and are traditionally stuffed with a variety of fillings, from cheese to meat or tomato sauce to peas.

Although this version is stuffed with cheese, we recommend heating up some marinara sauce as a dip for an extra level of flavor.

MAKES 16 RICE BALLS

3 cups low-sodium chicken broth

Kosher salt

1 cup Arborio rice

2 tablespoons pine nuts, toasted

2 ounces shredded mozzarella cheese

2 ounces shredded fontina cheese

2 tablespoons fresh Italian parsley, chopped

2 large eggs

½ cup grated Parmesan cheese

1½ cups breadcrumbs, divided

Vegetable oil, for frying

Red Gravy (page 299), to serve

BEER PAIRING: BARLEYWINE

1. In a medium saucepan over medium-high heat, bring the broth and ¼ teaspoon salt to a boil. Stir in the rice, reduce heat to low, and simmer until tender, approximately 20 minutes.

2. Spread the rice on a parchment-lined baking sheet and cool completely.

3. Combine the pine nuts, mozzarella, fontina, and parsley in a bowl and set aside.

4. In a large bowl, beat the eggs, and then stir in the cooled rice, Parmesan, and ⅔ cup breadcrumbs. Shape the mixture into sixteen 1½-inch balls.

5. Put the remaining breadcrumbs in a shallow bowl. Press your finger into the center of each rice ball, insert 2 teaspoons of the mozzarella mixture, then pinch the filling to enclose. Roll the balls in the breadcrumbs and place on a parchment-lined baking sheet. Cover loosely and refrigerate at least 1 hour. If you're planning on refrigerating overnight, roll the rice balls once more in breadcrumbs just before frying.

6. Heat ½-inch of vegetable oil in a large saucepan over medium heat until a deep-frying thermometer or candy thermometer reads 350°F. Working in batches, fry the rice balls, turning, until golden brown on all sides, about 4 minutes.

7. Remove and let drain on a towel-lined plate.

8. Season with salt and serve with heated Red Gravy or marinara sauce.

OYSTER PO' BOY

RECIPE BY ED KOWALSKI

In 1929, New Orleans restaurateurs (and former streetcar conductors) Benny and Clovis Martin opted to offer free sandwiches to former colleagues engaged in a four-month-long strike against the streetcar company. The restaurant workers started referring to the strikers as "the poor boys," and the sandwiches were soon being called the same.

A staple of New Orleans cuisine, the most common po' boys consist of fried seafood (most often shrimp, clams, or oysters, but we've seen calamari and octopus used as well) on crusty French bread, dressed with lemon juice, melted butter, and sliced pickles. A Louisiana-style hot sauce (such as Tabasco) is optional, but a great idea.

MAKES 4 PO' BOYS

2 pounds shucked fresh oysters

1 cup plus 1 tablespoon milk

1 tablespoon water

¼ teaspoon ground cayenne pepper

2 eggs

1 cup all-purpose flour

½ cup corn meal

½ teaspoon freshly-ground black pepper

1 teaspoon kosher salt

Vegetable oil for frying

2 12-inch long loaves French bread, ends trimmed and cut in half

1 stick unsalted butter, melted

1 to 2 lemons, quartered

24 dill pickle slices

Hot sauce (like Tobasco), optional

1. Drain the oysters and place in a small bowl. Cover with 1 cup of milk and soak for approximately 15 minutes. In a medium bowl, whisk together remaining milk, water, cayenne and eggs. In a separate bowl, sift together the flour, corn meal, black pepper, and salt; set aside.

2. Heat oil to 360°F.

3. Drain oysters from the milk. Working in batches, dip oysters in the egg mixture, then the flour mixture, coating evenly. Remove to a plate and repeat until all oysters are coated.

4. Fry oysters in batches, being careful not to overcrowd. Cook until golden brown, about 2 minutes. Remove to a paper towel to drain, repeat with remaining oysters.

5. To serve, slice bread horizontally, leaving a "hinge." Slather a generous amount of the remoulade on the inside, and fill generously with oysters. Drizzle with melted butter and squeeze lemon juice over the oysters. Top with 6 pickle slices per sandwich, plus hot sauce.

BEER PAIRING: LAGER

SCOTCH EGGS

Scotch eggs have gotten a bum rap stateside. First ignored, then "reclaimed" and "reinterpreted" by shitty, expensive gastropubs. Won't you provide a loving home to this wonderful dish today?

MAKES 4 EGGS

6 large eggs, 2 beaten

⅔ pound ground pork

⅓ pound spicy pork chorizo

2 teaspoons ground, roasted arbol chiles

1 teaspoon ground ancho chile

1 teaspoon cinnamon

1 teaspoon hot Hungarian paprika

1¼ cups bread crumbs

2 cups all-purpose flour

Oil, for frying

1. Place 4 eggs in a small saucepan; add cold water to cover. Bring to a boil. Remove from heat, cover, and let stand for 3 minutes. Carefully drain, then fill pan with ice water to cool eggs. Gently crack shells and carefully peel under cold running water. Place eggs in a bowl of cold water; cover and chill until cold.

2. Place ground pork in a large bowl, add chorizo, ground chiles, cinnamon, paprika, and ¼ of the bread crumbs and mix evenly. Divide into 4 equal portions.

3. You'll need 3 more shallow bowls. Place flour in one, bread crumbs in another, and 2 beaten eggs in another.

4. Start by flouring your hands. Pat 1 portion of sausage into a thin patty over the length of your palm. Lay 1 soft-boiled egg on top of sausage and wrap sausage evenly around egg, sealing to completely enclose. Repeat with remaining sausage and eggs.

5. Roll the meat-covered egg in the flour, making sure to dust evenly, and then shake off any excess. Coat your dusted egg in the egg wash, then roll in the bread crumbs.

6. Heat oil to 350°F. Fry eggs, turning occasionally and maintaining oil temperature of 325 to 350°F, until sausage is cooked through and breading is golden brown and crisp, 5 to 6 minutes. Use a slotted spoon to transfer eggs to paper towels to drain.

BEER PAIRING: LAGER

RECIPE CONTINUES

SCOTCH EGGS VARIATIONS

Sukotchieggu (Asian Scotch Eggs): This recipe is what happens when an evicted Chinese restaurant leaves a secret, ancient curse and some leftover ingredients for the ironic hipster bar taking its place. For your sausage base, evenly mix 1 pound of ground pork with 4 tablespoons of soy sauce, 1 tablespoon of five-spice powder, and ½ tablespoon ground mustard. Finely crush ⅓ cup of wasabi peas and mix with ⅔ cup of panko, use mixture to replace the breadcrumbs. For an easy dipping sauce that really compliments the flavors in the Scotch egg, combine some Japanese mayo and hoisin sauce. The sauce should be 2 parts hoisin to one part mayo.

BEER PAIRING: JAPANESE WHEAT ALE

Curry Scotch Egg: Every so often a sober brain acts stoned and a recipe like this is born. In a large bowl, evenly mix 1 pound of ground pork, 1 tablespoon turmeric, 1 tablespoon curry, and 1 teaspoon fresh ground black pepper. Stick with 1¼ cups bread crumbs. For an easy dipping sauce; combine the pulp of 1 large mango, ¼ cup of honey, and the juice of 1 lime in a food processor.

BEER PAIRING: INDIA PALE ALE

BOUDIN BALLS

When travelling through Louisiana you'll see boudin balls at gas stations and restaurants that are devoted to them. Don't be dismayed by the use of pork liver in this dish; it adds a slight earthiness but is not overpowering. This popular treat is typically served with Creole mustard and remoulade but we suggest trying it with our Honey Sriracha Mayo (page 285) and Porter Beer Mustard (page 294).

MAKES 20 BALLS

1 pound pork shoulder steak, cut into 1-inch cubes

¼ pound pork liver, cut into 1-inch cubes

½ cup onion, diced

1 poblano pepper, seeded and diced

2 jalapeños, seeded and diced

¼ cup celery, diced

1 clove garlic, chopped

2 tablespoons salt

1 tablespoon pepper

2 teaspoons chili powder

2 teaspoons cayenne pepper

½ cup chopped green onion

½ cup finely chopped parsley

2 cups cooked white rice

2 eggs, beaten

1 cup flour

1. Start the night before. In a stock pot, mix meat, onion, peppers, celery, garlic, salt, pepper, 1 teaspoon chili powder, and 1 teaspoon cayenne. Pour water to cover meat and simmer 30 minutes.

2. Strain the meat, pepper, and onions and reserve liquid. Rinse the meat with cold water.

3. Coarsely grind the meat, peppers, and onion. Place in a large bowl. Add the green onions, parsley, and cooked rice to mixture. Slowly mix in 1¼ cups reserved liquid.

4. Cover and chill overnight.

5. Preheat oil to 350°.

6. Mix 1 teaspoon cayenne and 1 teaspoon chili powder with panko. Place eggs and flour in separate bowls.

7. Form the meat and rice mixture into twenty 2-inch balls, dredge in flour, dip in eggs, and cover in panko. Fry 4 to 5 minutes until golden brown. Remove with a slitten spoon and cool 2 minutes.

BEER PAIRING: VIENNA LAGER

THEME PARK CHURROS

Theme parks are man-sized hamster mazes designed to separate you from your money. The steadfast among you can resist purchasing the eleven dollar beer, the forty dollar t-shirt, and the bullshit skip-the-line pass. But none can resist the siren call of the churro. It's 95 degrees, you hate everyone, and you just saw a kid turn green on the teacups. But even with all that, a piping-hot churro straight out of the fryer smells like manna from heaven. So enjoy our version. It's so much easier.

MAKES 12 CHURROS

6 tablespoons unsalted butter

1 teaspoon kosher salt

1 teaspoon vanilla extract

1 stick cinnamon

2¼ cups water

2¼ cups flour

2 eggs

2 cups brown sugar

1 tablespoon ground cinnamon

Canola oil, for frying

1. In a medium saucepan, bring the butter, salt, vanilla, cinnamon stick, and water to a boil over medium heat.

2. Remove the cinnamon stick and gradually add the flour, whisking constantly, until the lumps disappear and a smooth dough forms. Remove from heat, transfer to a bowl, and let cool.

3. When the dough has cooled enough to not cook them, whisk in the eggs one at a time and stir until the dough is smooth. Do not eat the dough.

You're eating the dough, aren't you?

4. Fill a piping bag with dough and fit it with a star tip.

5. Combine the sugar and cinnamon in a brown paper bag and have it ready to finish the churros when they come out of the fryer.

6. Bring the canola oil to 400°F. Working in batches, carefully pipe the dough into the oil in 6-inch lengths. Be careful not to overcrowd the fryer.

7. Fry until the churros turn golden brown, about 2 minutes, then carefully remove with tongs and drop into the paper bag. Shake until evenly coated.

8. Serve to your guests before trying to sell them nine dollar rain ponchos. Cackle malevolently.

BEER PAIRING: OATMEAL STOUT

ONES

½ teaspoon ga..c powder

Chimichurri (page 284), to serve

Grated fresh Parmesan, to serve

1. Heat oil to 325°F and prepare a large bowl of ice water.

2. Add the plantain slices in batches and fry 2 minutes per side, until golden brown.

3. Remove and place on a parchment or paper towel-lined cookie sheet.

4. Place a spatula on top of one of the plantains and smack it with your hand to press it to ½ inch thickness. Repeat with the rest of them. Don't try to do more than one at a time, or you'll end up with half-assed, sorta-smashed plantains that fall apart.

7. Drop the plantains into the water and let them soak for 60 seconds. We'd say 1 minute, but we want you to count out each individual second. Keep them in any longer and they'll begin to disintegrate. Remove and carefully pat dry.

8. Fry the smashed, soaked plantains in the oil (returned to 325°F) for 2 more minutes per side, until puffed up and golden brown. Remove to paper towels, newspaper, or paper bags.

9. Season the tostones with salt and garlic powder while they're piping hot from the fryer, then grate Parmesan over top and add chimichurri. Eat to your heart's content, because they're no good as left overs.

BEER PAIRING: LAGER

RED SAUCE CALAMARI

You're used to having calamari served to you by an indifferent waitress at the red sauce place in your town, but people from South Africa to the Middle East swear by this tasty fried squid. When made well, it's a multi-tentacled work of art. When made not-so-well, it's still pretty delicious. Start practicing today and become the preeminent fried squid artist in your zip code.

MAKES 4 SERVINGS

2 pounds mixed tiny squid and thinly sliced tentacles

1 cup buttermilk

1 tablespoon kosher salt, plus more to taste

2 teaspoon black pepper

1½ cups unbleached all-purpose flour

Peanut oil, to fry

1 lemon, sliced into wedges, to serve

Red Gravy (page 299), to serve

1. Place the squid in a snug container and pour over the buttermilk. Let sit for at least 30 minutes.

2. Heat oil to 375°F.

3. Mix the salt, pepper, and flour in a large bowl.

4. Add the squid to the flour and toss to coat thoroughly.

5. When oil is ready, remove squid from the flour mixture and shake off excess.

6. Fry the squid for 30 seconds. (Seriously. Most of the calamari you have and don't like is cooked too long. Squid turns tough and rubber band-ish incredibly quickly.)

7. Remove, season with salt, and serve with lemon wedges and warm Red Gravy.

BEER PAIRING: SESSION IPA

FRIED GIARDINIERA

This is a trick we learned from Chicago hot dog legend Doug Sohn in the sunset days of his encased meats empire. And for that, we'll forever be grateful. The spicy tang of the Giardiniera cuts through the fried richness like 1980's Chuck Norris through the enemies of freedom. It's made us completely re-evaluate how willing we are to fry condiments. You're next, bacon jam.

MAKES 4 SIDE SERVINGS

2 cups Super 16-Bit Giardiniera (page 281)

1 cup unbleached all-purpose flour

1 tablespoon kosher salt

Peanut oil, to fry

1. Drain the giardiniera in a colander over a stack of paper towels or grocery bags (you don't want the oil in your pipes, and your landlord certainly doesn't). Let sit for 15 minutes, shaking frequently, until the excess oil has drained onto the paper. Discard the paper.

2. Heat oil to 350°F.

3. Mix the flour and salt in a medium bowl. Add the giardiniera, shake to coat thoroughly, and remove, shaking off excess.

4. Fry giardiniera in batches, turning frequently, until golden brown, 3 to 5 minutes.

BEER PAIRING: KOLSCH

THE PLOW & HAG FISH AND CHIPS

British pubs always have the greatest names. Just place any two everyday people, items, or occurrences together. This is the horrible name of our fantasy pub with awesome food and an off-putting sign. Rejected names included the Rifle & Fishwife, the Dog & Butler, and the Toilet & Thatcher.

Almost as great as the oddly named pub is the tradition of whitefish and chips straight from the fryer with a shaker of malt vinegar on the side. We're proud to be Americans, but this is maybe the most perfect bar dish in the entire world. A lot of places pride themselves on secret beer batters passed down through the generations, but soda water actually gives you the carbonation you need. Use a beer if you like, but you won't taste it in the final result.

Traditionally, this was a dish you could get wrapped in day-old newspaper. But UK health regulations no longer allow that. Sounds like someone needs a little freedom.

MAKES 2 BASKETS OF CHIPS

2½ pounds russet potatoes, peeled and cut into the wide, flat chips (about 4 inches x ½ inch) and placed into cold water

1 cup unbleached all-purpose flour, plus 1 cup to dredge

1¼ teaspoons baking soda

1 tablespoon lemon juice

1 tablespoon kosher salt, plus more for the chips

1 teaspoon black pepper

1 cup soda water

4 cod or haddock filets

Malt vinegar, to serve

Lemon wedges, to serve

1. Heat oil to 325°F and oven to 250°F. Remove the chips from the water, shake off excess, and carefully lower into the oil. Fry gently for 3 minutes, until poached but not brown or fried. This is just your first go-round. Relax. Remove to a wire rack in a single layer and let cool.

2. Whisk 1 cup of flour, baking soda, lemon juice, salt, and pepper together in a large bowl.

3. Slowly whisk in the soda water until it forms a consistent, thick batter without lumps.

4. Pat the fish filets dry and dredge thoroughly in the cup of flour. Shake off excess and coat with the batter.

5. Slowly lower the filets into the hot oil one at a time, holding each for 10 seconds or so as they descend into the oil so it doesn't hit the bottom of the fryer or pan and stick to the vessel.

6. Fry for 8 to 10 minutes, until browned and cooked through, and remove to a wire rack in the oven.

7. When the filets are fried, turn the oven up to 375°F. Line a large bowl with a couple of paper towels and keep the salt close at hand.

8. Fry your chips another 3 to 4 minutes, until crispy and golden brown.

9. Remove the chips from the oil, shaking off excess, into the bowl. Season the fries, then pull a Houdini on the paper towels to give them an even coating.

10. Line a plate or basket with some newspaper (GOD SAVE THE QUEEN!) and serve the fried filets on top of the chips. Serve with malt vinegar, lemon wedges, and, if you're British, some nice room-temperature beer.

BEER PAIRING: PINT OF BITTER, LUV! (ESB)

EMPANADA DOUGH

This is the base dough for every kind of empanada we make. And you can put almost anything in an empanada to create something delicious. Shrimp? Indeed. Potato and cheese? You got it. Skittles? No, man. That's gross. Have some self-respect.

MAKES 20 EMPANADAS

3 cups all-purpose flour

2 teaspoons sugar

1 tablespoon baking powder

¼ teaspoon salt

½ cup lard

1 egg

1 tablespoon cider vinegar

¾ cup chicken stock

1. Sift flour, sugar, baking powder, and salt in a large bowl.

2. Using your hands or a pastry knife, knead the lard into the flour. You'll want to work it in so there are no large chunks of lard.

3. In a separate bowl, whisk together egg, vinegar, and chicken stock. Then slowly pour and mix into the flour mixture. It should start to look like dough now.

4. Remove dough from bowl and place onto a floured surface. Knead for around 15 seconds; too long and you'll make the dough tough.

5. Put dough back into the bowl and refrigerate for at least 1 hour before making empanadas.

6. Preheat oil to 350°F.

7. Roll thin on a lightly floured surface and cut into 4½- to 5-inch disk. A bowl or large cup works great for this.

8. Place 2 to 3 tablespoons of filling into center of disk and fold over. Seal with a fork and fry in hot oil until golden brown.

SEAFOOD EMPANADA

Imagine yourself sitting on a cliff overlooking the Atlantic Ocean in Argentina. You'd have a cold beer in one hand, an empanada in the other. Feel the sea breeze and the warmth of the sun on your face. Feels great, doesn't it? Of course, this is only your imagination, back to reality of bills, family, a car that keeps breaking down, and a lawn that needs mowed. This dish is your vacation.

MAKES 20 EMPANADAS

2 tablespoons butter

1 medium yellow onion, diced

1 clove garlic, chopped

2 cups shrimp

¾ cup lump crab meat

½ pound small scallops

½ teaspoon smoked paprika

½ teaspoon cumin

1 heirloom tomato, chopped

Oil, for frying

1 batch Empanada Dough (page 76)

2 tablespoons cilantro, chopped

1. In a saucepan, sauté onions in butter. Add the garlic, cook for a minute until fragrant, then add shrimp, crab, and scallops with paprika, cumin, and tomato for 5 minutes. Remove from heat and mix in the cilantro.

2. Preheat oil to 350°F.

3. Drain excess liquid from seafood mixture.

4. Working in batches, roll out dough on lightly floured surface and cut into 4- to 5-inch disks. Place 3 tablespoons of filling in the center of each disk, then fold over and seal with a fork.

5. Fry empanadas for 3 minutes or until dark golden brown. Remove and serve with chimichurri.

BEER PAIRING: SAISON

CHICKEN EMPANADAS

We've all been there. We cooked a chicken and still have half of the thing left over. Sure you can make tacos with it, or a soup. *Boring!* You do know that frying is way cooler than soup, right? Shred that chicken, wrap delicious dough around it, and make a damn empanada with those leftovers.

MAKES 15 TO 20 EMPANADAS

1 small onion, chopped

1 clove garlic

1 tablespoon butter

2 cups shredded chicken thighs

3 tablespoons sour cream

½ teaspoon chipotle chili powder

¼ teaspoon salt

½ teaspoon cumin

½ 12 oz. can green chili, chopped

1½ teaspoons fresh oregano, chopped

1 cup shredded Chihuahua cheese

Oil, for frying

1 batch Empanada Dough (page 76)

1. In a saucepan, sauté onion and garlic in butter until translucent. Add shredded chicken, sour cream, chili powder, salt, cumin, and heat through for 6 minutes. Take off heat, then add green chili and oregano. Once chicken is cool, combine with cheese in a large bowl.

2. Preheat oil to 350°F.

3. Working in batches, roll out empanada dough and cut into 5-inch circles. Fill each one with 3 tablespoons of filling, fold over, and seal using a fork.

4. Fry for 3 minutes and serve.

BEER PAIRING: BELGIAN SAISON

HAWAIIAN EMPANADA

It's an empanada filled with ham, pineapple, and cheese. In a way, it's a lot like the Hawaiian pizza you enjoyed as a kid, except you get to eat twenty of them.

MAKES 20 EMPANADAS

Oil to fry

3 cups shredded mozzarella cheese

2 cups ham, chopped

2 cups pineapple, chopped

1 batch Empanada Dough (page 76), cold

Chimihurri

1. Preheat oil to 350°F.

2. Mix together the cheese, ham, and pineapple in a large bowl.

3. Working in batches, roll out the dough on a lightly floured surface and cut into 4- to 5-inch disks. Place 3 tablespoons of filling in the center of each disk, then fold over and seal with a fork.

4. Fry the empanadas for 3 minutes or until dark golden brown. Remove and serve with chimichurri.

BEER PAIRING: AMERICAN BLONDE ALE

'MERICA EMPANADAS

Inspired by the great American dessert of apple pie, these empanadas are a sweet way to finish a meal. Tart Granny Smith apples surrounded by a sweet peanut butter sauce that will have you screaming like an eagle.

MAKES 15 TO 20 EMPANADAS

½ cup unsalted butter, divided

½ cup dark brown sugar, divided

4 Granny Smith apples, peeled and cut into bite size pieces

1 cup peanut butter

½ teaspoon salt

½ cup heavy cream

Oil for frying

1 batch Empanada Dough (page 76)

1. Melt ¼ cup butter and 1 tablespoon brown sugar over medium heat; add apples. Cover, stirring every minute, until apples are tender, about 12 to 14 minutes. Remove from butter with slotted spoon and place in a bowl. Cover the bowl and allow to cool.

2. In a saucepan over low heat, place the peanut butter, ¼ cup butter, remainder of the brown sugar, and salt. Stir to combine. Remove from heat and add the cream. Mix until smooth, then add the apples and cool.

3. Preheat oil to 350°F.

4. Making 4 to 5 empanadas at a time, roll the dough on a lightly floured surface and cut into 4- to 5-inch circles. Place 3 tablespoons of filling in the center, then fold over and seal with a fork.

5. Fry empanadas for 3 minutes or until dark golden brown. Remove and serve.

BEER PAIRING: FUCK IT, IT'S AMERICA. EAT IT WITH A BOURBON.

SWEET POTATO EMPANADAS

Like potatoes, but sweet. Sorry, we don't have good stories for all the empanadas.

MAKES 15 TO 20 EMPANADAS

1 cup onion, chopped

2 cloves garlic, minced

1 tablespoon butter

2 cups cheddar, shredded

3 cups sweet potatoes, steamed and diced

1 teaspoon chili powder

1½ teaspoons cumin

1 batch Empanada Dough, cold (page 76)

Oil, for frying

1. In a souce pan, sauté onions and garlic in butter in a saucepan until translucent.

2. In a bowl, mix together cheddar and potatoes and spices, then mix in sautéed onions and garlic.

3. Preheat oil to 350°F.

4. Making 4 to 5 empanadas at a time, roll the dough on lightly floured surface and cut into 4- to 5-inch circles. Place 3 tablespoons of filling in the center, then fold over and seal with a fork.

5. Fry empanadas for 3 minutes or until dark golden brown. Remove and let oil drain off before eating. Serve with chimichurri.

BEER PAIRING: SESSION SOUR

FRIED RAVIOLI

This is a dish beloved in St. Louis that the general public mostly finds mystifying. Which, to be fair, is the unfair knock on a lot of the city's food. But provided you're not making your own pasta from scratch and then throwing it into a deep fryer (because why?), this is a nice little change of pace and a hell of a bar snack. The Cardinals still suck, however, and their pleated-khaki fans are only slightly better.

One might pair this with marinara, but we really dig it with our spicy, cheesy, rich vodka sauce.

MAKES 4 SERVINGS

2 eggs, beaten

½ cup whole milk

All-purpose flour, to dust

Italian breadcrumbs, to dredge

24 frozen cheese ravioli

Oil, for frying

Grated Parmesan, to serve

Chopped flat-leaf parsley, to serve

Warm Red Gravy (page 299) or Vodka Sauce (page 300), to serve

1. Mix the beaten eggs with the milk and place in a shallow dish.

2. Lay out the flour, egg/milk mixture, and breadcrumbs, in that order in seperate bowls.

3. Heat your oil to 350°F.

4. Coat the ravioli in the flour (shaking off excess), egg mixture (ditto), and bread crumbs (and a third time).

5. Fry the ravioli in batches for 1½ minutes, until golden brown.

6. Remove to a wire rack as they finish. Garnish with Parmesan and parsley and serve with Red Gravy or Vodka Sauce.

BEER PAIRING: BERLINER WEISSE

FRIED CHICKEN

Frying chicken is the most useful of all techniques. If you can make moist, crisp fried chicken, we're confident in predicting that you can fry or cook most anything given a crack or two at it. And if you can't eat all of the chicken (we haven't yet mapped the boundaries of our consumption ability), it goes into anything and everything else. It's even good eaten cold at a graveyard with a domestic lager, as John C.'s Southern family was wont to do on Sundays. This was before cable had quite so many channels, and way before Nashville had a football team.

MAKES 8 PIECES

1 chicken, cut into 8 pieces

4 cups buttermilk (or pickle brine)

2 cups unbleached all-purpose flour

2 tablespoons kosher salt

2 teaspoons black pepper

Oil, for frying

4 eggs, beaten

1 cup whole milk

Hot sauce, to serve

Buttermilk biscuits or rolls, to serve

1. Place the chicken pieces into a snug-fitting container. Pour the buttermilk or pickle brine over and let sit 2 hours, up to overnight.

2. Mix the flour, salt and pepper. Divide between two shallow dishes. Add a few tablespoons of buttermilk to the flour.

3. Heat oil to 325°F.

4. Remove the chicken from the buttermilk or brine, pat dry, and dredge in flour mixture, shaking off excess.

5. Coat the chicken in the egg mixture, shaking off excess over the remaining dish of flour.

6. Coat the chicken in flour and lower into the fryer. Fry in batches for 12 to 14 minutes, until a digital thermometer reads 160°F. Remove to a wire rack.

7. Serve with hot sauce and rolls or biscuits.

BEER PAIRING: DOUBLE IPA

NASHVILLE HOT CHICKEN

If we'd written this book a year or two ago, we'd be talking about how Nashville hot chicken was an obscure local favorite we can't get enough of. A population influx and widespread acclaim for local joints including Prince's and Hattie B's means that it's less of a secret local favorite and more of a genuine Southern food phenomenon.

Every place guards their recipe like the original Coca-Cola formula, but no secrets are safe from ManBQue. And we're damned sure that our shot at this Southern classic is legit.

If you're looking for a super-spicy kick, add additional ¼ teaspoon of cyanne or even ghost powder to the finishing sauce until you melt like one of the Nazis in *Raiders of the Lost Ark*.

MAKES 8 PIECES

1 chicken, cut into 8 pieces

4 cups buttermilk, divided

1 cup hot sauce, divided

2 cups unbleached all-purpose flour

2 tablespoons kosher salt

2 teaspoons black pepper

2 teaspoons cayenne pepper, plus 1 tablespoon

4 eggs, beaten

1 cup whole milk

Oil, for frying

3 tablespoons brown sugar

4 slices white bread, to serve

Buttermilk biscuits, to serve

Sour pickles, to serve

1. Place the chicken pieces into a snug-fitting container. Mix the buttermilk with ½ cup of the hot sauce and let sit at least 2 hours, up to overnight.

2. Mix the flour, salt, pepper, and 2 teaspoons cayenne. Divide between two shallow dishes. Add a couple of tablespoons of buttermilk to the flour.

3. Mix the eggs with the milk and ¼ cup of the hot sauce.

4. Heat your oil to 325°F.

5. Remove the chicken from the buttermilk/brine, pat dry, and dredge in flour, shaking off excess.

6. Coat the chicken in the egg mixture, shaking off excess over the remaining dish of flour.

7. Coat the chicken in flour and lower into the fryer. Fry in batches for 12 to 14 minutes, until a digital thermometer reads 155°F. Remove to a wire rack.

8. Ladle ½ cup of the hot oil into a skillet over medium heat. When it begins to shimmer, add the 2 tablespoons of cayenne, 2 tablespoons of hot sauce, and the brown sugar. Stir to combine.

9. Finish the chicken in the sauce and serve immediately with white bread, biscuits, and sour pickles.

BEER PAIRING: DOUBLE IPA

TRIPLE-PEACH FRIED PIES

You know those hand pies you see in every drug, grocery, and convenience store that are as delicious as they are bad for you? People still make them from scatch in the South. This is actually part of the citizenship test in certain parts of the country. We used three types of peaches to achieve maximum peachiness.

While we do appreciate the irony of saying this in a "Fry Your Own Pie" recipe, we recommend starting with some pre-made pie dough. Good lord, does it save some hassle.

MAKES 12 PIES

1 tablespoon unsalted butter

1 cup diced peaches

3 tablespoon sugar

¼ cup peach preserves

½ teaspoon cayenne pepper

2 teaspoon cornstarch

1 tablespoon peach schnapps

1 teaspoon cinnamon

1 portion of pie dough, rolled out into a 16 x 11-inch sheet (or equivalent surface area), refrigerated

Vegetable oil, to fry (or lard, if you're feeling awesome)

1. Melt the butter over medium-high heat in a saucepan and sauté the peaches and sugar for 2 minutes, stirring regularly until the sugar dissolves. Add the preserves, cayenne, cornstarch, schnapps, and cinnamon and cook for another 2 minutes. Remove from heat.

2. Cut the dough into 3½-inch diameter circles and place 2 teaspoons of the peach filling onto the center of the dough. Fold over, pinch closed, and set on a plate. Repeat with the remaining dough and refrigerate for 30 minutes.

3. Heat your oil (or lard, come on, try lard, you never do anything fun) to 350°F. Fry pies in small batches for 1½ to 2 minutes per, turning frequently. Remove to a rack of towel-lined plate to dry.

BEER PAIRING: BELGIAN TRIPEL

AMERICA'S FAVORITE VEGETABLE

French fries, owing to some spectacularly dumb USDA classification standards, are officially America's favorite vegetable. This leads people to question why they should bother taking their precious time at home to make something so ubiquitous and cheap. And it's a fair question, to which we ask you to remember the number of times that the cooks at your local fry haven:

- Forgot to salt your fries

- Undercooked your fries into a soggy mess

- Overcooked your fries into crunchy abominations devoid of pillowy potato texture

- Tried to charge you extra for sauce

- Were closed on Sunday to protest gay marriage

By becoming master of your own fry domain, you can guarantee the best results every single time, experiment with new sauces, seasonings, and techniques, and avoid the pitfalls of commercial fry vendors.

We could give you fifteen slightly different recipes here, but after searching wisdom far and wide, and even going to the Frietmuseum in Belgium (I mean, we were already nearby and they serve beer), we've figured out that every fry recipe is a small variation on one theme: par-cooking sliced potatoes, cranking up the heat, and finishing them to a crisp golden-brown.

We know that a lot of places leave their skin on to joyously announce the fact that they make hand-cut fries in house, but we find that going skinless leaves us with a better end product. Ignore this note if you're striving to open a burger place or bar with "gourmet," "farm-to-table," or "artisan" used without irony on the menu.

Here's your absolutely perfect, repeatedly tested, *oh my god how are we going to get all this oil out of our test kitchen*, base recipe for classic Belgian fries. Since France and America can't play nice when it comes to this dish, we're assigning it to a neutral party.

MAKES 3 POUNDS OF FRIES

3 pounds russet potatoes, peeled and cut into sticks that are ½-inch wide and ½-inch thick, then dropped into a bowl of cold water

2 quarts peanut oil, to fry

Kosher salt, to season

RECIPE CONTINUES

1. Heat your oil to 325°F in a deep fryer, or a large, deep, heavy pot. Please don't try this in a shallow cast iron pan, a big skillet, or any other vessel where the oil barely covers the tiny batches of fries you're coaxing along. The temperature will drop too much, they'll turn oily, and your finished product will leave you wistful for the drive-through.

2. Remove the potatoes from the water, shake off excess, and carefully lower the fries into the hot oil. Be careful to avoid any spatter. Fry the potatoes in small batches (about one or two wire skimmers worth at a time, depending on your cooking vessel) for 5 minutes, until lightly colored. Bring the oil back up to 325°F between every batch, adjusting the burner if necessary.

3. Remove to a paper towel-lined plate, newspaper, or a paper grocery bag and let cool in a single layer.

4. When you've par-cooked your fries, either package them up and freeze in small batches for later or turn the oil up to 375°F to finish. Line a large bowl with a couple of paper towels that cover the bottom in one continual piece.

5. Fry 1 to 2 minutes, agitating frequently, until the fries are crispy and golden brown. Remove in batches and place in the bowl. Season them generously with the salt NOW NOW NOW NOW while the hot oil is still on the surface to greedily accept the delicious sodium.

6. When the fries have been piled up and seasoned, aggressively swipe the towel away to mix the seasoning in consistently. You've got a bowl of fries! Congratulations! Serve with your favorite dipping sauces.

THE WONDERFUL WORLD OF FRIES

Once you've made the classic, there are other places to go. We wrote a book about it, but it turned out the title infringed on an existing work by Dr. Seuss. Oh well.

FAST FOOD FRIES

Fast food fries are thinner, crispier, and saltier than the classic version, which is why entire generations think it's the apex of the art. The great Kenji López-Alt did a whole series on this on Serious Eats that we recommend you read, if even just for fun. The main takeaways:

1. Cut the fries uniformly ¼-inch thick (he used calipers, even!) for the perfect crust-to-potato result.

2. Boil the fries for 10 minutes with a tablespoon of white vinegar and a tablespoon of salt per quart of water.

3. Fry in 400°F oil for just under 1 minute, then freeze overnight.

4. Finish straight from the freezer in 400°F oil for 3½ minutes. Viola—a perfect replica.

CURLY FRIES

You'll need a curly fry cutter, which is a uni-tasker in every sense of the term. Curly-cut them, follow the usual par-cooking procedure, then dredge them in Cajun-seasoned flour before the second fry. Serve in a paper cup and it's the state fair with fewer neck-tattoos!

WAFFLE FRIES

Another style, another special cutting tool. This time it's a cross-cutter, which you'll get with a decent mandoline, or you can buy it as a standalone. It's not quite so uni-tasking here, as a cross-cutter is also the secret for delicious crispy homemade chips. Follow the usual procedures, but give them an extra 30 to 45 seconds in the hotter oil to finish, and be sure to serve them with plenty of sauces. What's the point of making a potato dolphin net unless you're going to imprison a whole lot of duck or BBQ sauce with it?

SWEET POTATO FRIES

In the interest of directness, we need to inform you that sweet potato fries are never quite crispy unless they're burned or turned into sad oven-baked shadows of their true selves. It's the tradeoff for the sweet taste that pairs so well with aiolis of all kinds. Finish these at a gentler 350°F and keep a close eye on them as they cook. Taste the first few and adjust your timing as needed.

BRITISH CHIPS

We actually cover this in our Fish and Chips recipe (page 74), but suffice to say, you want to cut wider chips for maximum malt vinegar application area and a more potato-y flavor. In addition, you may also want to replace the first par-fry with a 10-minute vinegar and salt boil, akin to what Mr. López-Alt taught us about fast food fries.

LEFTOVER FRIES

You know how leftover fries from a restaurant always suck? They don't have to. Pour ¼ inch of oil into a wide sauté pan. Heat over medium heat until just shimmering, then add your fries. Toss them in the pan or with tongs every 10 to 15 seconds for a minute or two, until hot and crispy. Remove, add any additional seasoning you might want (they're probably already salty), and marvel at your ability to raise the dead. You need never leave fries out of the doggie bag again.

GET SAUCED!

If the Europeans do one thing right, it's offering a rainbow of delicious dipping sauces for their fries. Meanwhile, we're over here drowning them in ketchup like overgrown toddlers with bills and blood pressure issues. Ditch the 57, just for now, and try one or all of these on your fries.

GARLIC AIOLI

1 cup mayo

2 cloves garlic, minced

1 teaspoon lemon juice

1 teaspoon black pepper

CURRY SAUCE

1 tablespoon olive oil

1 cup diced yellow onion (about ½ onion)

1 cup peeled, diced apple (about 1 apple)

2 cloves garlic, minced

¼ cup demi-glace

¼ cup brown ale

½ teaspoon curry powder

¼ teaspoon black pepper

1. Sauté the onion and apples for 5 minutes, until soft. Add the garlic and cook another minute, until fragrant.

2. Add the demi-glace, brown ale, curry, and pepper. Bring to a simmer and let cook for 20 to 30 minutes.

3. Remove from heat, carefully (or immersion) blend, and strain.

MAYOKETCHUP

½ cup mayo

½ cup ketchup

½ teaspoon Worcestershire sauce

SAUCE ANDALOUSE

1 cup mayo

2 tablespoons tomato paste

1 tablespoon onion, minced

2 tablespoons bell pepper (red and/or green), minced

2 teaspoons lemon juice

½ teaspoon anchovy paste

SAMURAI SAUCE

1 cup mayo

¼ cup harissa or sambal oelek

TARTAR SAUCE

1 cup mayo

1 tablespoon lemon juice

2 tablespoons chopped cornichons

1 tablespoon grated white onion

1 glove garlic, minced

1 teaspoon chopped fresh chives

KATSU PORK

Katsu is our lesson that even in world of infinite street food dishes, you can find commonalities between Hokkaido and Iowa. Delicious breaded pork, rich sauce, and plenty of beer to drink it with are the tenets of this classic Izakaya dish, but you'd imagine that ethos would appeal to Hawkeye football fans as well.

MAKES 4 CUTLETS

4 cups cold water

½ cup sugar

½ cup kosher salt

1 pound pork loin, cut into chunks 1 inch wide x 4 inches long x ½ inch thick

Peanut oil, to fry

Flour, to dredge

3 eggs, beaten

Panko bread crumbs

Katsu Sauce (page 274), to serve

Shredded cabbage, to serve

Thinly sliced red onion, to serve

1. Mix the cold water, sugar, and salt to create a brine. Add the pork and let bring at least 45 minutes, up to overnight.

2. Remove pork, pat dry, and heat oil to 350°F.

3. Thread the pork onto skewers running through the length of the chunks.

4. Dredge the pork in flour, egg, and panko, shaking off excess between each one.

5. Fry pork, in batches, for 12 to 15 minutes, until golden brown and the internal temperature reaches 145°F.

6. Remove, cool for 2 minutes, and serve with katsu sauce, cabbage, and onion.

IPA WINGS

We used a high alpha hop in the first version of this wing sauce. Naturally, everyone who sampled it was soon walking around with sour face except for the big hop lovers. Lucky for you, we've knocked the bitterness down considerably to be a well-rounded sauce. This also makes a great dipping sauce for Belgian fries (page 89).

MAKES ABOUT 32 WINGS

Oil, for frying

½ cup malty beer

Juice of 2 lemons

½ teaspoon Worcestershire sauce

¼ teaspoon pepper

4 ounces Hops Butter (page 289)

½ cup heavy cream

2 teaspoons arrowroot powder

3 pounds chicken wings, cut into flats and drumettes

¼ teaspoon low-alpha hop pellets, ground, to garnish

1. Preheat oil to 350°F.

2. In a saucepan over medium heat, add beer, lemon juice, Worcestershire sauce, and pepper, then boil for 5 minutes.

3. Lower heat to simmer, add hops butter and melt, then add cream and simmer for 3 minutes, stirring constantly.

4. Remove from heat. Mix the arrowroot with 2 teaspoons of water, stirring to create a slurry, and add to the sauce, stirring until thickened.

5. Fry wings for 10 minutes, until crispy and cooked through.

6. Remove wings from the fryer, toss the wings with the sauce, and garnish with ground hops.

BEER PAIRING: KÖLSCH

LE CORN DOG

This is maybe the most American of all foods in this book, mostly because, if you're running for office, you can't escape primary season in Iowa without a really unflattering picture of you taking down a corn dog. So it's really the only dish that's the food of both presidents and the lady at Wal-Mart whose scooter takes up the whole aisle.

Fresh corn-rich batter, crisp brown exterior, and just steaming enough on the inside to provide textural contrast. A properly made corn dog doesn't even need condiments. But, you'll have them anyway—it's your night.

MAKES 6 CORN DOGS

6 hot dogs, preferably skinless

1 cup yellow cornmeal

1 cup unbleached all-purpose flour

1 teaspoon baking powder

¼ teaspoon baking soda

1 teaspoon kosher salt

½ teaspoon smoked paprika

1½ cups buttermilk

1 egg, beaten

1 tablespoon honey

1 tablespoon peanut oil, plus more to fry

½ cup cornstarch, to dredge

1. Thread the hot dogs with skewers through the length of the dog. Heat oil to 375°F.

2. Mix the cornmeal, flour, baking powder, baking soda, salt, and paprika.

3. Mix the buttermilk, egg, honey, and tablespoon of peanut oil.

4. Stir the wet ingredients into the dry, taking care not to over-mix, until you have a smooth batter.

5. Dredge the skewered dogs in the cornstarch, shake off excess, and dip into the batter.

6. Fry the dogs 5 to 6 minutes, until deep brown and crispy.

7. Remove from fryer and serve immediately with Porter Beer Mustard (page 294) and/or Bacon Jam (page 282).

BEER PAIRING: BROWN ALE

FRIED AVOCADO TACOS

Our slogan is "Meat. Beer. Rock & Roll". But that doesn't mean we live by it every day. Most days yes, but we hear there's actually great food out there that doesn't have meat. Case in point, these fried avocado tacos. Maybe someday we'll also learn there are beverages besides beer or music outside of rock. But today is not that day.

MAKES 8 TO 10 SIX-INCH TACOS

¾ cup all-purpose flour

3 eggs, beaten

2½ cups panko

1 teaspoon cumin

1 teaspoon chili powder

2 avocados, pitted and cut into ½ inch cubes

1 cabbage, sliced

1 red onion, sliced and soaked in water

2 cups peanut oil, to fry

8 to 10 corn tortillas, 6 inches round

Pico de gallo, to serve

1 cup Monterey Jack cheese, shredded, to serve

Tequila Lime Crema (page 300)

1. Preheat oil to 350°F.

2. Place the flour, eggs, and panko in three separate bowls. Mix the cumin and chili powder into the panko.

3. In batches of 6, dredge avocado pieces in flour, dip them in the egg, shake off the excess, then coat with panko.

4. Fry the avocados in oil for 2 to 3 minutes, until golden brown. Transfer with a slotted spoon to a towel-lined plate. Work in batches until all the avocado pieces have gone to their golden-brown reward.

5. Lay the avocado, cabbage, and red onion onto their respective tortillas. Top with the pico de gallo, cheese, and crema.

BEER PAIRING: RYE BEER

THE SOUTH SIDER

Bridgeport is on the near south side of Chicago where the White Sox play. It's a close-knit community of Irish, Italian, and Lithuanians and home to five Chicago mayors. The presence of the Chicago Machine is strong in this area and it must create an appetite. The breaded steak sandwich is a unique invention from here. It's a thin, breaded steak that's fried, then smothered with red gravy and topped with mozzarella cheese. The "small" sandwich is typically the size of your forearm, which helps power the cops, firefighters, and city workers who can be found eating it.

MAKES 4 SANDWICHES

2 cups peanut oil, to fry

3 eggs, beaten

1 teaspoon salt

1 teaspoon pepper

2 cups dry Italian bread crumbs

½ cup panko

¼ cup Parmesan

Four ¼ inch-thick slices of top round steak

1 cup all-purpose flour

¼ cup milk

Red Gravy (page 299), to top

1 baguette, quartered and sliced lengthwise

2 cups shredded mozzarella cheese

Sweet peppers, hot peppers, and/or
  giardiniera, to top

1. Preheat fryer oil to 350°F.

2. Mix the eggs, milk, salt, and pepper in shallow dish.

3. Combine the bread crumbs, panko, and Parmesan in second shallow dish.

4. Pound the steaks with a meat tenderizer mallet, then pat dry.

5. Coat the steaks with flour, submerge in egg wash, shake off excess, then coat with breadcrumb mixture.

6. Fry each steak for 4 minutes.

7. Remove steaks as they finish to a towel-lined plate and let cool for 1 minute.

8. Dip the steaks in red gravy, lay onto the sliced bread, then top with cheese and peppers.

9. Finish by closing the sandwich. Geologically-(meatologically?) speaking, you'll have delicious things in this order: steak, mozzarella, peppers, steak, and bread that's dripping with red gravy. If something has gone wrong, consult the nearest scientist.

BEER PAIRING: IPA

NATIVE AMERICAN FRY BREAD

RECIPE BY ADAM PALMER

This dish is an inspiring example of the power of making the best of what you're given. At the same time, it's also a stone cold bummer. When the US government forced the various native populations onto reservations, they were provided Army rations to keep them from starving in new and unfamiliar environs. The fry bread—soft, sweet, and adaptable—became part of the tribal identity, with each nation showing identifiable deviations in their recipe. You can find them all over the Southwest as both a delicious snack and a killer tortilla.

MAKES 14 PIECES

10 ounces (2½ cups) self-rising flour (plus more for forming)

2 cups buttermilk

Vegetable oil, to fry

Honey Butter (page 288), to serve

1. Sift the flower into a bowl and add the buttermilk gradually, stirring continually, until a thick dough forms.

2. Turn the dough out onto a floured surface and begin to knead. Dust your hands with flour and knead continuously for 10 minutes, then switch to a coating of oil on your hands.

3. When you can handle the dough without it sticking to your hands, rub the dough with oil and place it in a covered container in a warm place and let sit for at least 3 hours.

4. Heat the vegetable oil to 325°F.

5. Turn the dough out onto a clean surface and pinch off a ball. Flatten it with your hands, like you would a disc of pizza dough. Tear a small hole in the middle of the dough—this will ensure more even frying.

6. Drop the dough into the oil and cook 2 to 3 minutes, until golden brown on both sides. Use chopsticks to turn the bread without tearing it.

7. Repeat with remaining dough, making sure to return the oil temperature to 325°F before frying new dough. Leftover dough can be placed in a plastic bag and refrigerated up to 4 or 5 days.

8. Sear with honey butter.

BEER PAIRING: ENGLISH BARLEYWINE

CHICKEN-FRIED BACON

RECIPE BY GUS PASCHALIS

No, we don't eat like this every day. And six strips will usually cover it for a gathering, because in addition to being delicious, it's incredibly rich. But you know you want to try it. And before you ask, "chicken-fried" refers to the process (which is like frying chicken), not the ingredients (which do not include chicken). We get that question a lot.

It seems counterintuitive for something you're battering and frying, but use a decent bacon. It'll finish with some chew, so you'll get a lot of smoky, porky goodness. If you're one of those people who can't stand chewy bacon, par-bake the slices and let them cool before you coat them.

We like to serve this with hot sauce and a Sriracha Mayo, but go nuts and try whatever you like on the side. Short of broken glass, anything you dip this into is going to be awesome.

1. Pat the bacon dry.

2. Beat the eggs with the salt.

3. Heat your fryer to 375°F. We like peanut oil for this, but do whatever.

4. Mix your flour, salt, pepper, and cayenne, and place in a shallow bowl.

5. Dip the bacon in the egg wash and coat it with the seasoned flour.

6. Fry the bacon for 2 to 3 minutes, depending on how well your fryer is calibrated, and suddenly you've got delicious chicken-fried bacon. How do you feel? We bet it's "like an AMERICAN."

BEER PAIRING: DOUBLE IPA

MAKES 6 SLICES

6 strips regular-cut bacon

2 eggs

½ teaspoon salt

Peanut oil, for frying

2 cups flour

1 teaspoon salt

2 tablespoons black pepper

½ teaspoon cayenne pepper

Hot sauce, to serve

Honey Sriracha Mayo (page 285), to serve

BROAD SHOULDER WINGS

These wings are our tribute to the 7,000 Chinese restaurants in Chicago. We discovered this sauce's flavor profile while visiting a place on the north side while searching for the best wings in Chicago. The flavor's not soy, it's not teriyaki; it's hot and sweet, gingery and sesame, and truly unique like the city itself.

MAKES ABOUT 32 WINGS

⅓ cup water

⅓ cup sugar

¼ cup soy sauce

1½ tablespoons rice vinegar

1 tablespoon roasted sesame oil

1 tablespoon honey

¾ inch fresh ginger root, finely grated

2 teaspoons Sriracha

5 cloves garlic, minced

2 teaspoons cornstarch

3 pounds chicken wings, cut into flats and drumettes

½ cup thin-sliced green onions

1 tablespoon sesame seeds

1. Combine the water, sugar, and soy sauce in a small saucepan over medium heat and stir until sugar is dissolved.

2. Add the rice vinegar, oil, honey, ginger, Sriracha, and garlic. Simmer for 8 minutes.

3. Slowly stir in the cornstarch and stir. When the sauce thickens, remove it from the heat.

4. Toss wings with sauce and top with sliced green onion and sesame seeds.

BEER PAIRING: EUROPEAN PALE LAGER

CHICAGO MEETS BUFFALO WINGS

Traditional Buffalo sauce is wonderful by itself; it's also a kickass base for laying in more flavor. This sauce adds sweet and heat from habanero and slight smoke from chipotle chili without making that last jump to become one of those burn-your-face-off wing sauces.

MAKES ABOUT 32 WINGS

1 tablespoon arrowroot powder

3 pounds chicken wings, cut into flats and drumettes

1 cup unsalted butter

2 cloves garlic, minced

1 cup cayenne hot sauce

½ habanero pepper, minced

1 tablespoon Sriracha

½ teaspoon chipotle chili powder

¼ teaspoon chili powder

¼ teaspoon paprika

⅛ teaspoon pepper

⅛ teaspoon salt

1. Mix the arrowroot and ½ tablespoon of water in a bowl to create a slurry and set aside.

2. Melt the butter and garlic in a small saucepan over low heat. Just before the butter is completely melted, add the hot sauce.

3. Add the habanero and spices and lower heat to a simmer, stirring occasionally.

4. Once the sauce begins to steam, remove from heat and stir in the arrowroot. Keep stirring like a mad man so that the sauce doesn't separate before the arrowroot sets up and thickens.

5. Preheat your fryer to 350°F.

6. Fry your wings for 10 minutes, until cooked thoroughly and crispy.

7. Remove the wings to a bowl and toss with sauce to coat.

BEER PAIRING: IMPERIAL IPA, SUCH AS GREEN BULLET TRIPLE IPA—GREEN FLASH BREWING CO.

KOREAN HOT CHICKEN WINGS WITH PEANUTS AND SCALLIONS

RECIPE BY BRANDON FROHNE

We first met Brandon while eating our fill of Hot Chicken in Nashville and were blown away by the food culture of the city. We naturally asked him for his favorite street food recipe, and he gave it to us.

MAKES 4 PORTIONS

2 cups buttermilk

1 tablespoon minced garlic

2 teaspoons Tabasco

1 tablespoon kosher salt

1 teaspoon black pepper

1 pound chicken wings, separated into flats and drumettes (tips discarded)

1 cup kochukaru (Korean chili flakes)

½ cup soy sauce

¾ cup chopped mango

½ cup rice wine vinegar

½ cup honey

¼ cup ginger, grated

½ cups garlic, minced

¼ cup sesame oil

Juice of 4 limes

½ cup toasted benne seeds (or sesame seeds)

1 tablespoon butter

Peanut oil, for frying

1 cup rice flour

½ cup all-purpose flour

¼ cup cornstarch

½ cups crushed peanuts, to serve

½ cup green onions, diced, to serve

1. In a bowl, mix the buttermilk, garlic, Tabasco, salt, and pepper. Pour over wings in a snug container or zip-top bag and allow to marinate in the refrigerator overnight.

2. The next day, combine the kochukaru, soy, mango, vinegar, honey, ginger, garlic, sesame oil, lime juice, and toasted benne or sesame seeds in a medium pot. Bring to a simmer over medium heat and cook for 15 minutes, stirring occasionally.

3. Remove the sauce from the heat and stir in the butter. Mix until incorporated.

4. Heat oil to 350°F.

5. Mix the rice flour, all-purpose flour, and cornstarch in a medium bowl.

6. Remove wings from marinade, shaking to remove excess buttermilk. Roll in the flour mixture and place in the fryer for 6 to 8 minutes until cooked to an internal temperature of 165°F.

7. Remove from fryer and place on a sheet pan. Using a pastry brush, brush wings with the sauce and sprinkle crumbled peanuts and scallions over the top.

BEER PAIRING: MAIBOCK

SMOKED SALMON AND BACON POPPERS

These are the poppers you wished that dive bar next to your house served. Jalapeño smothered in beer batter greatness and stuffed with smoked salmon and a crunchy cream cheese. They're the real deal.

MAKES 12 POPPERS

12 jalapeño

3 ounces smoked salmon, sliced into 12 pieces

1 pound cream cheese, at room temperature

2 cups all-purpose flour

½ tablespoon olive oil

1½ teaspoons baking powder

½ cup milk

¼ cup pilsner beer

¼ teaspoon salt

Peanut oil for frying

¼ pound bacon, cooked (page 175) and finely chopped

1. Gently score the skin of the jalapeño (this will help the batter stick). Slice the top of the jalapeño open, leaving the stem attached. Remove the seeds.

2. Mix the chopped bacon and chream cheese.

3. Fill each pepper with a slice of smoked salmon and 1 tablespoon of cream cheese mixture.

4. Preheat oil to 350°F.

5. Mix 1 cup of the flour with the olive oil, baking powder, milk, beer, and salt in a bowl. The consistency should be similar to pancake batter.

6. Dredge the peppers in a bowl filled with the remaining cup of flour. Shake off excess, then dip in batter.

7. Fry 6 minutes until golden brown. Remove to a towel-lined plate and let cool for 7 minutes.

BEER PAIRING: AMERICAN PALE WHEAT ALE

WENCESLAS SQUARE SANDWICH

Beside the beauty, history, and beer, Prague has excellent street food. Just a few blocks away from the heavy tourist area of Old Town Square is the busy, resplendent shopping district Wenceslas Square. While drinking your way from Prague Castle across the Charles Bridge to enjoy a view of the astronomical clock in Old Town Square, you can really work up an appetite. At the north end, a few street vendors serve fried cheese sandwiches. They're big breaded cheese sticks on a bun with a little mayo, and they're the best damn beer food in the city.

MAKES 6 SANDWICHES

1 clove garlic, minced

1 cup breadcrumbs

¼ cup panko

1 cup flour

2 eggs, beaten

1 pound Edam cheese, cut into 6 even slices (typical wire cheese slicer cuts to perfect thickness)

Oil for frying

6 brioche buns

Mayo to spread

1. Preheat oil to 400°F.

2. Combine garlic, breadcrumbs, and panko in shallow bowl. Put the flour in a separate shallow dish and eggs in another. Dipping time.

3. Dredge cheese in flour, wet with egg, and cover with breadcrumb mixture.

4. Fry for 30 seconds, remove, and let oil drain off.

5. Place the cheese into bun, top with mayo and party on.

BEER PAIRING: CZECH PILS

LINE COOK CHICHARRONES

RECIPE BY JAMES GOTTWALD

The same people that taught us the wonders of the Philly Cheesesteak and the magic of the Roast Pork Grinder showed us this neat little trick to create a killer snack from the pork roast trimmings. They say they won't put it on the menu because they can't figure out what to call it (Pork Scraps? Pig Chips?), but we wouldn't be surprised if they were saving the good stuff for themselves.

MAKES ABOUT 1½ POUNDS

1½ to 2 pounds pork trimmings

½ cup reserved rub from the Philly Roast Pork Grinder (page 208)

Honey Sriracha Mayo (page 285), to serve

1. Preheat oil to 350°F.

2. Chop the trimmings into roughly uniform pieces, about ½ to ¾ inch long.

3. Toss the pork with the rub, coating it generously.

4. Fry the coated pork for 5 to 6 minutes, until deep red and crispy.

5. Remove to a towel-lined plate, let cool 2 minutes, and serve with Sriracha Mayo.

BEER PAIRING: AMERICAN IPA

FRY LIKE A SCOTSMAN

The Texas State Fair gets all the credit for freakish deep-fried creations (bubblegum, cola, your hopes and dreams), but Scotland is renowned for its love affair with fried food of extremely questionable nutritional value. Here's how to batter and fry the food of your dreams.

This is your all-purpose "Should I really be frying this? Yes, I should. It's for science" batter. You may notice it's basically pancakes without the last step. You need something hardy to close around your food and protect it from the ravages of the fryer. You need something soft and sweet to complement, but not overpower, your ingredients. Is there anything you can't do, pancakes? We love you.

4 eggs, separated

2 cups all-purpose flour

½ teaspoon baking powder

¼ teaspoon salt

1½ cups whole milk, divided

½ cup butter, melted

Oil, for frying

1. Whip the egg whites and set aside.

2. Stir the flour, baking powder, and salt together. Whisk in 1 cup of the milk, the melted butter, and the egg yolks. Beat it until it's as uniform and yielding as a post-apocalyptic dystopian society. Whisk in the rest of the milk.

3. Fold in the egg whites until combined. It's time to dip.

4. Get your oil to 375°F. Remind yourself one more time to be really careful. It would be a shame to lose a body part over stunt-gluttony.

5. Coat your foods generously in the batter and lower into the oil. Don't just drop it in, as you might either splash hot oil or inadvertently dunk the food so hard it hits the bottom of the fryer and glues itself there.

6. Turn your food regularly for 2 to 3 minutes. Given the irregular shapes and delicate coating, a pair of disposable wooden chopsticks work *extremely* well to turn the food.

7. After 5 minutes, your batter should be crispy and golden brown. Remove, drain excess oil on a rack or a towel-lined plate, and you're ready to feed some extremely hungry people.

WHAT CAN YOU FRY NOW? SO MANY THINGS:

Oreos. (Or Hydrox. Do they still make Hydrox? You know that Hydrox came first? Fun fact.)

Snickers or Mars bars. Depending on your general feelings vis-à-vis nuts.

Twinkies. KING OF THE CRAP FOOD!

NOT Kit Kats. We found out the hard way that they just kind of stiffen up and the wafers harden. Live and learn.

FRIED GREEN TOMATOES
(THE FOOD, NOT THE LIFE-AFFIRMING MOVIE)

This is the perfect change of pace for that time of year when everyone's late-summer harvest is making you re-think your relationship with seasonal fruits and vegetables. When you absolutely can't stand another locally-sourced salad buoyed on the quality and freshness of its ingredients, it's time to make some junk food and dunk it in bacon spread.

This is a great "but I don't have a fryer!" recipe, because it works perfectly in a cast iron pan with a half-inch of oil.

5 green tomatoes, sliced ½ inch thick

Sea salt, to taste

Black pepper

3 eggs, beaten

Vegetable oil, to fry

All-purpose flour, to dredge

2 cups panko, to dredge

Honey Sriracha Mayo (page 285), to serve

Bacon Jam (page 282), to serve

Diced heirloom tomatoes, to serve

1. Season the tomatoes on both sides with salt and pepper.

2. Beat the eggs with ¼ cup water to make an egg wash.

3. Heat your oil to 350°F.

4. Dip the tomatoes in the flour, then the egg, then the panko, shaking off the excess between each station.

5. Drop tomato slices carefully into the oil and fry 1½ minutes each, in batches. Remove to a rack or towel-lined plate.

6. Serve hot with sriracha mayo, bacon jam, and diced tomatoes.

BEER PAIRING: PALE ALE

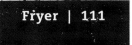

FRIED PICKLES

Another Southern dish recently made good, fried pickles are on absolutely every menu. Look down—you might be eating some right now and not even know it.

MAKES 4 PORTIONS

½ cup unbleached all-purpose flour

½ cup yellow cornmeal

1 teaspoon baking powder

½ teaspoon salt

¼ teaspoon baking soda

1 egg, beaten

1 cup buttermilk, plus more if needed

16-ounce jar dill pickles, drained

Peanut oil, to fry

1. Mix the flour, cornmeal, baking powder, salt, and baking soda. Heat your oil to 350°F.

2. In a separate bowl, mix the egg and buttermilk.

3. Stir the wet ingredients into the dry to form a smooth batter. Add more buttermilk if necessary.

4. Pat the pickles dry and dredge in the cornstarch.

5. Dip the pickles in the batter and gently lower into the fryer.

6. Fry 3 to 4 minutes, until golden brown. Remove to a paper towel, newspaper, or paper bag to drain, then serve immediately.

BEER PAIRING: AMERICAN IPA

FRIED CHEESE CURDS

Wisconsin, to us, is three things:

1. Delicious cheese and craft beer

2. A whole bunch of lakes to go enjoy those two things near

3. Football teams we'd rather not mention

Cheese curds, for those of you not familiar with dairy country, are unseasoned cheddar curds made from adding rennet to fresh pasteurized milk. They're a lot like cheddar, with a firmer (they squeak!) texture. Battering and frying them is the surest way to fall in love with them forever.

MAKES 4 SERVINGS

1 cup unbleached, all-purpose flour, plus more to dredge

1 teaspoon baking powder

½ teaspoon salt

¼ teaspoon baking soda

1 cup soda water (or beer, if you want to use it)

1 egg, beaten

1 tablespoon hot sauce

½ pound fresh cheddar cheese curds

Peanut oil to fry

1. Mix the flour, baking powder, salt, and baking soda.

2. Whisk soda water, egg, and hot sauce together.

3. Heat your oil to 350°F.

4. Dredge your curds in the flour, shake off excess, then dip into the batter to coat.

5. Fry the curds in batches until golden brown, about 2 minutes, and remove with a wire skimmer to a paper towel, newspaper, or paper bag.

6. Serve immediately.

BEER PAIRING: AMERICAN PALE ALE

POTATO CHIPS

Trust us, this is another cheap and ubiquitous dish that you'll really be surprised by when you make it at home. Nothing like warm chips straight out of the fryer. If you can waffle-cut them, preferably with a mandoline, you'll get more crunch with less cooking. If not, then just roll with the thinnest slices you can manage—⅛ inch or smaller. Please don't cut yourself.

Once you've got your technique down, you can make all your favorite chips—vinegar powder is readily available online for you Salt and Vinegar chip people, dried fish and shellfish for shrimp cracker fans, or just dump every single spice in and try for Zapp's Voodoo flavor.

MAKES 4 SERVINGS

2 russet potatoes, peeled and sliced exceptionally thin, then placed into a bowl of cold water

Peanut oil, to fry

Kosher salt, to season

Freshly ground black pepper, to season

1. Let your potato slices soak for 30 minutes. Heat oil to 350°F.

2. Remove some potato slices from the bowl and shake off excess water.

3. Fry the slices in batches, agitating frequently, for 2 to 3 minutes, until golden brown.

4. Remove and season immediately. Repeat with remaining slices, keeping an eye on the oil temperature and adjusting if necessary. Keep seasoning the chips straight out of the fryer.

5. Toss the batches of chips together to distribute the seasoning and textures evenly, then serve.

BEER PAIRING: AMERICAN PALE ALE

WHITE TABLECLOTH BBQ CHIPS
(AND LAMB!)
RECIPE BY MATT DANKO

Raw lamb and potato chips? Damn straight raw lamb and potato chips. Matt Danko runs a phenomenal seafood restaurant in Chicago, and we asked him to give us his cheffy interpretation of street food flavors. This is great on both a tiny porcelain plate in your dining room or in a paper boat on your front porch.

MAKES 6 SERVINGS

1½ pounds of lamb loin with fat cap intact

¼ pound butter

½ pound of fingerling potatoes, sliced thin into a bowl of cold water

Peanut oil, to fry

Kosher salt, to taste

Black pepper, to taste

2 tablespoons grape-seed oil

1½-ounce package dried shrimp, ground and passed through a mesh strainer

1 medium turnip, diced into ⅛-inch cubes

Chili flake, to taste

1. Remove the fat from the lamb loin and set aside. Cut ¼-inch medallions from the loin, stacking them 4 to 5 pieces high as you go. When you've sliced the entire loin, cut the medallions into ¼-inch strips, turn them 90 degrees, and cut them crosswise. Should give you a coarsely chopped ground meat texture. Was this a complex way to tell you to cube it? Maybe, but now you know exactly how we do it.

2. Place the lamb into a bowl and cover the surface of the lamb directly with plastic wrap. Then place a second piece over the mouth of the bowl and refrigerate. We're all about preventing oxidation.

3. Cube the fat you saved from the loin and place it into a medium saucepan. Add the butter and 2 tablespoons of water and cook over medium heat 3 to 5 minutes, until it becomes clear and you can see the bottom of your pot easily. Strain through a coffee filter into a bowl or jar, cover, and reserve somewhere warm where it won't solidify while you finish the recipe.

4. Preheat oil to 300°F. Remove the chips from the water and pat dry.

5. Fry the chips in batches 1 to 2 minutes, until the chips are golden brown. Remove from the oil and season immediately with salt and pepper. (Optional: if you've got a cold smoker, use it on the chips for 2 minutes per side to get a great smoky taste. Smoked sea salt also works.)

6. Remove the lamb from the refrigerator and mix with the salt, pepper, grape-seed oil, diced turnips, and chili. Stir gently to combine.

7. Brush some of the reserved lamb fat onto warm plates and divide the lamb tartare on top. Garnish with the ground shrimp, chili flakes, and serve.

BEER PAIRING: OYSTER STOUT

GREAT LAKES FISH FRY
(FANCY VERSION)

RECIPE BY MATT DANKO

Around the Great Lakes, summer is a time when everyone gets together, rounds up some super-fresh, super-delicate whitefish, and boils or fries it for Friday night community gatherings. You load up a paper plate, crack a beer, and maybe pass on the sketchy-looking macaroni salad. Eat until the sun's gone and you're getting eaten alive by mosquitos, and go home to do it all again tomorrow until eventually it's winter and you have everything.

We've given this proud tradition the fancy treatment, because why not? ManBQue's lucky to have guys around to provide contrast to our natural "let's dump chili in a chip bag" inclinations.

MAKES 8 SERVINGS

2½ pounds skinless whitefish filets

1¼ cups (about 5.3 ounces) all-purpose flour

4 teaspoons kosher salt, divided

2 large eggs, plus 4 egg yolks

1 cup unsalted butter

Peanut oil, to fry

1 cup plain yogurt

2 tablespoons lemon juice

1 teaspoon Spanish paprika

½ teaspoon smoked cinnamon

¼ teaspoon garlic powder

1 tablespoon ground coriander

½ teaspoon cumin

⅛ teaspoon saffron

Lemon zest, to garnish

Pickled lemon verbena, to serve

1. Grind the fish in a food processor until the texture is uniformly smooth.

2. Add 1¼ cups of water to a small saucepan and bring to a boil. Add the flour and stir until you've got a smooth paste, then remove from the pot and let cool on a small sheet pan.

3. Once the flour mixture has cooled, add it to the fish puree in the food processor and pulse until the mix is once again smooth. Add 2 teaspoons salt, eggs, butter, and yolks, and grind until homogenous. If your eggs look like they're cooking, you skipped the flour-cooling step. Didn't you? DIDN'T YOU?

4. Coat a sheet pan with flour. Place the batter in a piping bag with a #9 tip, or into a large zip-top bag and cut yourself a corner hole that resembles 1¹⁄₁₆ inches as much as possible. Pipe into 2-inch links down the length of your tray and set in the fridge for 30 to 45 minutes to chill. The time generally depends on how much crap you have in your fridge. Maybe get rid of that hard lemonade because you're not a sorority girl during rush week.

5. Bring a large pot of salted water to a simmer and lower your links into the pot. The batter will sink, then rise to the surface. After it rises, give it 1 minute to cook, then remove to a towel-lined plate to dry.

6. Return the links to the fridge and let them chill completely. You can wrap and freeze any extra for future fish fries at this point.

7. Heat oil fryer to 350°F. Meanwhile, mix the yogurt with the lemon juice, paprika, cinnamon, and garlic powder. Set aside. Then mix the remaining 2 teaspoons salt with the coriander, cumin, and saffron.

8. Fry the links for 2 minutes, agitating frequently, until golden brown. Remove and seaon with coriander spice mixture.

9. Serve with yogurt and verbena, garnish with lemon zest, and serve.

BEER PAIRING: BIERE DE GORDE

WOK

People have been making masterful food in woks since well before the dynastic ages of China. We've been doing it for . . . (checks watch) . . . like eight years. But it's going really well!

Remember everything we've told you about buying other pieces of kitchen equipment? How you should look for sturdy, solidly built pieces? This is literally the opposite of all that. Your wok should be made of thin, heat-reactive metal (aluminum or carbon steel), have some texture on the inside to hold pieces of food in place, and be light enough for you to move on and off the heat or swing at an intruder like a flaming cudgel of justice. Cast iron woks, stainless steel woks, and woks with delicate Teflon coating are all pretty useless in our opinion. Might as well adapt to one of your many other pans and make the best of it.

As a side note, one fun trick we've discovered is lighting a chimney starter half-full of charcoal and using that as an outdoor wok burner. That's how you get the serious heat that authentic places use on their food. Even better: If you can use a cutting tool to create an access vent in a non-galvanized metal bucket, you've got a mobile wok station ready to go.

BACON LIME FRIED RICE

RECIPE BY LUKE GELMAN

This dish has almost everything people love unconditionally (eggs, bacon, rice) in it. At your next party, it's time to blow a few minds with your wok skills. Or you can make it for yourself and ignore your friends, which may have happened once or twice in our development process.

MAKES 2½ CUPS

5 strips bacon, cut into ½-inch lardons

2 eggs

¼ cup corn kernels, frozen

2 cups cooked white rice

5 tablespoons soy sauce

3 tablespoons lime juice

3 tablespoons chopped cilantro

1. Cook your bacon in a wok over medium heat until the fat is rendered and the pieces begin to crisp. When they're done, push them up to hang out on the side of your wok.

2. Drop your eggs into the bacon grease and scramble in the pan, stirring until mostly cooked.

3. Drop your frozen corn in the pan as well and cook for another 30 seconds.

4. Drop the rice into the pan, add the soy sauce and lime juice, and mix. Let the rice cook until the bottom starts to get a little crispy. Toss once more and remove from the heat.

5. Dump the bacon lime fried rice into a bowl and sprinkle the cilantro over the top. Finally, your friends will truly love you. Sure, it's conditional, but do you care?

BEER PAIRING: FARMHOUSE ALE

HONG SHAO ROU

This is a traditional Chinese comfort food cooked with pork belly braised in soy, sugar, and Shaoxing wine. This recipe takes some time, but it's not difficult and it's even better late at night. The great thing about this dish is it's always left us craving it the next morning, which has made us cook it again and again. It'll be a perfect comfort food for your household.

MAKES 2 SERVINGS

2 inches ginger, peeled, divided

4 green onions, 2 chopped, 2 sliced

1½ pounds pork belly, cut into 1 inch cubes

1 tablespoon oil

2 tablespoons dark brown sugar

¼ cup dark soy sauce

¼ cup Shaoxing wine

1 cinnamon stick

2 pods star anise

1. Bring 3 cups water to a boil, cut ginger in half lengthwise, and add half the ginger and 1 sliced green onion. Add belly and cook for 4 minutes, then remove and set aside. Drain wok and wipe dry.

2. Thinly slice the other half of the ginger and heat the oil in wok to medium heat. Cook the ginger for 30 seconds, then add the pork belly and brown, tossing often, for 3 minutes.

3. Add the sugar, soy, and wine over meat and cook for 5 minutes.

4. Add 2½ cups of water, cinnamon stick, one sliced onion, and star anise. Cover and simmer for 45 minutes.

5. Uncover, remove the cinnamon, star anise, sliced onion, and any large chunks of ginger. Increase the heat to high to reduce liquid to 3 tablespoons, stirring frequently. It will take about 30 minutes.

6. Garnish with remaining green onion. Serve in a bowl or on a steamed bun.

BEER PAIRING: CHINESE LAGER

PORK BELLY GYOZA

MAKES 36 DUMPLINGS

1 pound pork belly, cubed to 1 inch

1½ teaspoons kosher salt

¼ pound bacon, diced

1 large egg, beaten

2 tablespoons chicken stock (or pork stock if you've got some)

2 teaspoons sake

2 teaspoons rice vinegar

2 teaspoons soy sauce

½ teaspoon sugar

16 scallions, sliced thin

Gyoza wrappers

Vegetable oil, to pan-fry

1. Spread pork out on a baking sheet, and place in the freezer for 25 minutes.

2. Toss pork with salt and grind using a coarse die. Toss the ground pork with the bacon, egg, stock, sake, vinegar, soy sauce, and sugar. Grind a second time, then stir in sliced scallions.

3. Fill the dumpling wrappers with 1 teaspoon of the pork mix. Moisten the edges, fold over, and crimp.

4. One optional step is to steam the dumplings for 5 minutes. It's not required, but steaming and then frying creates an awesome contrast between the slippery/chewy inner dumpling skin and the crisp/oiled outer skin. Give it a shot if you've got the time. You can even steam the dumplings ahead of time, refrigerate them, and finish them in the oil.

5. Coat your wok with vegetable oil and heat over medium-high. Cook the dumplings for 90 seconds per side, until browned and crispy on the outside.

BEER PAIRING: JAPANESE WHEAT ALE

HOT DOG GYOZA!

You may not have known this, but if you met any of us for longer than a minute, you'd know we were two-time Hot Dog Champions of Chicago. Our coronation came both times at a charity event set up by a local news site and judged by local food critics, food historians, and encased meat legend Doug Sohn. Real restaurants and formally trained chefs compete in this, which leads us to believe we got holy-shit-lucky twice in a row.

This recipe is from that second time, when we decided to juke the competition and bring a Japanese street food flair to the proceedings. We opened up the casings of our charity-assigned hot dogs, scooped out the delicious cured meat, and used it as a base for some Chicago-style gyoza. Mike Sula of the *Chicago Reader*, a respected writer with a master's in junk food, later told us he was impressed that it tasted exactly like it had been dragged through the garden. We had succeeded in making hot dogs the slightly-more-difficult way. SUCESS!

It's hard to believe, but we were not high in the slightest when we thought this up. We promise.

MAKES 24 DUMPLINGS

¼ pound bacon, diced

4 all-beef hot dogs (about ½ pound), casings removed

½ cup white onion, diced

¼ cup neon green pickle relish

2 tomatoes, fire-roasted (on the stovetop or under the broiler) and diced

24 gyoza wrappers

2 tablespoons peanut oil

Hot mustard, to serve

Celery salt, to serve

Sport peppers, to serve

1. Grind or process the bacon and the hot dog meat. Mix with the white onion, relish, and diced tomatoes.

2. Place 1 teaspoon of the hot dog mixture into the center of a gyoza wrapper, fold over, and crimp the edges. Repeat with remaining meat and wrappers.

3. Steam the dumplings in batches for 4 minutes, then remove and set aside.

4. Heat a wok over high heat and swirl with peanut oil. Pan-fry the dumplings in batches 2 minutes apiece, until crisp and slightly browned.

5. Serve drizzled with hot mustard, sprinkled with celery salt with peppers on top.

BEER PAIRING: BROWN ALE

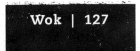

STRIP MALL PAD THAI

In the past couple of years, some really talented cooks have done well to bring the regional variations and unique textures of authentic Thai food to a wider audience. They're taking people past the unusually numbered dishes and select-a-size levels of spice to something new and exciting. We, on the other hand, are nowhere near as talented. So let's whip up some delicious Pad Thai that you'd be happy to eat while you wait for the dry cleaner next door to find your sweater. Remember, kids: "inauthentic" isn't a synonym for "bad" if you're doing it right.

MAKES 4 SERVINGS

¼ cup dark brown sugar

¼ cup white sugar

¼ cup tamarind pulp

½ cup fish sauce

½ cup Thai chili paste

1 tablespoon vegetable oil, plus 1 tablespoon

1 pound skinless chicken thighs, sliced into ½-inch strips

2 shallots, sliced

1 egg, beaten

6 ounces rice noodles

1 cup bean sprouts

¼ cup chopped toasted peanuts

2 teaspoons Thai basil, sliced thin

1 lime, cut into wedges

1. Mix the brown sugar, sugar, tamarind, fish sauce, and chili paste. Set aside.

2. Heat 1 tablespoon of oil over medium-high heat. Season the chicken thighs and cook 2 to 3 minutes, until browned slightly. Remove to a plate and wipe out wok.

3. Heat the remaining vegetable oil over medium heat in your wok, then sauté the shallots and cook 3 minutes, until soft.

4. Pour the egg into the pan and begin to scramble. As it comes together, return the heat to high and add the noodles and sugar/fish sauce mixture, tossing to coat.

5. Add the chicken, tossing to coat.

6. When the noodles begin to color slightly, fold in the bean sprouts and cook another minute.

7. Remove from heat and garnish with peanuts and Thai basil. Serve with lime wedges, preferably in a cool waxed paper container with some disposable chopsticks.

BEER PAIRING: HELLES BOCK

FIRE

FIRE

We fucking love cooking over fire. We wrote an entire book about it, even. But there's more than just the grill out there. The bane of Zeus has adapted to cooking situations everywhere, from pimento wood pits in Jamaica to late-night binchō-tan-burning grills in Sapporo. What kind of vessel should you use to bring flame to meat? Well, it happens we've created an entire flow chart to guide your decision. Enjoy!

HOW TO COOK ACTUAL, NO-BULLSHIT KOBE OR WAGYU BEEF

Much has been written on the subject of "authentic" Kobe beef vs. sorta-Kobe Wagyu beef. Much less has been written about how to cook it. Which is unfortunate, because it's the kind of really expensive ingredient that you'd be pretty mad to ruin on your first few tries. Fortunately, it's incredibly easy and forgiving. Go sell some plasma, buy the most marbled beef at the Japanese market, and get ready to make something delicious.

MAKES 4 APPETIZER PORTIONS

8 ounces heavily marbled Kobe or Wagyu beef

1 teaspoon peanut oil

Large-grained sea salt

Black pepper

2 tablespoons soy sauce

1 teaspoon mirin

½ teaspoon rice vinegar

1. Pat the steak dry and rub with peanut oil. Then, you salt. You salt that steak like you've never salted before. Not like you're packing it for an overseas voyage via sailing ship, but do make it look like it's been snowed upon. Add the pepper to your taste.

2. Place the steak on a rack and let it chill in the fridge for 45 minutes.

3. While the salt does its work on the steak, start a full load of coals (hardwood charcoal, if you have it) in the grill of your choosing. Open the vents all the way and get it hot enough to peel the paint off of a car. When the coals are caught and on their merry way, lay a cast-iron griddle or pan right on top of the coals.

4. Stir together the soy sauce, mirin, and rice vinegar. The meatheads among us cry out, "You don't need sauce for steak," and we cry back, "But it's nice to cut the richness sometimes."

5. It's time. Your reticence is the only thing that stands between you and the richest beef you've ever eaten. Don't worry—you've got this. Lay your precious cargo directly onto the hottest part of your coal-fired cast iron. Let it sit, but don't go anywhere. Flip it after 90 seconds.

6. Check the temperature after another 90 seconds. This is going to sound sacrilegious, but you're going to want to wait until the internal temperature is at 150 to 155°F to take it off. When a piece of beef is this well-marbled, cooking it to rare or medium-rare just cheats you out of delicious melted beef fat.

7. Remove the steak and let rest for 5 minutes. Slice it thin against the grain and serve with your sauce poured into shallow, tiny dishes. Luxuriate in it. Seriously, you've going to love this.

BEER PAIRING: BELGIAN BLONDE ALE

BACON S'MORES

RECIPE BY LUKE GELMAN

This one takes a little practice but you figure it out quickly. It is messy, salty, and terrible for you—in short, all the best things in life.

MAKES 6 BACON S'MORES

24 strips regular-cut bacon

12 graham crackers

12 marshmallows, cut in half

12 squares chocolate

1. To make each s'more, line a ceramic plate with two sheets of paper towel, then lay out four pieces of bacon in the shape of a plus sign, as follows:

- One laid down on the paper towel, vertically

- One laid horizontally across the middle

- Repeat, laying one horizontal slice next to the first piece, then one vertical against the other piece

- If you did this right, you'll have a 3 x 3 woven bacon grid

2. Lay three sheets of paper towel on the top, and weigh down with a second plate.

3. Microwave the bacon for 2 minutes to par-cook it. Don't cook it fully, or your marshmallows won't melt. Don't under cook, or it will become a greasy mess. Luckily, it's easy to hit that middle ground.

4. Carefully remove the bacon, pat dry, and let cool while you repeat the above steps. You'll get a lot faster as you go.

5. Assemble the s'mores—place a graham cracker square in the middle, then 2 pieces of marshmallow. Add 2 squares of chocolate, then the last graham cracker. Gently smoosh (why no, we didn't go to culinary school) the s'more together without breaking the graham cracker. Fold up the sides of the bacon from the bottom over the sides and tip and secure with a tooth pick. Again, you'll get faster as you go.

6. Find a kick-ass live fire, or just get a grill going. Using a grilling basket, tongs, or even a grill fork, cook the s'more for two minutes per flat side and 20 seconds per seam side—until the bacon is *juuuust* crisp around the sides.

7. Sing camp songs. Anything by Hall and Oates should do.

BEER PAIRING: ENGLISH BARLEYWINE

BALIK EKMEK

We know, you're wondering what the cool Turkish name for this dish is all about— it actually translates to "fish and bread." Sometimes a name tells you all you need to know about a dish. It's just a simple sandwich that complements the taste of fresh fish cooked quickly over fire. Give it a few years, and someone will slap an "artisan" on this Istanbul classic and have the stones to put "Market Price" next to it. Until then, let's just enjoy it.

MAKES 4 FISH SANDWICHES

1 cup mayonnaise

¼ teaspoon garlic powder

1 teaspoon ground sumac

4 6-ounce filets of cod, haddock, or another whitefish

2 tablespoons olive oil

2 teaspoons kosher salt, plus more to taste

1 teaspoon black pepper

4 soft French bread rolls, sliced

1 cup shredded romaine lettuce

Parsley, to garnish

Juice of 2 lemons

2 Roma tomatoes, thinly sliced

½ red onion, thinly sliced

1. Heat your grill to medium, and definitely remember to clean and oil the grates. Whitefish can be unforgiving.

2. Mix the mayonnaise, garlic powder, and sumac. Taste and adjust seasoning with salt. Set aside.

3. Brush the filets lightly with olive oil and season with the salt and black pepper.

4. Grill the filets until they go just over halfway opaque and flip carefully. A fish spatula helps a lot here. Cursing helps not at all, but it does make you feel better if something goes wrong. And if it does, you're putting it in a sandwich with toppings, not serving it to the President on a plate. Relax.

5. Remove the filets and let them rest a minute or two while you prepare the rolls.

6. Spread the mayo mixture on both sides of the bread and place lettuce on the bottom of the rolls.

7. Lay the fish into the split rolls and top with parsley, a spritz of the lemon juice, then the tomatoes and onions. There you have it—fish and bread (and other things).

BEER PAIRING: AMERICAN WILD ALE

BALTIMORE PIT BEEF

RECIPE BY STEVE MUHLBAIER

The native barbecue style of Baltimore isn't something that a Texan, Tennessean, or North Carolinian would recognize. It's a hotter, faster cooking process. It's most often a charcoal fire. And rather than the fall-apart meat of the Southern states, Baltimore pit beef is only cooked to rare or light medium rare. It inspires devotion—on HBO's *The Wire*, a guy going up for several murders he didn't commit "confesses" in full in exchange for a pit beef with extra horseradish.

Let the purists turn their noses up all they want—we'll be over here, eating pit beefs until we are wheeze-breathing like latter-day Marlon Brando.

MAKES 12 SANDWICHES

½ cup chopped fresh garlic

½ cup kosher salt

¼ cup fresh cracked black pepper

¼ cup Montreal steak seasoning

¼ cup Dijon mustard

4 pounds bottom round roast

12 white buns

2 white onions, sliced thin

Prepared horseradish, to serve

1. Mix the garlic, salt, pepper, Montreal steak seasoning, and Dijon mustard together and rub it generously all over the meat. Let it sit overnight.

2. Set up grill for indirect cooking, with a water pan on the cool side. Sear the meat on all sides over direct heat for 2 minutes per side, then move it over the water pan to begin indirect cooking.

3. Cook for about 1 hour, or until the internal temperature reaches 130°F. You may have to factor in more time—the larger the cut of beef the longer it will take.

4. Remove the meat and let it rest for 15 minutes. Slice it against the grain as thinly as possible and serve on a roll with thinly sliced white onion and horseradish.

BEER PAIRING: AMERICAN PORTER

CHICKEN SATAY

RECIPE BY STEVE MUHLBAIER

Thanks to this Malay classic, the phrase "street food" conjures up the image of meats on sticks, eaten standing up. It's just a simple sauce, some really humble slices of meat, and maybe a little garnish, but it's something you end up dreaming about nine years and an entire hemisphere later.

MAKES ABOUT 36 SKEWERS

5 pounds boneless chicken thighs, cut into
   1-inch strips

2 cups soy sauce

2 cups sweet chili sauce

1 cup lime juice

½ cup sambal oelek

¼ cup Sriracha sauce

2 tablespoons grated fresh ginger

2 stalks lemongrass, split length wise and cut
   into quarters

1 tablespoon sesame oil

½ cup chopped green onion

1. If you're using wooden skewers, soak them for at least 2 hours, then thread the chicken onto the skewers.

2. Add the soy sauce, sweet chili sauce, lime juice, sambal, Sriracha, ginger, lemongrass, and sesame oil to a saucepan over medium-high and bring to a boil. Remove from heat and let stand for 45 minutes before placing in the refrigerator to cool.

3. Divide sauce—pour half of it over the chicken skewers in a container or zip-top bag and let marinate overnight. Reserve the other half for basting.

4. Preheat your grill for medium-high direct heat cooking.

5. Grill the chicken 3 to 4 minutes on each side, making sure to move the skewers to a cooler part of the grill if the sauce begins to burn. Baste chicken with remaining half of your sauce throughout cooking process.

6. Remove the skewers from the grill as they finish and garnish with green onion.

BEER PAIRING: BROWN ALE

CHICKEN TIKKA KEBABS

RECIPE BY STEVE MUHLBAIER

MAKES ABOUT 24 KEBABS

3 pounds chicken breast, cubed to 1 inch

2 pounds red onion, chopped

2 pounds tomatoes, chopped

5 poblano peppers, chopped

4 tablespoon garam masala

2 tablespoons hot paprika

1 tablespoon ground coriander

2 tablespoons kosher salt

1 tablespoon crushed red chili flake

1 teaspoon turmeric

4 cups plain yogurt

½ cup cilantro chopped

Warm naan bread, to serve

1. If you're using wooden skewers, soak them in water for at least 2 hours. Then thread the chicken, onion, tomato, and peppers through the skewers.

2. Stir together the remaining ingredients, except chopped cilantro, in a mixing bowl. Place the kebabs in a snug container or carefully in a large zip-top bag. Pour the liquid over and let marinate overnight.

3. Preheat your grill to medium-high. Grill kebabs until the chicken and veggies get a nice char and the chicken reaches 160°F.

4. Remove kebabs and garnish with cilantro. Serve on naan.

BEER PAIRING: RYE IPA

BUFFALO CHICKEN SAUSAGE

Are Buffalo wings not convenient enough for you? Sure, they're mobile, but having to deal with bones is such a pain! (Black and white infomercial showing wing incompetency.)

One of the first recipes conceived with our first sausage stuffer was a Buffalo chicken recipe. Since we were new to the sausage-making world, we added ingredients that shouldn't go in sausage and used collagen casings. It was terrible, but the idea was there, dammit! Top the greatly improved version with our Blue Cheese Ale Sauce (page 284) and you may never eat Buffalo wings again.

MAKES 8 SAUSAGES

6 pounds chicken, deboned and meat cut into 1 inch cubes (keep 2 tablespoons fat and 2 tablespoons skin)

½ tablespoon smoked paprika

2 teaspoons salt

1 teaspoon pepper

2 cups Buffalo sauce (page 103)

Pork casing, soaked

8 high-quality brat rolls

Blue Cheese Ale Sauce (page 284)

1. After deboning chicken, place chicken on a baking sheet and rub with paprika, salt, and pepper. Then place in the freezer for 45 minutes.

2. Using a coarse setting, grind the chicken into a bowl. (Tip: Place a larger container with ice underneath the bowl to keep everything cold.)

3. Mix Buffalo sauce into the ground chicken.

4. Prepare sausage stuffer and make some fucking sausage.

5. Age sausage uncovered in the refrigerator for 24 hours. Dry and flip the sausages periodically.

6. We recommend simmering the sausage in a beer bath for 8 minutes and then brown them on the grill. Let them cool a few minutes before putting onto the bun and topping with Blue Cheese Sauce.

BEER PAIRING: IPA

WING-BAK: CHICKEN WARRIOR

MAKES ABOUT 36 WINGS

4 cloves garlic, chopped

2 tablespoons fresh ginger, minced

½ cup lime juice

½ cup kosher salt

1 cup vegetable oil

½ cup water, hot

¼ cup Sriracha sauce

½ cup sambal oelek

3 tablespoons fresh ginger, grated

1 cup soy sauce

2 cups peanut butter

4 cups hoisin sauce

2 cups roasted peanuts, chopped

5 pounds chicken wings, cut into flats and drumettes

½ cup cilantro, chopped, for garnish

¼ cup toasted white sesame seeds, for garnish

1. Mix the garlic, ginger, lime juice, salt, and vegetable oil, and pour over the chicken wings in a container or zip-top bag. Let the wings marinate for 4 hours.

2. Add the water, Sriracha, sambal, ginger, and soy sauce to a saucepan and bring to a boil. Remove from heat, add the peanut butter, and mix until smooth.

3. Add the hoisin sauce and chopped peanuts to the sauce.

4. Set up grill for direct heat cooking. Grill the wings, turning frequently, until the skin is crispy and the meat is cooked to an internal tempature of 160°F, about 10 to 12 minutes.

5. Remove, toss with the sauce, and let rest for 5 minutes. Garnish with the cilantro and sesame seeds.

BEER PAIRING: BELGIAN PALE ALE

KUNG PORK

RECIPE BY LUKE GELMAN

You can theoretically Kung Pao anything. The term itself is just descriptive of the Szechuan seasoning style, and it translates to the super-badass phrase "palace guardian" if you're wondering. We chose to Kung some delicious ground pork. We are pleased at the result, and it has become the new guardian of our refrigerator palaces.

MAKES ABOUT 12 SAUSAGES OF FURY

FOR THE SAUSAGES:

5 pounds ground pork

2 tablespoons soy sauce

1 tablespoon sesame oil

1 tablespoon sugar

½ cup super-chunky peanut butter

2 tablespoons crushed red pepper

1 tablespoon minced ginger

1½ tablespoons minced garlic

6 feet rinsed and prepared hog casings

TO SERVE:

1 head Napa cabbage, shredded

2 medium carrots, grated

2 bell peppers, julienned

1 jalapeño, stemmed and sliced thin, core removed

½ cup rice wine vinegar

1 tablespoon tamari soy sauce

1 tablespoon fresh ginger, grated

1 teaspoon lime juice

¼ teaspoon lime zest

½ teaspoon crushed red pepper (optional)

¼ cup super-chunky peanut butter

12 brat or sub rolls

1. Combine all of the sausage ingredients in a large mixing bowl. Mix lightly until evenly distributed. Place the mix into your freezer for about 1½ hours, until the meat is firm, but not frozen.

2. Pass the meat through the grinder using a coarse grind plate.

3. Stuff the ground mixture into your casings, using a standalone stuffer, mixer attachment, or a small rural village full of determined matrons.

4. To make the slaw, toss the cabbage, carrot, bell pepper, and jalapeño together.

5. Mix the rice vinegar, sesame oil, tamari, ginger, lime juice, lime zest, red pepper, and remaining ¼ cup of the chunky peanut butter. Whisk together until thoroughly mixed. If you're not a fan of chunky peanut texture (you monster), use a food processor. Toss with the slaw and set aside.

6. If you're preparing the sausages ahead of time or you'd like to hedge the risk of your casings splitting, gently poach in simmering water or beer until they reach 145°F, then remove and let cool. Otherwise, move on to the next step.

7. Preheat fire to medium-high. Grill the sausages over direct heat for 4 to 5 minutes, until the interior reaches 160°F. Remove, let rest for 5 minutes, and serve on the buns with the slaw.

BEER PAIRING: BELGIAN GOLDEN ALE

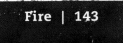

BEEF ENDS

Here in Chicago, we have a lot of places that use gigantic aquarium smokers to turn lowly, unloved, cartilage-filled rib tips into something addictive. A rib tip is an off cut typically discarded when the butcher is cutting country-style spare ribs. Rib tips are hard to find anywhere else. We adapted this recipe a bit so you can experience the simple joy of a well-made rib tip and readily available short ribs.

MAKES 4 POUNDS OF BURNT-END FAUX-RIB TIPS

Yellow mustard, to slather

4 pounds boneless beef short rib

2 cups of our BBQ rub (page 298), plus 2 tablespoons

1½ cups apple juice

¼ cup olive oil

MB(B)Q Sauce (page 273), to serve

1. A day or so before you'd like to cook, slather a thin layer of yellow mustard all over the short ribs. Really get it all over. Don't worry if you don't like mustard—a big part of its function is as glue for the rub. Generously sprinkle your rub all over the meat and put everything into a zip-top bag, then place the bag into your freezer. Trust us, it adds flavor down the line.

2. Preheat some coals, a grill, or a smoker to a relatively cool 225°F. Add a couple of handfuls of hickory, cherrywood, and/or pecan chips. Really, whatever hardwood you've got around.

3. Remove meat from the bag and add another generous layer of rub to the meat. Add enough so that the exterior still appears a bit dry, rather than a paste.

4. Place the meat over the fire while it's still cold. This will help with the smoke absorption.

5. Mix the apple juice, olive oil, and 2 tablespoons of rub in a spray bottle.

6. Give your meat a quick spritz after 1 hour. Give it another quick spritz after another hour and flip your meat over.

7. Once your meat has a nice mahogany bark to it, wrap it in aluminum foil and place it back in the smoker.

8. When your meat hits about 195°F, pull it from the smoker, remove the foil, and apply your favorite BBQ sauce.

9. Return to the fire and let the sugars in the sauce caramelize for 15 minutes.

10. Remove the meat, re-apply MB(B)Q sauce, and rest for 15 minutes.

11. Slice the short ribs and serve.

BEER PAIRING: CREAM ALE

BEEF JERKY

Thanks to national advertising and our insatiable hunger for meat, you're never more than four miles from a serving of beef jerky. People eat it for workout protein, long-haul trucking, and in loving memory of Macho Man Randy Savage (R.I.P.). It's too bad that most of what's out there is pretty awful—glopped with nauseatingly sweet sauce, made of what appears to be low-grade mummy flesh, or packaged with something they call cheese (but once opened, turns its gaze to you and the tells you the exact date of your death).

Here is how you make some delicious beef jerky over a fire: thin slices, a bold marinade, and plenty of time. Crack a beer, then drink it in front of the eleven other beers so they know what's coming. Settle in: It's fucking jerky time! (Fires revolvers into the air, buys Kenny Chesney tickets online.)

MAKES 2 ZIP-TOP BAGS FULL OF JERKY

2 pounds beef loin, trimmed

1 ounce curing salt

⅛ teaspoon liquid smoke

1 teaspoon crushed red pepper

½ teaspoon black pepper

1. Slice the loin, with the grain, into ⅛-inch strips.

2. Sprinkle the curing salt evenly between the slices, place on a rack over a foil-lined pan, and refrigerate for 5 days.

3. Remove, lightly brush with the liquid smoke, and season with the red and black pepper.

4. See how low your oven goes. Set it to that, unless you're lucky enough to have a dehydrator, in which case, follow the dehydrator's instructions. You can also fire up the smoker if you can manage to keep it around 140°F.

5. Use a spoon or foil ball to keep the oven door slightly ajar and let the meat sit on wire rack or screens for 6 hours. Check for firmness (it should be very firm, but if it snaps in two easily, it's over-dried), and set the clock for another hour if it's not ready. Depending on your meat, this can take up to half a day or longer.

6. Store in plastic bags for up to a month, or wrap tightly and freeze. Say a prayer for the Macho Man.

BEER PAIRING: ENGLISH PORTER

ELOTE WINGS

RECIPE BY PATRICK MCBRIDE

What's more American than a chef with an Irish last name making a Mexican specialty into a sauce for chicken wings? Eagles and monster trucks, presumably. But you can't eat those without getting into a whole bunch of shit with the Forestry Department.

MAKES 32 WINGS

12 ounces Mojo Criollo marinade

1 bunch cilantro, cut above the twist tie

4 cloves garlic

3 pounds wings, separated into flats and drumettes (tips discarded)

3 packets Sazon con Azafran

1 12-ounce package frozen sweet corn kernels (look for gold and white mix)

1 cup heavy cream

1 cup Cotija cheese

1 cup mayonayse

Salt and pepper, to taste

Tajin or chili powder, to taste

1. Combine the Mojo Criollo, cilantro, and garlic in a blender and liquefy.

2. Throw wings in a bowl and toss with the Sazon con Azafran until evenly covered and bright orange. Pour in marinade, cover, and refrigerate overnight.

3. For the sauce, heat the corn, then puree with cream, Cotija, and mayo.

4. Preheat grill medium direct heat.

5. Grill chicken 5 to 8 minutes, toss in sauce, sprinkle with salt and pepper, and extra Cotija and Tajin, and with chili powder.

BEER PAIRING: HELLES LAGER

BUTCHER'S HOT LINKS

If you've ever had the fortune to live by a good butcher who makes their own sausage, you know the joy of showing up to shop when they're sampling the newest freshly ground recipe. It's good to have a Meat Guy. Even in this era of chain groceries and insufferable hipster butchers, there are still honest-to-god Meat Guys doing fine work from Oregon to Georgia. This is our tribute to the house sausages produced by that noble, porky guild.

MAKES 1 LARGE, GLORIOUS HOT LINK, OR 16 REGULAR ONES

5 pounds ground pork

1 tablespoon minced garlic

1½ tablespoons cayenne pepper

2 teaspoons white pepper

1 tablespoon mace

1 tablespoon sage

23 grams salt (about 4 teaspoons, but more accurately 1% of total meat weight)

6 inch rinsed prepared hog casings

1. Combine the ingredients in a large mixing bowl. Mix lightly until everything is evenly distributed.

2. Place the mix into your freezer for about 1½ hours until the meat is firm, but not frozen.

3. Grind the meat through a coarse grind plate.

4. Stuff the sausage, pinching and twisting to create anything from one glorious spiral of meat heaven to 16 sausages that come in at just under a third of pound.

5. If you're cooking ahead, poach the sausages in beer or water until a thermometer inserted into the center reaches 160°F. Remove and let cook before you.

6. Grill over medium-high for 3 to 5 minutes, until well seared on either side.

7. Serve it by itself, in its own glorious bratwurst-y goodness. Bratwurst? More like bratBEST. Aw yeah.

BEER PAIRING: BOCK

IZAKAYA CHICKEN PIECES

Ever try to drink ten pints of light Japanese lager and sing a gender-swapped version of "I'm Real" with your best lady friend? It's hard work. You need the fortifying power of bar snacks to sustain you for another round of karaoke stardom. Quick, before the weird guy asks for Radiohead's "Creep" and fucks up the entire night!

MAKES 8 SKEWERS

1 pound assorted chicken pieces (thighs, legs, breasts)

¼ cup salt

¼ cup sugar

¼ cup tamari

2 tablespoons white miso

1 teaspoon mirin

½ teaspoon crushed red pepper flake

2 green onions, sliced thin

Toasted sesame seeds, to serve

1. Cut chicken into 1-inch cubes and thread onto soaked wood or metal skewers

2. Dissolve the salt and sugar in 1 quart of water. Add chicken pieces, cover, and refrigerate for 20 to 30 minutes.

3. Stir the tamari, miso, mirin, and red pepper together.

4. Prepare a medium heat fire. Remove your skewers from the brine and pat dry.

5. Grill your chicken skewers 6 to 8 minutes, until each piece registers 160°F. Brush with the sauce and return to the grill for 30 seconds per side, reapplying the sauce as needed.

6. Remove, garnish with green onions and sesame seeds, and serve immediately.

BEER PAIRING: PILSNER

GERMAN DÖNER

Germans know their beer, and as a result, they know drunk food better than most of the world. Even among all the beer-enhanced late night dishes in a country of enthusiastic drinkers, the döner is tops in Deutschland. After stumbling through the Bavarian village of Amberg, loudly mangling the lyrics to "Ein Prosit," we discovered that they do in fact go great with three liters of beer.

Döners are typically cooked on a vertical rotisserie, which are too pricey for the average cook. So we adapted to a typical kitchen scenario, because we're also not yet freewheeling millionaires. You'll need about 40 inches of butcher's twine for this, which is an awesome and macho thing to buy, as far as string goes. It's like the opposite of yarn.

MAKES 6 DÖNERS

2 chicken breasts (about 1½ pounds)

4 garlic cloves, minced

2½ tablespoons extra virgin olive oil, divided

¼ cup whole milk

2 tablespoons tomato paste

1½ teaspoons chopped fresh oregano, plus ½ teaspoon

1 tablespoon chopped thyme, plus ½ tablespoon

½ tablespoon yellow curry, plus ½ tablespoon

¼ teaspoon kosher salt, plus ½ teaspoon

¼ teaspoon black pepper, plus ½ teaspoon

½ teaspoon dried red pepper flakes

2 thinly-cut veal cutlets (about ½ pound)

Dill Tzatziki (page 295), to serve

6 pitas

1 head lettuce, shredded

2 tomatoes, cut into wedges

1 head red cabbage, shredded

1 white onion, sliced thin

Dill

RECIPE
CONTINUES

1. Place the chicken cutlets on cutting board and cover with plastic. Pound to ¼-inch thickness using the flat side of a meat mallet, a rolling pin, or an ironically-wielded hardcover vegan cookbook.

2. Place the meat in a snug-fitting container. Mix the garlic, olive oil, milk, tomato paste, oregano, thyme, curry, salt, pepper, and red pepper flakes in a medium bowl. Pour the liquid over the meat, cover, and refrigerate for at least 4 hours, turning occasionally.

3. Combine the remainder of the olive oil, oregano, thyme, curry, salt, and pepper in a small bowl.

4. Lay four 5-inch lengths of butcher's string on a cutting board. Place chicken breast over them and cover with half of the olive oil mixture from the bowl. Top with the veal, roll it up carefully, and tie the strings. Repeat with second chicken breast.

5. Set up two-zone fire, with a hot side and a cooler side. Grill the roll, browning over direct heat and moving to the cooler side until cooked to 165.

6. Let the meat rest for 5 minutes, then slice thinly into ½-inch strips.

7. Spread tzatziki on the pita, and top with the meat, lettuce, cabbage, tomato, and onion.

BEER PAIRING: KRISTALWEIZEN

TANDOORI CHICKEN WINGS

3 pounds chicken wings, cut into flats and drumettes

½ cup plain yogurt

2 tablespoons fresh lemon juice

1 tablespoon minced garlic

1 tablespoon powdered ginger root

1 tablespoon ground cumin

2 teaspoon garam masala (or 1 teaspoon ground coriander)

½ teaspoon chili powder

¼ teaspoon ground cardamom

¼ teaspoon ground cloves

¼ teaspoon fresh-ground black pepper

2 teaspoons salt

Vegetable oil, to brush

1. Using a fork, generously poke the chicken wings. Using sharp knife, make small cuts all around the chicken so the marinade can penetrate. Set aside.

2. In a medium bowl, combine the yogurt, lemon juice, garlic, ginger, cumin, garam masala or coriander, chili powder, cardamom, cloves, black pepper, and salt. Mix well and add your chicken wings.

3. Coat the chicken evenly and rub the marinade into the chicken flesh. Cover and refrigerate for at least 4 hours, and no more than 30.

4. Remove wings from the marinade, shaking off excess.

5. Oil your grill, prepare a medium fire, and grill your wings for 15 minutes, turning frequently.

6. Remove and serve.

BEER PAIRING: DUNKEL BOCK

BRATS FOR ALL!

And that's because baths are perfect for days when you have a crowd coming over but you're not sure when they're coming. You can rage at your friends and their flakiness, or you can let these brats ride over indirect heat for an afternoon so people can eat when they want. The flakier your friends are, the more delicious the onions lurking in the bottom of the bath will get.

We use this recipe to dispose of the crappy light-struck green bottles of skunky beer in the back of the fridge that someone brought so they could drink your local brew conscience-free.

MAKES 12 BRATWURSTS

4 tablespoons olive oil

5 yellow onions, halved and sliced

4 tablespoon Dijon mustard

½ teaspoon salt

1 teaspoon pepper

12 bratwurst

6 beers from that Island of Misfit Beers in the back of your fridge

12 sliced deli rolls

Bavarian Sweet Mustard (page 282), to serve

1. Preheat a two-zone fire.

2. Position the foil pan over the hottest part of the fire. Heat the olive oil and sauté onions for 4 minutes.

3. Add the Dijon mustard, salt, and pepper to the onions, toss, and brown for 2 minutes.

4. Rest the brats on the onions and pour the beer over.

5. Bring to simmer, move to the cooler side, and simmer slowly until the brats hit 145°F.

6. As your guests are ready, take the brats out of the bath and sear them over direct heat for 2 minutes per side.

7. Serve on deli rolls with sweet mustard and top with beer-bathed onions.

BEER PAIRING: PILSNER

CHINATOWN WINGS

Visiting Michelin-starred places is nice, but we tend to take inspiration from the everyday food that lives in the cardboard leftover boxes in our fridges. Take these wings, for instance—inspired by these Hunan cumin-crusted short ribs known as *ziran paigu*. The marinade goes great on a lot of non-wing proteins, so give it a shot on whatever member of the food chain you've got in the fridge.

MAKES ABOUT 32 WINGS

2 green onions, sliced down the center

5 slices of ginger, peeled

1 teaspoon anise seed

¼ cup soy sauce

¼ cup dry sherry

1¾ teaspoons salt, divided

2 cups water

3 pounds chicken wings, cut into flats and drumettes

½ cup butter

6 cloves garlic, minced

½ cup brown sugar

½ teaspoon ground white pepper

1 tablespoon grated ginger

2 tablespoons cumin seeds, coarsely ground/crushed

3 Thai red chili peppers, diced

3 scallions, sliced thin, to garnish

1. Combine the green onion, ginger slices, anise seed, soy sauce, sherry, 1 teaspoon of the salt, and water. Pour over the wings and let marinate for at least 4 hours.

2. Prepare your fire and oil the cooking surface.

3. Melt the butter in a small saucepan over medium-low heat. Sauté the garlic in the butter for 2 minutes, then add the brown sugar, white pepper, grated ginger, cumin, chili pepper, and remaining salt. Stir until the brown sugar is melted and remove from heat.

4. Cook the wings for 5 to 7 minutes per side, until they are cooked through and skin is crisp.

5. Toss the wings with sauce, then garnish with scallions.

BEER PAIRING: AMERICAN BROWN ALE

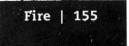

CURRY WEISSWURST

European culinary tradition is a funny thing—you can put a currywurst on a roll, stir curry into some ketchup, and absolutely drench the whole works, but actually marrying curry to veal sausage is somehow an offense to tradition. But we've never been big on tradition. Sometimes bastardizing traditional recipe leads to great flavors.

MAKES 12 6-INCH SAUSAGES

1¼ pounds pork shoulder, cubed

1¾ pounds veal chuck, cubed

½ pound pork back fat, diced

2 teaspoons ground white pepper

1 tablespoon curry

1 tablespoon paprika

3 tablespoons kosher salt

½ teaspoon ground mace

¾ cup nonfat milk powder

Natural pork casings, soaked

1. Lay the meat on a sheet pan in a single layer and put into the freezer for 30 minutes, until the meat is firm but not frozen through.

2. Toss the meats and fat together, attach the fine disk, and grind together into a chilled metal bowl placed over ice water.

3. Mix in the spices and milk powder, and grind a second time. Mix again and grind a third time.

4. Put the casings on the funnel feeder and stuff the sausages, twisting into 6-inch links.

5. Simmer or steam the sausages until they reach an internal temperature of 145°F to parcook. Finish immediately or refrigerate.

6. Grill or griddle for 2 minutes per side to finish, then serve with a pretzel roll and sweet Bavarian Sweet Mustard (page 282).

BEER PAIRING: WHEAT BEER

HARISSA LAMB LOLLIPOPS WITH MINTED YOGURT SAUCE

RECIPE BY JASON GILMORE

MAKES 7 TO 8 LOLLIPOPS

1 rack of lamb, cut into lollipops (one bone and a piece of meat)

1 cup Harissa (page 286)

5 ounces Greek yogurt

1 tablespoon lemon juice

1 tablespoon lemon zest

1 tablespoon chopped mint leaves

Salt and pepper, to taste

1. Spread the harissa on the lamb lollipops and marinate for 4 to 24 hours.

2. In a smal bowl, mix yogurt, lemon juice, zest, and mint leaves together. Cover and chill.

3. Prehead grill for medium direct heat.

4. Remove lamb lollipops from the harissa and grill until meat reaches an internal temperature of 145°F.

5. Remove to a wire rack and cool for 3 minutes and serve with minted yogurt sauce.

BEER PAIRING: BLACK IPA

HULI-HULI CHICKEN

Remember the carbonized hot dogs and charred meat-pucks of your youth? What if the church picnics, the Little League banquets, and the Rotary fundraisers of your youth featured tangy, fragrant char-grilled chicken busting with juice? It's reason 1,409,382 that the Hawaiians have a leg up on the rest of us.

It's not that Hawaiian dads are any better at putting meat to fire, but the soy-forward marinade brines the chicken and the fresh citrus (seriously, use fresh stuff) puts it over the top. Great street food doesn't have to be complicated, or secret. Just do it right once and start building your own mystique as a chicken whisperer.

MAKES 1 ENTIRE (8 PIECES) OF CHICKEN

½ cup tamari soy sauce, plus ½ cup

¼ cup white wine

2 tablespoons yellow mustard, plus 2 tablespoons

1 tablespoon sesame oil

6 thin slices ginger root

1 cup crushed fresh pineapple and juices

1 chicken, cut into pieces (breasts, tenders, legs, wings)

¼ cup ketchup

¼ cup honey

Juice of 1 lemon

1. Mix ½ cup tamari, white wine, 2 tablespoons yellow mustard, sesame oil, ginger root, and crushed pineapple.

2. Pour the marinade over the chicken in a snug, nonreactive container. Let marinate for 2 to 4 hours, turning frequently.

3. Prepare a two-zone fire (one hot side directly over the heat, one side with no fire underneath).

4. Strain the pineapple from the marinade, reserve, and discard the marinade.

5. Start your sauce by mixing the remaining ½ cup tamari, ketchup, honey, lemon juice, and reserved pineapple. Bring to a boil and reduce to a simmer while your fire heats up. Stir frequently and let reduce 5 to 10 minutes, until thickened.

6. Grill the chicken, skin-side up, for 10 minutes, turning frequently, until a thermometer inserted into the thickest part reaches 150°F. The wings will finish first, and the legs last. Take care not to overcook and dry out the breast, which is the cut most vulnerable to the heat.

7. As they reach temperature, flip the chicken pieces skin-side down nearer the heat. Brush the top (non-skin side) of the chicken pieces with the sauce and let cook for 60 to 90 seconds, until seared but not charred.

8. Flip the skin back onto the cooler side and brush the skin side with the sauce. Cover and let cook 30 to 45 more seconds, then remove to a platter. Serve with rice, fruit, and a whole lot of beer.

BEER PAIRING: HEFEWEIZEN

PINEAPPLE BOATS

You'll have to take our word for it, but please believe that we went to a lot of different cities and tried the best, most authentic version of everything to find the best dishes for this book. That being said, one of the things we really fell in love with along the way was this method of cooking and serving—a straight-up 1950s tourist dish they still serve at the Kona Hilton to this day. We added a little savory to it, but if you're serving a bunch of Brady Bunch Goes Hawaiian re-enactors in your home (WHY?!), this will hit it out of the park.

MAKES 8

2 pineapples, quartered through the core

8 tablespoons butter

¾ cup white wine

¼ cup tamari

1. Starting at the bottom (non-leaf) edge of each pineapple quarter, cut horizontally beneath the core to separate from the flesh. Don't sever the core at the top (leaf side) - it's going to keep the top of your pineapple from drying out.

2. Cut the flesh underneath the core vertically every half inch, cutting to (but not through) the husk. Everything should still be attached when you're done.

3. Melt the butter is small saucepan and stir in the white wine and tamari. Keep warm.

4. Preheat a fire two-zone fire (like, say, your Huli Huli fire).

5. Wrap the pineapple leaves in aluminum foil to keep them from catching fire.

6. Grill the pineapple over indirect heat for 10 minutes, basting twice with the sauce.

7. If the edges of the pineapple haven't begun to caramelize, move directly over the heat. If they have, then stay the course. Baste again and cook another 5 minutes.

8. Remove from the heat, carefully take off the foil, and hold covered in a warm oven until it's time to serve.

BEER PAIRING: AMERICAN IPA

FIG AND PIG SANDWICH

RECIPE BY JASON GILMORE

Roulade. Go ahead and say it out loud: roo-lawd. Sure does sound fancy, but you've probably cooked one before. It means meat that's been filled and rolled. In this case, capicola and figs. This roulade makes a great sandwich, and even a better one when a barrel-aged beer is used in place of the porter for the glaze.

MAKES 6 SANDWICHES

15 dried figs

4 ounces balsamic vinegar

12 ounces porter

1 tablespoon dark chili powder, divided

3 ounces maple syrup

4 ounces hot capicola

1 pork loin

Porter Beer Mustard (page 294)

3 cups baby arugula

6 hoagie rolls

1. Halve and stem the figs and cover with Balsamic vinegar. Allow to soak 12 to 24 hours.

2. Remove figs from the vinegar and mash into a paste. (Save the vinegar, it's good!)

3. In a small saucepan, bring the porter and half of the chili powder to a boil. Reduce heat and simmer until the beer has reduced by about half. Add the maple syrup and season with salt and pepper. Remove from head and keep warm

4. Butterfly and pound the pork loin into a ¼-inch thick rectangle. It should be around 7 inches wide.

5. Place a layer of hot capicola on what will be the inside of the roulade.

6. Cover the Capicola with the fig paste and season the inside of the roulade with half of the chili powder.

7. Roll the pork loin back up and tie it with butcher's string.

8. Place the loin over hot coals and sear 2 to 3 minutes per side. Once the pork is seared, move it to a cooler part of the grill and baste it with the porter maple glaze. Continue basting every five minutes until the internal temperature of the loin reaches 145°F.

9. Remove from the grill and let rest for 10 minutes.

10. Cut off the string and slice thin. Place onto hoagie roll, with arugula and mustard.

BEER PAIRING: ALTBIER

HARISSA BUTTER GRILLED OYSTERS

RECIPE BY JASON GILMORE

MAKES 24 OYSTERS

1 stick of butter, at room temperature

¼ cup Harissa (page 286)

2 tablespoons butter

1 cup panko bread crumbs

2 dozen oysters

2 lemons, cut into wedges

1. Mix butter and ¼ cup of harissa.

2. Roll the compound butter into a log in parchment paper and return to the refrigerator to re-harden.

3. Meanwhile, melt the 2 tablespoons butter in a pan and add the panko breadcrumbs. Toast until golden brown.

4. Shuck oysters and leave them in the half shell.

5. Place the oysters over medium direct heat on the grill, toping them with a pat of the harissa butter. When the liquid in the oysters begins to bubble, they are heated through.

6. Remove from grill. Top the oysters with the toasted breadcrumbs and serve with lemon wedges.

BEER PAIRING: RAUCHBIER

SMOKED PORCHETTA

They say it takes a village to raise a child. Now imagine if that child was a pork loin wrapped in a pork belly and smoked for hours. We grabbed our pig-lovingest friends and came together to create a big fat park roll smoked with a mixture of applewood and hickory. We're so proud of our little piggy.

MAKES 1 PORCHETTA

3 tablespoons fennel seeds

1 teaspoon juniper berries

1 teaspoon whole coriander

2 tablespoons crushed red pepper flakes

2 tablespoons sage leaves, minced

1 tablespoon fresh rosemary, minced

1 tablespoon fresh oregano, minced

3 cloves garlic, crushed

⅓ cup extra-virgin olive oil

1 2 to 3 pound center-cut pork loin, excess fat trimmed

1 5 to 6 pound skin-on pork belly

1. Toast the fennel seeds, juniper, coriander, and red pepper over medium heat in a dry skillet until fragrant, about 2 minutes. Remove from heat and let cool, then fine grind.

2. Add the fresh herbs to the ground spices and grind again. Then add garlic cloves and grind. Finally, add the olive oil and mix into a paste.

3. Place the loin over the belly and trim so that the meats are roughly uniform in size, with the belly slightly longer.

4. Lay the pork belly skin-side down and score a grid ¼ inch deep on flesh side of the belly. Flip it over and poke a dozen holes or so in the skin. Tenderize skin with the pyramid side of a meat tenderizer, making three passes over the skin.

5. Rub the spice paste on the inside of the belly and loin. Roll it up carefully from the shorter sides of the meat. Truss the roll with butcher's string, wrapping the string around the meat at every 1½ inch interval.

5. Place the porchetta in your refrigerator, uncovered, for 24 hours. Take the meat out of the refrigerator 2 hours before smoking.

6. Preheat your smoker to 225°F.

7. Smoke at 225°F until internal temperature reaches 150°F, which will take anywhere from 5 to 7 hours, depending on the size and fat distribution of your meat. When the temperature hits 145°F, preheat grill to medium-high direct heat.

8. Time to crisp up the skin. Take the pork from the smoker and place it onto the grill. Grill, slowly rotating as the skin turns dark brown and crispy, for about 10 minutes.

9. Remove and let rest for 30 minutes.

10. *You did it, man!* Double pig meat! All your enemies will rue the day they crossed you! Maybe make a delicious Pigwich (page 269) out of it? That'll show them. That'll show ALL OF THEM.

BEER PAIRING: WEIZENBOCK

SMOKED PORCHETTA CONSTRUCTION

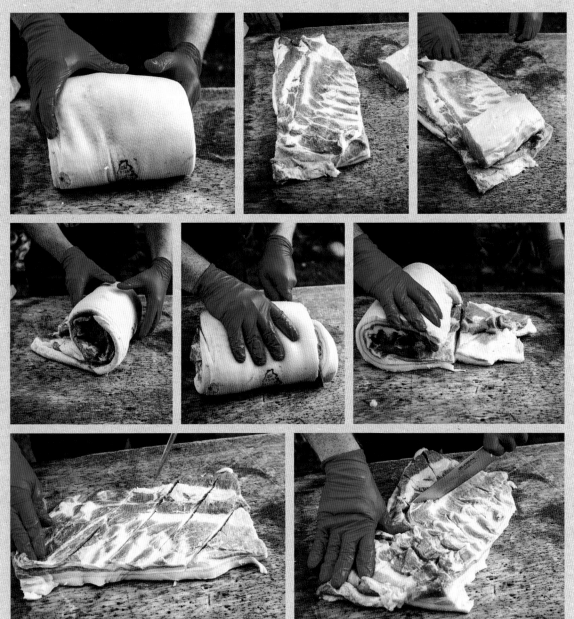

VOLTRON: THE SANDWICH

RECIPE BY GERRY MCLOUGHLIN

We took the best things we liked from banh mi (pickled vegetables), tortas (bolillo rolls), and churrasco (skewered meat) to create this ultimate sandwich that fights for justice and freedom. In space.

MAKES 4 SANDWICHES

1 cucumber, peeled and sliced thin

2 jalapeños, sliced thin

1 medium red onion, sliced thin

1 cup rice vinegar

1 cup sugar

1 cup water

¾ cup olive oil

1 tablespoon cilantro, chopped

1 tablespoon flat leaf parsley, chopped

1 garlic clove, chopped

1 lime, juiced

½ tablespoon dried chipotle powder

½ tablespoon paprika

½ tablespoon brown sugar

½ tablespoon cumin

1 teaspoon kosher salt

1 teaspoon ground black pepper

¼ teaspoon onion powder

⅛ teaspoon cayenne powder

2 pounds steak tenderloin, cut into 1 inch-wide strips

4 bolillo rolls, split

2 tablespoons fresh cilantro leaves

1. Place the cucumber, jalapeños, and red onion in a heat-proof container.

2. Mix the rice vinegar, sugar, and water in a saucepan over medium heat. Bring to a boil, stirring frequently, until the sugar dissolves. Remove from heat, pour over vegetables, and cover for at least 20 minutes. Cover and refrigerate.

3. Combine the olive oil, lime juice, chopped cilantro, garlic, and parsley. Pour over steak and let marinate for at least 2 hours, preferably overnight.

5. Mix the dry ingredients, remove steak from the marinade and rub with seasoning. If you're using wood skewers, soak them in water for at least 20 minutes, because…you know, wood and fire. Either way, skewer and pre-heat your grill for medium direct heat.

6. Grill the skewers for 3½ minutes per side.

7. On bolillo bread pile up the steak, top with pickled vegetables, and garnish with cilantro.

BEER PAIRING: AMERICAN PALE ALE

HA HA HA HA HA
YOU LOSE IDIOTS WINGS

Ever attend a barbecue competition? They're a whole lot of fun, but they do attract the odd obsessive weirdo. And sometimes those people make fun of the fact that you showed up with two tiny cheap smokers and a staggering amount of beer. And then you drink too much, leave the wings on the pit, and arise just in time to beat all of them with these wings. That's a mostly true story!

Anyway, if and when that happens to you, the important part is to be gracious and act like you've been there before. Hence the title of this recipe. As you'll note from this, barbecue judges like sweet.

MAKES ABOUT 32 WINGS

3 pound chickens cut into flats and drumettes

2 cups black pepper

¾ cup kosher salt

¼ cup seasoned salt (Lawry's, Tiger, etc. Your pick.)

½ cup sugar

¼ cup dark brown sugar (plus ½ cup)

¼ cup granulated garlic

¼ cup granulated onion

¼ cup smoked sweet Hungarian paprika

8 tablespoons butter

1 cup brown sugar

1½ cups MB(B)Q Sauce (page 273)

Peanut oil, to brush

1. Mix the pepper, salts, sugars, garlic, onion, and paprika in a bowl and shake to combine.

2. Coat wings in the spice rub and let them sit overnight.

3. Awaken, open a beer, and get your smoker to a reliable 225°F.

4. Add the wings and a pan of ice (for humidity, so the wings take on more smoke), and smoke for about 90 minutes, until they're just about at 165°F.

5. Heat a separate grill for direct heat. Scrape and oil the grates. Prepare for grate-ness, if you will.

6. Mix the butter, brown sugar, and barbecue sauce in a medium saucepan.

7. Rub the wings with the peanut oil and grill over direct heat for 90 seconds to 2 minutes, until the skin is crisp.

8. Remove the wings, toss with a quarter cup of the sauce, adding more until you've reached your happy level of sauce saturation. Pack into a Styrofoam box and send it out into the world. You're so proud of your little champions. Hopefully you saved enough for yourself.

BEER PAIRING: IPA

GRILLED FISH TACOS

RECIPE BY ED KOWALKI

Wanna know what's a huge bummer? Bad fish tacos. More often than not, it's a couple fried fish sticks thrown into a soggy flour tortilla and topped with lettuce and some kind of salsa. By the time it gets to your table, condensation and/or fryer oil have rendered the tortilla totally inedible, and you have to eat the damned things with a fork. A *fork!* No more. Today we reclaim the art form.

MAKES 8 TACOS

1 pound white flaky fish like mahi mahi, tilapia, or wahoo

¼ cup canola oil

Juice and zest of 1 lime

1 tablespoon ancho chile powder

1 jalapeño pepper, coarsely chopped

¼ cup fresh cilantro leaves

8 6-inch flour tortillas, warmed

Grilled Fruit and Sweet Corn Salsa (page 296)

1 head radicchio, shredded

Sour cream, to garnish

1 large red onion, thinly sliced, to garnish

Green onions, thinly sliced on a bias, to garnish

Cilantro leaves, roughly chopped, to garnish

1. Place the fish in a medium-sized bowl. Whisk together the oil, lime juice and zest, chili powder, jalapeño, and cilantro and pour over the fish. Marinate for 15 to 20 minutes.

2. Set up a grill for direct, medium-high heat. Clean and oil the grate.

3. Remove fish from marinade and place on grill. Grill for approximately 4 minutes, then flip and grill for 30 seconds. Remove from heat and let rest for 5 minutes, then flake fish with a fork.

4. Divide fish among the warmed tortillas and top with salsa, radicchio, sour cream, onions, and cilantro.

BEER PAIRING: PILSNER

OVEN

Every budding cook who obsesses over the latest hot chefs and restaurants—and, god forbid, self-applies the title "Chef" to their Twitter account despite working in insurance and blogging on the side—wants to cook with hot, sexy techniques. Sear this steak! Char that tuna! Liquid nitrogen these meatballs because I watch too much YouTube and I don't know what the fuck I'm doing! Meanwhile, you'll just be sitting here making incredible food with your old reliable oven.

The bad news is that ovens don't look good on TV, and oven recipes don't really do anything on TV. Jon Taffer and Gordon Ramsey can't call an oven stupid and make it cry. So it's left behind the food TV tidal wave for the rest of us to figure out.

The good news is that with a minimum of prep, a few neat tricks, and the time to wait out the result, you can make a week's worth of delicious food while mostly sitting on your ass being unproductive. Since meat proteins stop denaturing after 222°F, the oven gives you the advantage of sitting right on that sweet spot and cooking some of the most tender, most delicious meat of your life without having to figure out the vagaries of a smoker's hot and cool spots or do guesswork on feeding in the fuel. That said, these times and temperatures also translate for hardwood smoking, if you're so inclined. We might even call you a hero.

If you're looking for an oven, go for something electric. Gas has to cycle on and off to hit a target temperature, while electric ovens keep a steadier temperature. If you find yourself falling in love with the control and timing of oven cooking, you're just a short walk from the *sous-vide* obsession that we're are currently struggling with. All great passions begin with delicious meats.

BACON
(JUST REGULAR-ASS BACON)

This is an incredibly stupid recipe. The reason we put it in here, though, is that we're not yet convinced that every human being with the capability to read English knows of the bacon-in-the-oven technique yet. It's good to have on hand for recipes that assume you have perfectly-cooked bacon.

One day soon, you'll be talking to a food-minded friend of yours, and you'll say, "I can't believe these assholes wrote and published a recipe that's just putting bacon in the oven at 400°F for 15 minutes to get perfectly crisp bacon and beautifully rendered fat." And at that moment, you'll realize we did it on purpose to help you learn. And you'll shed a single tear, create the Edward James Olmos *Stand and Deliver* Award for Rad Teaching, and present the inaugural award to us.

1. Preheat oven to 400°F.

2. Line half sheet baking pan with parchment paper and lay 8 slices of bacon, evenly spaced apart. Bake until crispy, around 15 minutes. Set aside.

3. Stand (at the table) and deliver (bacon).

BEER PAIRING: AMERICAN IPA

CANDIED BACON

Candied bacon had a moment in the sun a few years back, but it seems like people got kind of pissed that they kept burning it in search of crispy *and* sweet bacon. That's just the problem—you can't really have both. The sugars and the bacon fat kind of work against each other.

Instead, double down on the fatty, porky taste complementing your sweet, smokey spice rub. Grab thicker-cut bacon, drown it in rub, and take it out of the oven just as it achieves perfect chewy, sweet porkiness. Our favorite honky tonk in Chicago (incidentally named *Honky Tonk*) treats it like this and lays it over the top of a cheap, cold glass of beer. No one's ever gotten pissed at that.

MAKES 1 POUND OF DELIGHTFUL BACON TREATS

1 cup dark brown sugar

1 teaspoon mustard powder

1 teaspoon smoked sweet paprika

½ teaspoon cayenne pepper

1 pound thick-sliced bacon, cut in half

1. Preheat oven to 350°F.

2. Mix the brown sugar, mustard, paprika, and cayenne.

3. Dredge the bacon in the spice rub, set on a wire rack over a foil-lined pan, and bake for 10 minutes. Remove from the oven, flip, and bake an additional 10 to 15 minutes. Remove and serve hot.

BEER PAIRING: AMERICAN BARLEYWINE

CUBAN MOJO PORK

This is a great "week's worth of sandwiches" recipe from a reasonably cheap cut of meat. Use it on our Cubano (page 28), Medianoche (page 30), and anything else suffering from a lack of pork.

A caveat about the pork—if it's from a reputable butcher, cooking it to 145°F (instead of the long-held 165°F) is a completely reasonable thing to do. Even the FDA says so. But if this is cheap meat, err on the side of caution. And maybe find a new Meat Guy.

1 4-pound boneless pork loin

2 teaspoon smoked sweet Spanish paprika

Cuban Mojo Sauce (page 288), to marinate

1. Preheat oven to 400°F.

2. Slice halfway through the pork loin, opening it like a book. Repeat that on either side of the original slice, then again through the remaining ridges, until you've flattened out the pork.

3. Rub both sides with the paprika, then with the mojo sauce.

4. Lay the sliced loin flat over prepared lengths of butcher's twine, to truss, and distribute any loose garlic pieces over the top of the pork.

5. Roll the loin up tightly and tie off. Place on a rack over a foil-lined sheet pan.

6. Roast the pork for 1½ hours, until the internal temperature reaches 145°F. Remove and rest for 15 minutes.

7. Remove the string and slice or shave thin. Serve with black beans, rice, and plantains, or as part of a Cubano.

BEER PAIRING: DOPPLEBOCK

CHEESE-RICH OCEAN INLET BISCUITS

This is a recipe we've had for some time, forwarded to us by someone who likely stole it from one of those "Restaurant Secrets!" websites, who stole it from Darden Restaurants, who took it from the original beach seafood shack owners, who overthrew the sovereign government of Cheddar Bay to unearth the secrets in the first place. So much bloodshed and they just give them away. The horror.

MAKES ABOUT 12 BISCUITS

4 tablespoons frozen butter, grated, plus 4 tablespoon melted butter

2½ cups drop biscuit mix

1 cup grated sharp cheddar

½ teaspoon garlic powder

¾ cup cold whole milk

¼ teaspoon parsley

1. Preheat oven to 400°F.

2. Work the butter into the biscuit mix with your fingertips, until it's evenly distributed into pea-like clusters. Don't overwork and melt it with your hands.

3. Add the cheddar and garlic powder, then stir in the milk until just combined. Clumps are fine—these are not pretty biscuits.

4. Drop the biscuits onto a greased baking sheet a ¼ cup at a time, leaving space in between for the magic of baking. Otherwise you'll end up with an unsatisfying network of codependent biscuits.

5. Bake 15 minutes, then check on their progress. If you can do it without opening the oven, that's probably ideal.

6. If the biscuits are still pale, keep baking for another couple of minutes. If they look a fine tribute to maritime biscuitry, then take them out of the oven.

7. Brush the biscuits with the melted butter and season the biscuits immediately after with the parsley and garlic powder.

CORNISH PASTY

This dish is from Michigan by way of Cornwall—Cornish miners developed the dish in Wales and brought it over to the Looks Like a Mitten State during the Cornish Diaspora of the eighteenth and nineteenth centuries. Listen to us, dropping terms like "Cornish Diaspora" in a meat pie recipe. It's like an episode of *Frasier* in here.

You can make a whole bunch of these and easily reheat them. It's a great dish to take to work. Like, say, in a mine.

MAKES 4 PASTIES

1 russet potato, diced

1 large carrot, diced

1 medium yellow onion, diced

½ pound of ribeye, trimmed and cut into ½-inch cubes

2 teaspoons Worcestershire sauce

1 teaspoon Marmite (optional)

2 teaspoons kosher salt

1 teaspoon black pepper

4 8-inch rounds of puff pastry

1 egg, beaten with 1 tbsp of water

1. Preheat the oven to 400°F.

2. Place the potato, carrot, and onion in a medium saucepan, cover with water, and bring to a boil. Let cook 90 seconds, then drain and spread out to cool on a sheet pan.

3. In a large bowl, mix the cooled vegetables with the beef, Worcestershire, Marmite, salt, and pepper. Toss to evenly coat.

4. Divide the meat mixture evenly between the four pastry circles. Fold over, crimp the edges, and lay out on an oiled baking sheet.

5. Beat the egg with 1 tablespoon of water. Brush the pasties with egg wash and place in the oven for 15 minutes.

6. Lower the oven temperature to 350°F and bake for another 30 minutes. Remove, let cool, and serve immediately. Then hi ho, hi ho, it's back to work you go.

SESAME STEAK MANAPUA

Hawaii stands at the crossroads of a dozen-plus different culinary traditions. It's not all Spam, fish cakes, and poi, though there's nothing wrong with…like two of those. Manapua is a local take on the Chinese bao and can be either baked or steamed. We're making a soft, sweet milk bread version that will come out of your oven like the flourish of a really delicious magic trick.

MAKES 16 BUNS

½ cup sesame oil

2 tablespoons roasted sesame oil

⅔ cup soy sauce

½ cup sugar

10 garlic cloves, minced

1½-inch length of ginger, peeled and grated

1 teaspoon dried chili flakes

1½ pounds beef tenderloin, cut into 1-inch cubes

10 radishes, julienned

½ cup water

½ cup sugar

1 cup rice wine vinegar

8 green onions, charred (on a grill or over your stove burner) and sliced

¼ cup plucked cilantro

1 portion Hawaiian Milk Bread dough (Page 287)

2 eggs

2 tablespoons whole milk

1 tablespoon toasted sesame seeds

RECIPE CONTINUES

1. In a zip-top bag or other container large enough for the meat, combine the sesame oils, soy, sugar, garlic, ginger, and chili flakes. Pour over the meat and marinate for at least 4 hours.

2. Place the radishes in a heatproof container with a lid. Make the pickling liquid by mixing the water, sugar, and rice wine vinegar together in saucepan. Bring to a boil, stirring to dissolve salt and sugar. Remove from the heat, and pour over the radishes. Cover and let sit at room temperature for at least 4 hours.

3. Remove the meat, discard marinade, and grill 3 minutes per side, until rare.

4. Coarsely chop the cooked beef, green onions, and cilantro. Drain the radishes. It's almost time to stuff some buns.

5. Split the dough into 16 equal parts. If you don't have a scale because of some mistaken superstition that they'll steal your soul, then the easiest way to do this is to roll the dough into a ball, split it in half with a knife, then roll those halves into balls and split those in half. Then again, and again, until you're left with 16 dough balls roughly the same size.

6. Measure even portions of meat, green onions, cilantro, and radishes before you start rolling. This will make rolls uniform and ensures you won't run out of filling.

7. One by one, roll dough balls flat into 5-inch diameter circles and place filling in the center. Draw the dough around the filling and crimp closed at the top. Place crimped-side down on parchment-lined baking sheet. Repeat with the remaining buns.

8. Loosely cover the sheet with plastic wrap and let rise for 1 hour.

9. Preheat your oven to 400°F.

10. Make an egg wash by beating the eggs and milk. Uncover the buns brush with egg wash, and sprinkle with sesame seeds.

11. Place baking sheets in oven and immediately turn the temperature down to 350°F. Bake until golden brown, about 18 minutes.

12. Remove, let cool for 5 minutes, then see how many you can eat at once.

BEER PAIRING: SPICED BEER

YUCATAN PORK

RECIPE BY EFRAIN CUEVAS

With large, cheap cuts of meat, if it's worth cooking, it's usually worth cooking a lot of for use in everything from Tamales (page 227) to Steamed Bao (page 245). Our slow-cooked version of the Mexican *cochinita pibil* is the apex of this "let's cook a whole ton of this and eat for a week" philosophy. Try it in everything you make. We'd argue that even a milkshake would be improved by the presence of fragrant, savory pork.

If you look at this and wonder where in the hell you're supposed to find banana leaves or annatto seeds, they're both at the nearest Mexican grocery store, the leaves are in the freezer section. We already called for you, even. Both are sub-two-dollar ingredients, and both will last you a few times cooking this.

MAKES ABOUT 6 TO 7 POUNDS OF PORK

8-9 pound pork butt

½ cup freshly squeezed orange juice

¼ cup fresh lime juice

⅓ cup apple cider vinegar

10 cloves garlic, peeled

3 tablespoons ground annatto seed

2 tablespoons kosher salt

1 tablespoon dried oregano

2 teaspoons black pepper

1 package banana leaves, defrosted

1. Preheat your oven to 300°F.

2. Puree the orange juice, lime juice, vinegar, garlic, annatto, salt, oregano, and pepper in a blender.

3. Line the bottom of a large, deep roasting pan with a banana leaf. Lay another, larger one on top of that, with the ends sticking out from either end. Place one more large leaf perpendicular to the last one, with the criss-crossed leaves sticking out of both ends of the pan.

4. Drop the pork into the leaves, pour over the marinade, and fold over to encase.

5. Cover pan with foil and roast for 5 hours until fork tender.

BEER PAIRING: LAGER

BEEF ON WECK

Beef on Weck is one of those really simple recipes that's consistently delicious enough to get a cult-like regional following. We're always fascinated by these not-quite-famous city classics. Ever hear someone call a Buffalo Wild Wings "BW3"? It's because they started out as Buffalo Wild Wings & Weck. Sadly, the Weck proved less popular than sweet, face-scaldy chicken and watery Bud Light, so it was dropped.

The dish itself is a thin-sliced top round, served on a kummelweck roll with horseradish and dragged through the beef jus. A kummelweck is just a Kaiser roll studded with pretzel salt and caraway. The Buffalo bar owner who invented this was clearly trying to sell a lot of beer to some very thirsty people, and damn if it isn't great beer food.

Depending on the size and quality of your roast, you may or may not get quite the amount of jus you're going after. No worries – if you come up short at the end, just put the roaster on the stovetop and stir in some butter, white wine, and/or demi glace with the roast trimmings.

MAKES 12 SANDWICHES

3 pounds top round roast, trussed

2 tablespoons peanut oil

¼ cup kosher salt, plus more

3 tablespoons black pepper

2 tablespoons caraway seed

2 tablespoons pretzel salt (or the coarsest salt you can find)

1 tablespoon cornstarch

12 Kaiser rolls

Prepared horseradish, to serve

1. Preheat your oven to 325°F and brush the roast with the peanut oil. Cover generously with salt and pepper, truss for even cooking, and place on a rack over a foil-lined roasting pan.

2. Cook for 1½ hours (25 to 30 minutes per pound is a good rule. Check the internal temperature with a meat thermometer and remove from the oven at 130°F.

3. Remove the meat from the oven and let rest. Meanwhile, raise the oven temperature to 350°F.

4. Mix the caraway seeds and salt in a small bowl and set aside.

5. Bring a cup of water to a boil in a small saucepan. Mix the cornstarch with a tablespoon of water to create a slurry, then pour the slurry into the boiling water. Cook, stirring, for about 1 minute until it thickens and can coat a spoon.

6. Place the Kaiser rolls on a baking sheet and brush with the thickened cornstarch mixture. Sprinkle the tops of the rolls with the salt/caraway mixture and bake 3 to 5 minutes, until the cornstarch mixture dries and affixes the seasoning to the rolls.

7. Slice the beef thin and pour the pan drippings into a small bowl. If there isn't quite enough, mix with demi-glace and/or white wine in a small saucepan and bring to a brief simmer.

8. Split the kimmelweck rolls, drag the tops through the jus, and serve with horseradish.

BEER PAIRING: PORTER

BIG KAHUNA
PORK BELLY BURGERS

RECIPE BY KEN HAYNES

In asking after the origins of this dish, we were presented with a detailed series of footnotes on the recipe's development. Clearly, they were written by a madman. But if you believe everything you hear, then the recipe and dish is/was:

- Inspired by the etching found on a tablet in the burial chamber of a Pharaoh, at the foot of a statue glorifying a mischievous demi-god

- Banned in all but three NATO countries

- Able to unlock any door in the world

- Originally part of the first draft from the rebel barons responsible for the creation of the Magna Carta

- Partially to blame for low voter turnout in the 1996 presidential election

- Roughly the size and shape of a proper hat for an organ grinder's monkey

- Equivalent to thirty armies in a standard game of *Risk*

ENJOY!

MAKES 30 MINI BURGERS

¼ cup Sriracha

10 cloves garlic, smashed

6 tablespoons diced fresh ginger

6 scallions, white part only, sliced

½ medium onion, diced

2 tablespoons fresh thyme leaves

3 tablespoons soy sauce

2 tablespoons Dijon mustard

4 teaspoons rice vinegar

4 teaspoons sugar

8 cloves

2 teaspoons ground allspice

3 teaspoons black peppercorns

2 teaspoons ground coriander

2 teaspoons ground cinnamon

1 teaspoon ground nutmeg

1 teaspoon kosher salt

3 pounds pork belly, skin removed

30 slider buns or Hawaiian rolls

Pickled Pineapple Relish (page 293), to serve

Sliced white onion, to serve

RECIPE
CONTINUES

1. Mix the marinade ingredients (everything from the Sriracha to the salt) and whisk to combine. Place the belly in a snug container or large zip-top bag and pour over marinade. Let marinate at least 4 hours, or up to overnight.

3. Roast (or smoke!) the pork belly at 225°F for 1 hour and 15 minutes per pound or until the internal temperature comes up to 160°F. Take it to 180°F or 190°F if you've got the time. That's just meltier pork for you, captain.

4. Allow the meat to rest for 15 minutes before slicing into 3-inch strips against the grain, and then again into bite-sized pieces.

5. Optional: Crisp on a griddle or in a skillet with 1 tablespoon of oil for that incomparable street meat texture.

6. Serve a couple of slices of pork on each roll, garnished with the relish and onions.

7. Eat that burger. Make another. Eat *that* one. Repeat until blindness sets in.

BEER PAIRING: WEIZENBOCK

NO. 4½ BROCCOLI SUB

That's right. We—the people who made a life-size replica of the Stanley Cup out of meat—have thrown our lot in with a sub sandwich featuring a vegetable as the main ingredient. You'd have to imagine that this is some kind of kickass sandwich to make us take leave of our senses. And you'd be right. We were skeptical as any when we were convinced to take a visit to NYC's No. 7 Sub. They have meat on the menu. It's right there, next to the broccoli-heavy sandwich people are trying to trick us into ordering! Our actual words were "Broccoli sub? But why?"

But the thing is, it works. We've forgotten hundreds of mediocre meat-filled subs, but we'll always remember this sub's sneak attack of pure flavor.

We don't have the years of experience to claim that this is the real deal, but we'd say we're 4.5/7ths of the way there.

MAKES 4 SUBS

1 15-ounce can of lychees, pitted and chopped

3 cloves garlic, minced

1 shallot, diced

¼ teaspoon sesame oil

1 teaspoon raw sugar

2 dried Thai birdseye chilis, chopped

2 green onions, green and white parts, sliced thin

1 cup white vinegar

1¼ pounds broccoli, cut into florets

¼ cup crushed peanuts

¼ cup pine nuts

Mayonnaise, to spread on the rolls

4 Italian rolls, split

⅓ pound salted ricotta (ricotta salata), grated

Fried Shallots (page 274)

RECIPE CONTINUES

1. In a medium bowl, mix the chopped lychees with the garlic, shallot, sesame oil, sugar, chilis, green onions, and vinegar. Set aside.

2. Steam the broccoli in a steamer basket or (GASP!) the microwave for 4 to 5 minutes, until soft and just cooked.

3. Toast the peanuts and pine nuts in a dry skillet over medium-low heat, tossing frequently, until toasted—about 5 minutes.

4. Preheat your broiler, and line a baking pan with foil and a wire rack to build your sandwich empire upon. Split the sub rolls, spread both sides with mayo, then place the bottoms on the baking sheet rack. Build each sandwich by evenly dividing, in order, half the toasted nuts, the broccoli, the lychee mix, the rest of the nuts, and the ricotta.

5. Broil for 2 to 3 minutes, until the cheese begins to melt and the bread crisps a bit around the edges.

6. Remove from the oven and finish the sandwich with shallot rings and the top half of the bread. Press down, slice in half, and go to town.

BEER PAIRING: BELGIAN WILD ALE

FARMHOUSE PIZZA DOUGH

Once upon a time, we needed to use a not-so-great-tasting home-brewed beer in a recipe, because drinking it was an unpleasant prospect. Mistakes happen, and we roll with the punches. And since a typical home brew batch is 5 gallons, we found ourselves substituting off-flavored beers for water in a whole lot of different recipes. The absolute best result was this damn tasty pizza crust, which got even better when quality beer was used.

After experimentation with many light lagers, stouts, and IPAs, the perfect beer was found: Sofie from Goose Island. So if you're making this yourself, look for a Belgian farmhouse ale.

MAKES FOUR 7-INCH PIZZAS, OR TWO 14-INCH PIZZAS

1¼ ounces package active dry yeast

3 cups all-purpose flour

1 teaspoon salt

1 cup bottled conditioned farmhouse ale

2 tablespoons olive oil

1½ tablespoons honey

¼ cup cornmeal

1. Agitate yeast sediment from bottom of bottle before pouring. Heat beer to 100°F and sprinkle the yeast over the top. Allow to sit and proof for 15 minutes.

2. Place 3½ cups flour in upright mixer bowl and add salt.

3. Using a dough hook on the lowest stir setting, slowly add the beer and yeast mixture, olive oil, and honey. Stir until all ingredients are evenly mixed.

4. Knead on low for 8 minutes. If the dough is sticking to bowl, add a tablespoon of flour at a time until it's no longer sticking. If the dough is flaking apart, add the beer that's left in the bottle a teaspoon at a time until the dough is no longer flaking.

5. Set the dough into a greased bowl (freeze half of the dough for later use, if you'd like) and cover with plastic wrap. Let rise at room temperature for 2 hours, then refrigerate overnight.

6. Remove the bowl from the refrigerator and let it warm for 30 minutes before rolling out. Split the dough into 2 even balls, then flatten each ball into a 14-inch circle on a surface dusted with cornmeal. Poke holes all over the crust using a fork.

GRILLED DUCK PESTO PIZZA

Honing in the skills to grill a pizza may take longer than figuring out how to execute the perfect steak. Many prefer to cook pizza on a stone or pan but our purist selves say throw it directly on the grill grates. Sure, you may burn some dough while figuring out timing, but who cares—you're making pizza on the grill.

MAKES A 14-INCH PIZZA

½ cup cornmeal

½ portion of Farmhouse Pizza Dough (page 193)

1½ cups fresh Pesto (page 292)

1 cooked, sliced duck breast

8 ounces fontina cheese, shredded

1. Preheat grill to medium.

2. Spread cornmeal over a clean surface, split the dough, and roll into two 7-inch circles. Smaller pizzas will make flipping much easier. If you have a stone you can do one 14-inch pizza.

3. Have all the ingredients next to the grill. Things are going to start happening fast. Step away for even a second and you'll court disaster. Oh, and clean and oil the grill grate.

4. Lay the dough directly onto the grate and cook for around 3 minutes. The dough will puff and release easily from grill.

5. Flip the dough, spoon on the pesto, then top with duck and sprinkle cheese over the pizza. Cover the grill to melt cheese and cook for another 2 to 3 minutes.

6. Remove from grill and rest for a couple of minutes, then slice and eat.

BEER PAIRING: TRAPPIST ALE

BRESAOLA WHOLE PEELED TOMATO PIZZA

Whole peeled tomatoes take the place of a traditional sauce for this recipe. Why more places don't use these is beyond us. This pizza is layered a little differently than a normal pizza with cheese, meat, then tomatoes, and spices. We use low moisture mozzarella since the tomatoes are nice and juicy. This will ensure that your crust stays crunchy.

MAKES ONE 14 TO 16-INCH PIZZA

Farmhouse Pizza Dough (page 193)

2½ cups shredded low moisture mozzarella

10 slices bresaola, cut into strips

1 28-ounce can whole peeled tomatoes, drained

1 clove garlic, minced

1 teaspoon oregano

¼ tablespoon olive oil

2 tablespoons fresh basil, chopped

¼ teaspoon black pepper

1. Preheat oven to 400°F.

2. Roll out pizza dough and place on pizza pan, then heat in oven for 3 minutes until it starts to puff up.

3. Remove pizza from oven and add 2 cups mozzarella cheese onto crust and heat until cheese starts to melt, around 2 minutes.

5. Take pizza out again and add strips of bresaola, followed with whole peel tomatoes (be sure to break those babies open and spread them out) garlic, oregano, and olive oil topped with remaining mozzarella.

6. Heat until cheese is melted and crust is brown, 10 to 12 minutes. Add chopped basil and pepper and heat for 1 more minute.

BEER PAIRING: BELGIAN TRIPEL

PROSCIUTTO AND FIG PIZZA WITH ARUGULA

Stop putting tomato sauce on all your pizzas. Yes, we know it is a great base, but it's time to move out of your mother's kitchen and into your own. This pizza uses balsamic soaked figs as a base, topped with salty prosciutto, bitter arugula, and then a balsamic reduction made from the vinegar that you soaked the figs in. Full fucking circle.

MAKES ONE 14-INCH PIZZA

15 sun-dried figs, stems removed

1½ cups balsamic vinigar

1 batch Farmhouse Pizza Dough (page 193)

3 cups fontina cheese

6 slices prosciutto, cut up

2 cups baby arugula

1. Soak the figs in the balsamic vinigar overnight.

2. The next day, drain the balsamic into a saucepan. Simmering for 10 minutes, or until thick.

3. Preheat oven to 400°F.

4. While the oven is heating, pulse figs in a food processor until jam consistency.

5. Roll out pizza dough and place on pizza pan, then heat in oven for 3 minutes until it starts to rise.

6. Take out of the oven and spoon figs over the crust. Add the cheese and top with prosciutto. Bake for 14 minutes. During the final 30 seconds, add the arugula.

7. Remove from oven and drizzle balsamic reduction over the pizza.

BEER PAIRING: BARLEYWINE

JALAPEÑO POPPER PIZZA

John S. worked for four years at a pizza place, learning the trades of washing dishes, hosting, prepping salad bars, making pizzas, and finally retiring as the man who runs the oven. The restaurant pushed the envelope of what a pizza could be, back before pushing pizza envelopes was a trend. As what happens to most restaurants, the 20-year run came to the end. During the final month, John made a visit to say goodbye to the owners. The owner brought him back to the kitchen for a final walk through and let John's daughter make her first pizza on the same line he did many years before. Back at the table he noticed a new pizza appear on the buffet that day, the jalapeño popper pizza. The last slice he ate. This is his take on that pizza.

MAKES ONE 14-INCH PIZZA

8 ounces cream cheese, softened

1 tablespoon green taco sauce

1 batch Farmhouse Pizza Dough (page 193)

2 cups shredded Monterey Jack cheese

3 jalapeños, sliced

1 cup shredded cheddar

⅓ cup chopped cooked bacon

1. Preheat oven to 400°F.

2. Mix cream cheese and taco sauce in a bowl.

3. Roll out pizza dough and place on pizza pan, then heat in oven for 3 minutes, until it starts to rise.

4. Remove from oven and spread cream cheese mixture onto the crust.

5. Add Monterey Jack cheese followed by sliced jalapeños. Dab cheddar over each jalapeño. Top entire pizza with chopped bacon.

6. Cook pizza for 12 to 14 minutes, until crust is browned and all cheese is melted.

BEER PAIRING: SESSION IPA

PEAR AND GORGONZOLA PIZZA

So far we've shown you a pesto, whole peeled, cream cheese, and fig sauced pizza. You're probably wondering which page to turn to for the tomato sauce recipe. Welp, you're not going to find it. We've taken sauce out of the equation alltogether with this recipe. Cheese directly onto the crust!

MAKES ONE 14-INCH PIZZA

½ batch Farmhouse Pizza Dough (page 193)

2 cups mozzarella

½ teaspoon dried thyme

1 cup Gorgonzola

1 Bosc pear, sliced thin

¼ cup red onion, sliced and soaked in water for 30 minutes

1 tablespoon walnuts, chopped

1. Preheat oven to 400°F.

2. Roll out pizza dough and place on pizza pan, then heat in oven for 3 minutes until it starts to rise.

3. Take the pizza out of the oven and spread mozzarella evenly over the pizza, then sprinkle with thyme. Next add the gorgonzola in clusters, pear slices (get these close together as they'll shrink and you want pear in every bite), onions, and walnuts.

4. Bake for 14 minutes, or until crust is golden brown.

BEER PAIRING: DUBBEL

ITALIAN BEEF

Here's something with a fair amount of prep that you can make way ahead of time and throw together for a bunch of guests or a week's worth of food for yourself. Italian Beef is another one of those super-regional dishes (in this case, Chicago), that people will force you to eat when you visit their town. Then they'll argue about who has the best until feelings are hurt and someone throws a punch. It's fun that way.

Italian Beef came about as a way to feed a lot of wedding guests with a single roast and some cheap, filling local bread. Then people argue and someone throws a punch. Weddings are also fun that way.

One prep note that we feel compelled to share: if you want to do a quick and easy minor league version of this, get your deli to slice some regular roast beef as thin as humanly possible. Then just heat it in the gravy. We're all for going from scratch, but damn if the fake version isn't 85 percent there.

MAKES 6 BEEFS (YES, BEEFS!)

4 pounds bottom round roast

½ cup kosher salt

½ cup black pepper

1 tablespoon oregano

1 tablespoon thyme

2 teaspoons garlic powder

2 teaspoons onion powder

1 teaspoon marjoram

1 teaspoon basil

2 tablespoons peanut oil

2 beef neckbones

2 beef shanks

1 beef oxtail

1 onion, chopped

2 hearts of celery, chopped

3 carrots, chopped

4 cloves garlic, chopped

2 tablespoons tomato paste

1½ teaspoons oregano

¾ teaspoon thyme

½ teaspoon marjoram

¼ teaspoon basil

500 ml wine, plus a dash

2 tablespoons kosher salt

12 Italian rolls, split to the hinge but not cut in half, to serve

Super 16-Bit Giardiniera (page 281), to serve

1. Mix the salt, pepper, oregano, thyme, garlic powder, onion powder, marjoram, and basil.

2. Brush the roast with peanut oil and apply 1¼ cup of seasoning.

3. Preheat the oven to 250°F. Roast about 1 hour, or until the internal temperature comes to 125°F.

4. While the beef cooks, heat the peanut oil in a pot over medium-high and sear the neckbones, shanks, and oxtails, working in batches if necessary.

5. Remove seared meats, reduce the heat to medium, and deglaze with a splash of white wine, scraping up the stuck-on bits. Add the onions, celery, and carrots and cook 5 minutes, until soft.

6. Add the garlic and cook another minute, until fragrant.

7. Add the tomato paste and toss with vegetables to coat. Add oregano, thyme, marjoram, and basil and cook 30 seconds, until fragrant.

8. Add wine to cover, bring to a boil, reduce heat to a bare simmer, and let cook at least 45 minutes while you finish the dish. A dunk in the gravy is the very last thing, so no rush.

9. Remove the beef to a wire rack on a sheet pan in the refrigerator until cooled, then transfer to the freezer for 30 minutes, until firm.

10. Using your sharpest knife or the meat slicer gifted to you by your beloved richest aunt, slice that meat as thin as you possibly can. If you can read an issue of *Cat Fancy* through it, amazing accomplishment, but why are you reading that?

11. Set a colander over a large bowl and strain the solids out from your gravy. Taste the liquid for seasoning, adjust, and return to a simmer in the pot.

12. Assemble the sandwiches by stuffing the Italian rolls with the thin slices of meat. Make sure you don't split that roll in two, because that meat-juice-soaked hinge is going to be your last line of defense. Top with the Giardiniera, then take a pair of tongs, grab the sandwich from either side, and dunk it quickly in the juices.

13. Eat it fast and messy, then eat like two more. Praise one local sports team and mourn another in the next breath. This is the way of the world.

BEER PAIRING: DRY STOUT

ROPA VIEJA

We're not big fans of the Sunshine State (aka America's Wang) but to us, South Florida has one huge saving grace—the insane Cuban food I inevitably end up gorging myself on. Sure, people there may drive like extras in Mad Max, the heat may be unbearable, and their baseball team can burn in Hell for the 2003 NLCS. But there's something about good Cuban food in South Florida that's unmatchable; a crisp, savory Cuban sandwich; a plate of plantains fried twice and Hulk-smashed into the perfect snack; a cube steak breaded and fried with a side of earthy black beans.

The center piece of Southern Florida Cuban food is Ropa Vieja—long-simmered flank steak with peppers, onions, peas, and tomato that gets its name from its resemblance to tattered old clothes. The meat literally falls apart, a tender, earthy, flavorful dish that I could eat every day by itself, but which becomes something even more amazing with some rice and tostones. Clearly, we had to have it in our bag of cooking tricks.

We suggest tostones with a proper of Ropa Vieja. They're crispy and starchy, with a great texture and some freshly shredded cheese to provide some delicious contrast. Just make more than you think you'll be able to eat—a lack of tostones is an existentially terrifying thing.

MAKES 6 TO 8 SERVINGS

3 pounds flank steak

2 tablespoons peanut oil

2 tablespoons kosher salt, plus 1 teaspoon

1½ teaspoons black pepper, plus ½ teaspoon

Flour, to dust

2 white onions, chopped

2 medium carrots, peeled and chopped

3 cloves garlic, minced

2 stalks celery, chopped

1 bay leaf

1 teaspoon dried oregano

1 teaspoon cumin

1 green bell pepper, chopped

2 red bell peppers, chopped

2 orange bell peppers, chopped

16-ounce can whole tomatoes, crushed, juices reserved

1 cup red wine

3 ounces tomato paste

1 cup shelled peas (fresh or frozen)

½ cup sliced green olives

RECIPE CONTINUES

1. Brush steak with oil, season with salt and pepper, and dust with flour.

2. Heat 2 tablespoons oil in a large pot over medium-high and sear steak 2 to 3 minutes per side.

3. Remove meat and deglaze with a small amount of red wine. Add one onion and the carrots and cook 5 minutes, until soft.

4. Add garlic and celery, cook another 2 minutes.

5. Return meat to the pot. Add the bay leaf, oregano, cumin, salt, and peppercorns. Add the water - make sure it's enough to surround the meat, but not cover it entirely.

6. Bring the water to a boil, then reduce the heat and simmer, uncovered, for 2 hours.

7. Remove the meat and leave uncovered while you strain the liquid into a medium bowl. Discard the solids.

8. When meat has cooled enough to handle, shred it. You can use forks, but your hands do it faster. Just put your cigar between your teeth and tough it out. (Note: do not actually smoke over your food unless you work in a grade school cafeteria.)

9. In the same large pot, cook the remaining onion and bell peppers with a couple tablespoons of oil, for 5 minutes.

10. Add the meat, tomatoes with juice, 1 cup wine, 1½ cup braising liquid, tomato paste, and remaining salt and pepper.

11. Stir together and bring to a simmer. Continue to simmer for 30 minutes.

12. Stir in peas and olives and serve over white rice with Sweet Plantains (page 53) or Tostones (page 71).

ROPA VIEJA SANDWICH

If you follow the general template for the Cubano (page 28), but replace the interior with ropa vieja, Sweet Plantains (page 53), and black beans (page 222), you'll be very happy with the result. We guarantee it.

BEER PAIRING: SCOTCH ALE

OCTOPUSWICH!

RECIPE BY PATRICK MCBRIDE

It is, we are confident in stating, our only recipe that calls for a de-beaking.

MAKES 4 6-INCH SANDWICHES

6 small to medium-sized octopi, cleaned and de-beaked

Juice of 3 lemons

2 bunches Italian flat-leaf parsley, separated into stems and leaves

10 sprigs oregano, leaves removed from stems

3 cups dry white wine

2 tablespoons minced garlic (2 to 3 large cloves)

1 tablespoon salt

2 tablespoons red pepper flakes

1 cup extra virgin olive oil

1 pound clarified unsalted butter

1 fresh baguette, split

1. Heat a large pot of water to a rolling boil. Blanch the octopi for 90 seconds and remove. Reserve the liquid for braising.

2. Preheat the oven to 300°F. Place the octopi, lemon juice, parsley stems, half the oregano, the white wine, garlic, salt, red pepper, and olive oil in a large covered pan or Dutch oven for braising. Pour in enough reserved blanching liquid to bring the level to halfway up the octopi.

3. Braise, covered, for 2 hours.

4. Remove the octopi. Strain and reserve braising liquid.

5. Place the clarified butter in a large saucepan over medium heat with half of the parsley leaves, the remaining oregano, and remaining garlic. When it begins to boil, adjust the heat to a steady simmer. Simmer 5 to 10 minutes.

6. Meanwhile, clean and oil the grill's grate. Heat to medium-high.

7. Place the braising liquid in a blender, food processor, or immersion blender.

8. Blend the clarified butter into the braising liquid, adding slowly.

9. Grill each octopus 2 to 3 minutes, until the tendrils are crunchy and the hood (head) gets solid grill marks.

10. Remove and toss the cephalopods in your emulsified butter and braise until evenly coated.

11. Slather the remaining emulsion on your split baguette and grill until just toasted.

12. Cut the undersea friends diagonally to 1 inch thickness and place on the baguette. Drizzle with leftover emulsion and any remaining herb leaves. Add pepper if it floats your boat. GET IT? BOAT BECAUSE OCTOPUS! (cries for 30 minutes straight.)

BEER PARIRING: BELGIAN GOLDEN STRONG ALE

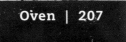

PHILLY ROAST PORK GRINDER

RECIPE BY JAMES GOTTWALD

MAKES ABOUT 8 SANDWICHES

1 5-pound boneless pork loin

1 cup sugar

1 cup kosher salt

¾ cup Hungarian paprika

2 tablespoons dried Greek oregano

2 tablespoons cayenne pepper

2 tablespoons dried basil

2 tablespoons granulated garlic

2 tablespoons garlic powder

2 tablespoons granulated onion

2 tablespoons red pepper flake

3 cups blanched broccoli rabe

3 cups julienned roasted red pepper

2 pounds provolone cheese

8 sub rolls

1. Trim the fat from the loin and set aside, working until the loin is mostly lean.

2. Reserve pork trimmings for the Line Cook Chicharrones (page 109).

3. Mix the dry ingredients in a large bowl. Reserve ½ cup of the rub for the chicharrones.

4. Halve the pork loin into two equal sections and apply the rub generously. Seriously, just cover the thing—it's gonna turn out great for you. Refrigerate overnight if you have the time.

5. Preheat the oven (convection is great if you have it) to 350°F.

6. Place the spice-rubbed pork loin sections on a baking rack set on a half-sheet pan. Bake to an internal temperature of 135°F, about 30 minutes. Remove and let rest for 15 minutes.

7. Slice the loin thin with a really sharp knife. It may still be a bit pink, which is ideal. Divide the slices into 8-ounce portions.

8. Get your oven back to 350°F. If it's still there, awesome. Grab a couple of half- or quarter-sheet pans and let's start building sandwiches. Lay out overlapping slices of pork directly on the pan in approximately the shape of the rolls you'll be using.

9. Spread the broccoli rabe and peppers over the pork, then tuck it in with a loving, cheesy blanket of provolone. Add a splash of beer or water to the edges of the pan to help the ingredients steam and bake for about 5 minutes, until the cheese is bubbling.

10. Using a long, wide spatula, slide the whole pork-scented pile onto a warmed split sub roll. Close up it up, roll it in deli paper, and cut in half.

BEER PAIRING: BIERE DE GARDE

SAUSAGE ROLLS

British people love making pastries from scratch—beef suet pies, scones, pasties—to the point where it can be a bit much to get into for the average home cook. When a recipe for a nice pub lunch has twelve steps and ten of them are about making puff pastry from scratch, it's time to call on some good old fashioned American laziness. Unless you're into baking to an ungodly degree, chances are FOODCORP LLC makes a better puff pastry than you do in your tiny apartment kitchen. No shame in that. It's time to maximize your talent the ManBQue way—make some delicious British sausage, get a puff pastry from the freezer section, and set to making one of the world's most delicious portable sausage snacks. It's like pigs in a blanket, dressed in a Fulham jersey and drinking room-temperature beer.

MAKES 16 ROLLS

1½ pounds ground pork

¾ pound (6 ounces) pork backfat or bacon, diced

3 ounces panko breadcrumbs

1 teaspoon black pepper

½ teaspoon dried oregano leaves

½ teaspoon dried basil

½ dried thyme

¼ teaspoon dried sage

¼ pound crumbled blue cheese

1 tablespoon kosher salt

¼ cup brown ale

2 feet rinsed, prepared pork casings

1 16 x 12-inch sheet puff pastry

1 egg, beaten

1. Gently mix the ground pork, pork fat or bacon, panko, salt, pepper, herbs, blue cheese, salt, and beer in a large mixing bowl with your hands until combined. Place in the freezer and let cool for 1½ hours, until firm but not frozen through.

2. Grind through corse plate, stuff the sausages into the casings, tying off at 6-inch intervals.

3. Preheat oven to 350°F.

4. Cut the puff pastry into 4-inch strips, then crosswise into 3-inch strips. You should have 16 strips of 4 x 3-inch puff pastry.

5. Wrap the sausages individually in the pastry sheets. Mix egg with 1 teaspoon water and bruch over pastry.

6. Place sausages on a greased baking sheet and cook for 45 to 55 minutes, flipping once, until golden brown and the sausage reaches 165°F.

BEER PAIRING: ESB

SOUTHERN CORNBREAD

Make this, if only so you can enjoy fighting with church picnic matrons and Southerners about proper cornbread technique.

MAKES 1 10-INCH PAN

2½ cups (11 ounces) all-purpose flour

1¼ cups (5 ounces) cornmeal

2 teaspoons salt

1 tablespoon baking powder

4 eggs

1 cup whole milk

½ cup bacon grease or vegetable oil, plus more to coat pan

1 cup sugar

1. Preheat the oven to 400°F with your cast-iron pan along for the ride.

2. Whisk together the flour, cornmeal, salt, and baking powder.

3. Whisk together the eggs, milk, grease, and sugar.

4. Add the dry ingredients to the wet, whisking to combine.

5. Remove the pan from the oven (carefully!) and add 1 to 2 tablespoons of the bacon grease. It should heat rapidly. Pour in your cornbread batter, which should sizzle a bit as it goes in.

6. Bake for 30 minutes. Remove and let cool before turning out and slicing.

BRAISED SAUERKRAUT

Cooking sauerkraut sands some of the rougher edges off of this divisive ingredient. Now you can put it on everything.

MAKES 1½ POUNDS

2 tablespoons vegetable oil

1 cup diced white onion

1 cup diced apple

1 russet potato, diced

1 pound canned or bagged sauerkraut, drained

4 juniper berries, crushed

½ teaspoon caraway seed

2 cups chicken stock

1. Preheat oven to 350°F.

2. Heat the vegetable oil in a pan over medium heat. Add the onions and apples and cook 10 minutes, until soft.

3. Add the potatoes and cook another 5 minutes.

4. Add the kraut, juniper, caraway, and stock. Bring to a boil, cover, and transfer to the oven for 1½ hours, until the liquid has evaporated. Serve with sausage.

BEER PAIRING: MARZEN

JALAPEÑO-INFUSED RIBS

RECIPE BY JOE RAKE

We're normally not big fans of letting boiling water anywhere near our ribs. The Rib Inquisition would execute us for even suggesting this. But damned if it isn't one fine way to make due in a city apartment without a smoker and represent yourself well at a cookout. In fact, a lot of the old man bars who do decent food have perfected the art of the oven rib. Serve it with a nice sweet sauce while you're at it.

MAKES 2 RACKS

7 large jalapeños, deseeded and sliced

4 cups water

½ cup apple cider vinegar

½ cup packed brown sugar

¼ cup vegetable or canola oil

1 garlic clove, smashed

2 tablespoons kosher salt, divided

2 tablespoons pepper, divided

2 racks of baby back ribs, approximately 2 pounds per rack, cut into 4 half-racks for easier handling

3 tablespoons brown sugar

1½ tablespoons paprika

1 teaspoon garlic powder

1. For the marinade, combine jalapeños, water, vinegar, sugar, oil, garlic, ½ tablespoon salt and ½ tablespoon pepper in a medium saucepan. Cover, bring to a boil, reduce heat and simmer for 5 minutes. Allow to cool, then marinate ribs in a closed container for 4 hours, or overnight.

2. Before grilling, you'll want to oven-roast the ribs. Pre-heat oven to 250°F.

3. Place the ribs bone down in a racked roasting pan. Then pour the marinade over top blanketing the ribs with jalapeños. Cover the roasting pan with aluminum foil.

4. Cook in the oven for 2½ hours. Ribs should be tender and need to be removed with tongs. Note: Ribs can be wrapped in foil, refrigerated, and grilled later or the following day.

5. Preheat grill to medium heat.

6. Combine brown sugar, paprika, remaining salt and black pepper, and garlic powder to make a dry rub. Apply rub generously ribs.

7. Place ribs on hot grill, bones up, for 4 to 5 minutes. Turn to bone-side down and grill for an additional 4 to 5 minutes.

BEER PAIRING: PALE ALE

SWEETCORN DIP

This is a great dip for those summer days when delicious sweetcorn is in season. Elotes, sweetcorn dip, maybe some cornbread. Life in the Midwest is exactly how you always pictured it.

8 ears of corn, in their husks

1 cup mayonnaise

1 tablespoon chipotle hot sauce

Juice of 2 limes

1 teaspoon salt

1 teaspoon fresh ground pepper

1 teaspoon sugar

¼ cup chicken stock

½ cup Cotija cheese, crumbled, divided

¼ cup cilantro, chopped, to garnish

1 teaspoon chili powder, to garnish

1. Preheat oven to 350°F.

2. Roast corn with husks on in oven (or grill) 30 minutes. Turn cobs halfway through for even cooking. Set roasted corn aside until cool enough to handle. Then shuck and cut the kernels off of the cob.

3. Mix mayonnaise, hot sauce, lime juice, salt, pepper, sugar, and chicken stock in saucepan over medium heat. Stir for 4 to 5 minutes until the mayonnaise is melted with the other ingredients. Add corn to sauce and warm through.

4. Pour mixture into a bowl and mix in half of the cheese. Refrigerate for 4 hours.

5. Garnish with remaining cheese, cilantro, and chili powder before serving.

BEER PAIRING: CZECH PALE LAGER

RUNZAS

RECIPE BY JAYME ADKINS-IRONSIDE

Imagine, if you will, a world where meat and cheese in a pastry doesn't foretell sad bachelorhood and intestinal distress. Runzas are a Nebraska thing, and we're all the richer for knowing them.

MAKES 12 BREAD POCKETS

1¾ cups (210 grams) unbleached all-purpose flour, plus 2¾ cups (330 grams)

½ cup (100 grams) sugar

5 teaspoons (½ ounce) active dry yeast

1 teaspoon (6½ grams) salt

¾ cup whole milk

8 ounces (2 sticks) unsalted butter, plus 2 tablespoon

2 eggs, beaten, plus 1 egg

1 tablespoon sesame oil

1¼ pounds ground beef

1 tablespoon kosher salt

1 tablespoon tomato paste

1 teaspoon Worcestershire sauce

1 teaspoon Marmite

1 tablespoon crushed red pepper

1 cup chopped white onion

3 shallots (about ½ cup) chopped

4 cloves garlic, minced

4 cups (about one medium head) chopped cabbage

1. Place the flour into the bowl of an electric mixer and add the sugar, yeast, and salt, stirring to combine.

2. Heat the milk, ½ cup of water, and butter in a small saucepan over low heat until the temperature reads about 120°F.

3. Add the heated milk to the dry ingredients and slowly stir in on low speed. Add the eggs when the mixture has cooled (you mainly just want to make sure they don't cook and scramble) and beat on high for 2 minutes.

4. Change out the beater for a dough hook, if you have it, reduce the mixing speed to low and add the remaining flour. Knead for 8 to 10 minutes, then turn out into an oiled glass bowl. Cover with plastic wrap and let rise for 1 hour, until it's doubled in size.

5. Heat the sesame oil in a large skillet over medium heat, add your ground beef and salt, and cook 3 to 4 minutes until browned. Add the tomato paste, Worcestershire, Marmite, and red pepper and remove from the pan.

6. Deglaze the pan with a bit of water and add the onions and shallots. Cook 5 minutes, until soft, then add the garlic and cook another minute.

7. Add the cabbage and cook 1 to 2 minutes, until wilted. Remove to a large bowl and mix with the ground beef.

8. Punch down the dough and divide it into 12 equal pieces (a scale is so useful for this). Roll the dough balls into squares, top with ⅓ cup of the meat/cabbage mixture, and pinch the edges closed with a fork.

9. Preheat your oven to 350°F and create an egg wash with your remaining egg and a teaspoon of water.

10. Line up your runzas-to-be on a baking sheet and brush them with egg wash. Bake for 20 to 25 minutes, until they're beautifully, almost pornographically, golden brown. They're ready, and so are you.

BEER PAIRING: BOCK

CAULDRON

Ever since three Scottish witches spurred Macbeth into a mad spree of regicide and clan warfare, people have been doing really cool things with pots full of bubbling liquid. You can steam a delicious, tender Chinese bao. You can spend a few hours letting a fatty piece of pork break down into delicious carnitas. You can even stuff a bunch of crabs in there and pretend you're a tyrant putting down an uprising of the Crab People (just us?).

Between a steamer insert (tamales) and some stackable bamboo accoutrements (bao), you can cook almost anything you want in a big ol' pot. And unlike the sleek, sexy, multi-clad sauté pans and copper sauceiers, you won't find a whole lot of overpriced "prestige" models to muddy your decision-making. Except those Francophone-enameled Dutch ovens, which are admittedly glorious. You find those heavy bastards at a garage or estate sale, or if you know a French chef who is selling off kitchenware to support a serious heroin addiction, you buy all of them and cherish them forever.

Look for something with a heavy bottom for good heat retention, and something that's big enough for the recipes you want to do. Trying to force five pounds of pork shoulder, plus liquid, into a 2-quart pot isn't going to end well for you. Size matters.

BELGIAN BEER MUSSELS

Mussels are one of those dishes that look more difficult to prepare than they actually are. Serving this super-easy, super-tasty dish to your friends a couple of times is how you start getting known as the talented cook in the group.

SERVES 4

1 tablespoon butter

1 shallot, finely chopped

1 cup Belgian beer

2 cups coconut milk

3 tablespoons red curry paste

½ teaspoon Sriracha sauce

2 to 4 pounds fresh mussels, cleaned

3 tablespoons basil, chopped

Toasted French bread, to serve

1. Melt butter in a 5-quart pot or Dutch oven and sauté shallots for 3 minutes, until translucent.

2. Pour in beer, coconut milk, red curry, and Sriracha. Increase the heat and boil for 5 minutes.

3. Add the mussels, cover, and steam 10 minutes, until they open.

4. Remove from the heat, add basil, stir, and cover again for 2 minutes.

5. Serve with frites (page 89) and crusty French bread to soak up that brothy greatness.

BEER PAIRING: BELGIAN BLONDE

CHESAPEAKE BLUE CRABS

RECIPE BY STEVE MUHLBAIER

Eating blue crabs in Maryland is part meal, part project. Since crabs are nature's tiny bank lockboxes, you need time, effort, and possibly a small hammer to extract the delicious, delicious meat within. So you pick a nice spot, spread out some newspaper, rip open a twelve-pack of something, and settle in for some serious eating.

Fun fact when you're buying the crabs: Males have underbellies that look like the Washington Monument, whereas female crab undersides resemble the U.S. Capitol Dome.

MAKES 12 CRABS

1½ cups of wheat beer

1 head garlic, with the top cut off

2 lemons, cut in half

1 tablespoon dried basil

2 tablespoons hot sauce

1 tablespoon cider vinegar

6 tablespoons Old Bay seasoning, divided

12 medium-sized male blue crabs

1. Add all ingredients except the crabs and 3 tablespoons of Old Bay to bottom of a large stockpot. Fill with water to just below the bottom of where the steamer insert reaches and bring briefly to a boil.

2. Place the steamer insert in the pot and add the crabs—using tongs, elsewise the crabs will have their revenge. Season the feisty bastards with the remaining Old Bay and slap the lid on the pot.

3. Bring the water to a boil to steam the crabs. Cook for 10 to 14 minutes. The shells of the crabs will turn a bright orange/reddish color when fully cooked.

4. Spread out some newspaper on your table, crack them open, and enjoy!

BEER PAIRING: SAISON

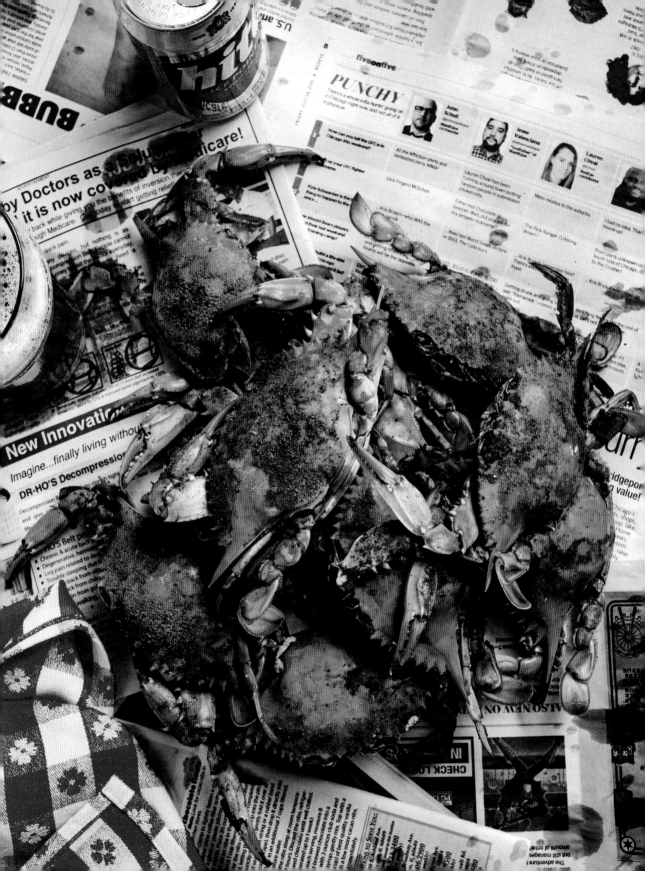

BLACK BEANS

Before starting, make sure to sort through the beans to remove any rocks. Black beans are notorious for harboring tooth-cracking stones. But, death-defying danger aside, you'll have a much better result by starting with fresh beans. These make a great side dish for almost anything, and they're fantastic when served with rice.

MAKES 12 SERVINGS

1 pound dried black beans, sorted and washed

1 cup chopped white onion

3 cloves garlic, chopped

3 bay leaves

1 tablespoon kosher salt

1. Place all ingredients into a crock pot, stir to combine, then add 6 cups of water.

2. Bring to a simmer, cover, and cook overnight, covered.

3. Remove the bay leaves, taste for seasoning, and add additional salt if needed.

SICILIAN-STYLE STUFFED ARTICHOKES

We have a complicated relationship with vegetables, and the artichoke in particular always looked like it wanted to hurt us. Imagine our surprise when we found out we could make a meal out of a steamed vegetable and also manage to eat a head of garlic at the same time.

You could theoretically serve this with a nice spicy mayo, but don't blame us if an Italian Nonna ziplines into your kitchen and starts whacking the crap out of you with a wooden spoon.

MAKES 4 SERVINGS

2 artichokes, stem and tips cut off

20 cloves garlic, minced

1½ cups chopped flat-leaf parsley

2 teaspoons kosher salt

2 teaspoons black pepper

2 teaspoons olive oil

½ lemon, sliced into wedges, plus two slices

1. Spread the artichoke leaves out and wash thoroughly. Let drain in a colander over the sink for 15 minutes.

2. Mix the garlic, parsley, salt, and pepper. Spread the leaves of the artichokes again and stuff the mixture between the leaves. Drizzle olive oil over the top.

3. Place in the steamer insert of a large pot, cover artichoke tops with lemon slices, and steam for 45 minutes.

4. Cut artichokes in half and serve, with lemon wedges.

BEER PAIRING: MUNICH HELLES LAGER

BRAISED PORK BELLY BANH MI SANDWICHES WITH NUOC MAU

RECIPE BY ED KOWALSKI

A friend turned us on to nuoc mau, a Vietnamese caramel sauce which makes this sandwich the best thing to come out of Vietnam since John Rambo.

MAKES 4 SANDWICHES

3 tablespoons sugar

2 tablespoons warm water

1 tablespoon canola oil

2 large shallots, minced

2 garlic cloves, minced

2 pounds pork belly, cut into 1-inch cubes

2 tablespoons fish sauce

½ teaspoon whole black peppercorns

½ cup unseasoned rice vinegar

¼ cup sugar

1½ cups water

1 cup daikon radishes, peeled and shredded

1 cup carrots, peeled and shredded

1 baguette, ends cut off and divided into 4 portions (sliced lengthwise)

1 jalapeño, thinly sliced, to garnish

½ cup cilantro, to garnish

1. Add sugar and water to a heavy-bottomed sauce pan. Heat the pan on medium heat and let the sugar melt and the mixture turn to a golden brown color. Keep stirring and watch for it to quickly turn to a golden brown color. It happens fast, so don't walk away.

2. If the mixture is too thick, slowly add additional water (1 tablespoon at a time) until the mixture is the desired consistency. Stir again with a wooden spoon to remove any hard lumps. Set aside. You've got nuoc mau. We're very proud of you.

3. In Dutch oven or large pot, heat the oil over medium until it simmers. Add the shallots and cook for about 1 minute, then add garlic and cook another minute, until both are fragrant.

4. Add the pork belly and sear on all sides, turning after about 2 minutes, 10 minutes in total to sear and brown all sides.

5. Stir in fish sauce and cook for another 5 minutes, then add water to cover.

6. Add the peppercorns and turn heat to low, cooking for an additional 10 minutes, stirring occasionally.

7. Add the nuoc mau, cover partially, and continue braising the pork over low heat for another 45 minutes to 1 hour, stirring occasionally, until the pork is tender.

8. While the pork is braising, combine the vinegar, sugar and water in a small saucepan. Bring to a boil over medium-high heat, stirring, until the sugar dissolves.

9. Place the shredded daikon and carrots in a heatproof vessel. Pour over the vinegar, cover, and let sit for 20 minutes.

10. Divide the pork belly evenly among the baguettes, top with the slaw, and garnish with cilantro and jalapeño.

BEER PAIRING: BIERE DE GARDE

BAR TAMALES

Here in Chicago, when you're drinking in a bar that doesn't have a kitchen, you're usually biding time for the Tamale Guy. He's a mysterious hero, a street food cipher, a lone sentinel of freedom who makes the rounds with two small coolers packed with homemade tamales just when you need them. He's got pork, he's got chicken, but you really want the peppers and cheese. Trust us.

MAKES 50 TAMALES

60 dried corn husks

2 pounds masa harina

2¼ cup stock

14 ounces lard

1½ teaspoon baking powder

1 tablespoon salt

2½ cups Chihuahua Cheese

2½ cups chopped jalapeño or serrano peppers

1. Soak husks in hot water for 45 to 60 minutes.

2. Mix the masa and stock.

3. Whip the lard until it forms peaks, then then add to the masa mixture, mixing vigorously.

4. Add baking powder and salt, and mix well. Take a piece of the masa mixture throw it in a cup of water—if it floats, it's ready to go.

5. Drain the husks and pat dry. Tear 5 to 10 of the lesser specimens into thin strips to secure your tamales.

6. Lay out a dried corn husk, then spread 2 tablespoons of the masa mixture over it in a vaguely rectangular shape. Spoon a tablespoon of cheese and a tablespoon of peppers into the middle. Adjust the ratio if you're a big serrano baby.

7. Roll the husk into a tubular shape, fold up the bottom, and secure with two strips of cornhusk. You don't need to fold both ends, as you're steaming them upright, but do whatever floats your boat. Having an assembly line for the remaining 49 will do wonders for your sanity, so call some friends and promise them beer.

8. Line a stock pot with a steamer insert and add enough water as to keep it below the steamer. Line the steamer with some of your spare husks. Annoying pro tip that totally works: A few pennies in the bottom of the pot will keep you alerted to when you run dry. As long as you hear the infernal chattering of the pennies, you've still got water in there.

9. Place the tamales open side up along the inside perimeter of the stock pot. Place extra husks on top the tamales and cover the pot. Steam for 1 hour, until the masa firms up and the husk peels away easily.

10. Pack into coolers with some hot sauce and prepare to make a bunch of money off of desperate drinkers.

BEER PAIRING: PALE LAGER

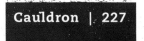

HOT DOGS
A NATIONAL ANTHEM YOU CAN EAT

There's nothing that unites Americans more than the love of encased meats. From the legendary Pink's in Los Angeles through Chicago and its eponymous natural-casing dog to the dirty water dogs of New York City, we are a proud nation united in hot dogs. Even our friends abroad in Norway, Iceland, South Africa, and Japan count them as an essential and beloved street eat.

With all those flavors from all those places, it's impossible to settle on a favorite. So let's go ahead and cook all of them. You earned it.

Wipe away that single tear and let's get looking. We love hot dogs. So fucking much.

Hot Dogs: The Hard-Hitting Questions

What should I look for in a hot dog?

Get something with a natural casing—it has a distinctive SNAP when you bite into it that makes the whole affair worthwhile. Skinless dogs are stuffed into synthetic casings, smoked, and removed from the casings. Same great meaty flavor, less-awesome texture, and zero natural snap. Kids actually tend to like them better, because they're easier to eat.

Not everywhere has the natural casing dogs, so don't feel bad about getting skinless. It won't affect the cooking any—this is a hot dog party, not neurosurgery.

But get the big 'ol bastards, right?

Actually, check the number of dogs per pound. Bigger isn't always better. Chicago-style dogs are traditionally eight to a pound, while our New York friends often get the slimmer ten to a pound franks. There's no right or wrong—you want the best ratio of toppings to meat. A quarter-pound dog (four to a pound) is a little too big for our tastes. The toppings tend to slide right off, and the larger-diameter hog casings (as opposed to lamb casings on the slimmer dogs) can be a little chewy.

Wait, I'm supposed to be afraid of hot dogs, right? They're mostly trimmings and off-cuts?

You'd be surprised. While there's plenty of cheap crap in the world of processed meats, brands like Sabrett's, Vienna Beef, and Casper's put out some fantastic hot dogs. We actually got to go on the production floor at Chicago's Vienna Beef factory to see how the sausage was made. This despite "see how the sausage is made" being the one thing you're *not* supposed to want to do.

At Vienna, and a lot of other top producers, there's nary a mechanically-separated meatstuff to be found. They use 95 percent lean bull meat, combined with brisket and navel cuts. Some producers also mix pork into the hot dogs, which is completely delicious in slightly different way.

The whole cuts are trimmed, mixed with the bull meat, and sent along through a vacuum chopper. Then that meat is emulsified the meat with beef fat, garlic extract, spices, corn syrup, ice, and sodium nitrite curing salt. This happens 4,000 pounds of meat at a time, after which they're stuffed into natural or artificial casings of varying sizes. After that, the newly formed dogs are smoked in cavernous temperature-controlled smokers. After that, they're packaged ready to eat, though they're much better if you heat them up first.

"What's different about the kosher hot dogs?

Kosher franks were traditionally held to a higher standard than regular hot dogs—only beef slaughtered and prepared in accordance with kosher dietary laws, no fillers, no pork. But with that comes skinless dogs or collagen casings, because natural casings qualify as organ meat, and are thus also a no-go. With people paying much more attention to what they eat these days, there are plenty of non-kosher producers that make similar quality products. But a lot of our friends who grew up on kosher dogs swear by the spice blend (deliciously garlicky), the quality of the beef, or some other nostalgia-colored perception. They're great for your cookout, whether it's kosher or not. Deep fry or char-grill to replace some of that natural casing snap.

What are "nitrate-free" hot dogs?

Uncured, or "nitrate-free" hot dogs are produced for people worried about the effects of sodium nitrate, the curing salt that preserves hot dogs and turns them that trademark pink color. Curing hot dogs prevents *clostridium botulinum*—a deadly bacterium that can kill the shit out of you and which rich people have injected into their faces—from forming in the meat. But nitrates aren't great for you in large doses, so some people try to avoid them entirely. Companies like Niman Ranch, Trader Joe's, and Whole Foods produce hot dogs without adding sodium nitrate to the mix. Some companies instead use natural sources of nitrate like celery powder, which are...you know, still nitrates. It's kind of a semantic thing. If you're that worried about hot dogs, we might recommend that you just don't eat hot dogs.

Cooking Your Hot Dogs

To Steam

Fill a pot of water to just below the line of the steamer insert. Add the dogs on top, bring the water to a boil, cover, and let steam 5 to 10 minutes, depending on the size of your franks. The big quarter-pound ones tend toward the 10 minute end, where the 10-to-a-pound dogs should be good and hot in 5 minutes.

To Simmer

This is where we want to belabor a very specific point, which is *NEVER BOIL YOUR HOT DOGS*. The delicious sodiums and spices will leak out, your casings will shrink and seize, and you'll have kind of a shitty dog at the end of things. Instead, bring a large pot of water just to a simmer, and slip the dogs in for an invigorating 4 minute warming bath. If you'd like that authentic New York City cart experience, change the water every presidential administration or so, charge your guests an exorbitant amount, and only offer warm Diet Pepsi to drink.

To Char-Grill

At some point in our lives, we're taught to make a dozen or so slashes through the dog so it doesn't explode under the intense heat of the grill. But we've found that by cutting two perpendicular slashes into the ends of the dog, the heat will cause those edges to vent the heat, crisp up, and bloom outward. So make your slashes, put them onto a grill over medium heat, and turn them frequently. The dog stays mostly intact, you've got a killer bite at either end, and it looks generally kickass. Don't worry about grill marks—you're tucking them into a bun and covering it with selected delicious toppings. No one's going to see them, unless they're eating a plain hot dog like Melvin from fifth-grade science class. Man, that guy was weird.

To Fry

Oh, this is going to be fun. If you're stuck with skinless dogs, frying can add some great texture to make up for it. Get your oil to 350°F, cut the ends like you're char-grilling, and drop that sucker in for 2½ minutes, turning frequently. Shake off excess oil, and you're ready to go. This is a great way to add a snap to a skinless dog.

To Microwave

Oh god, you're really doing this, aren't you? And it's not for a toddler? Alright, go ahead and grab the rock-hard package of frozen budget dogs from your '70s-era fridge/freezer. Slap those icy bastards into the sink to defrost. Maybe run a little cold water over things to speed up the process. Some food guy on TV said that's not a great idea, but you managed to survive the divorce, so hot dogs probably won't kill you either.

When they're good and soggy, pop them on a plate, make some slash marks so they don't detonate, and cover them with a paper towel. Microwave them for 45 seconds. Take the cooking time to crack open that plastic fifth of white label. I mean, it's 10:45 in the morning, but it's a weekend, right? Breakfast of champions, hoss!

You probably forgot to get buns, so take out a couple slices of white bread and your condiments. Garnish the dogs using the mustard, half-empty jar of salsa, or both.

Eat directly over the sink and contemplate how much easier life would be if you lost a finger at work. Not one of the important ones, just like a left ring finger or something.

Sigh loudly. Restart this chapter and consider one of the other prep methods. Actions have consequences, you know?

For Your Buns Only

A steamed hot dog bun is essential to the experience. It's why people enjoy ballpark hot dogs so much—a trip around the stadium wrapped in foil within a heated box brings the dog and bun together into a pillowy sweet bite that yields to the snap of the dog itself. It's meat poetry.

To steam your buns, place them between two sheets of parchment paper in a steamer (you don't want the condensed steam falling on them and making them soggy), cover, and let them go for 2 to 3 minutes. Carefully reach in to check. If they're soft and warm, they're good to go. It's the easiest thing to do, and it makes all the difference.

Hot Dog Styles: An Incomplete But Delicious Guide

ALL RECIPES MAKE UNLIMITED HOT DOGS FOREVER ON THE WINGS OF FREEDOM
(OR, MORE ACCURATELY, 8)

THE CHICAGO-STYLE HOT DOG

When you come to Chicago and order a hot dog "dragged though the garden," this is what you'll get in a perfect world. Poppyseed buns are authentic, but rare outside of Chicago, so don't feel bad substituting a replacement bun. Or even using ketchup—our populace is regularly (and incorrectly) pegged as psychos about that. Do what you want—it's your hot dog and this is America.

These are the world's most perfect expression of what a hot dog can be. We could eat two of these every single day. Imagine what a glorious (short) life that would be.

8 steamed poppyseed hot dog buns

8 steamed or simmered natural casing hot dogs

Yellow mustard, to serve

1 cup chopped white onion

Neon green pickle relish

2 plum tomatoes, halved and sliced thin

8 dill pickle spears

16 sport peppers

Celery salt, to serve

1. Top the dogs with a squiggle of yellow mustard, followed by the onion, relish, sliced tomato, pickle spear to one side, and sport peppers to the other. Give it a quick dusting of celery salt and you're ready to serve.

BEER PAIRING: PILSNER

THE DEPRESSION DOG

This is the other, and far less well-known, Chicago version of the hot dog. We still love it, because hot dogs are delicious and french fries only make them more amazing. If you're going for full authenticity, use smaller ten-to-a-pound natural casing dogs. Though if someone calls you on that particular detail, we'll be shocked.

8 steamed or simmered natural-casing hot dogs

8 steamed hot dog buns

Yellow mustard, to serve

Neon green relish, to serve

1 cup chopped white onion

16 sport peppers

1 batch French fries (page 89), to serve

1. Open a steamed bun, place your hot dog in, and add a squiggle of mustard. Then add the relish, onion, and peppers.

2. Top with an irresponsible amount of well-salted fries and serve immediately.

BEER PAIRING: STEAM BEER

IMPOSTOR BAGEL DOG

This is almost stupidly easy, but Professor Mark Reitman of Hot Dog University taught us this trick, so we're passing it on to you. You'll need a sandwich or hot dog wrapper, but your local hot dog stand or mom-and-pop fast food place should be nice about hooking you up. Otherwise you can buy hundreds more than you'd ever need in your life at a warehouse or restaurant store.

4 steamed natural-casing franks

4 steamed poppyseed hot dog buns

Mustard, to serve

1. Lay out a wrapper in front of you on a flat surface with one corner pointing toward you.

2. Lay a steamed bun at the bottom of the point, and a hot dog in the middle of the bun.

3. Quickly roll up the dog in the paper, pressing down firmly.

4. Unroll, slice into 8 pieces, *et voila*, pretty convincing fake bagel bites.

BEER PAIRING: COFFEE STOUT

MANHATTAN STREET MEAT DOGS

2 tablespoons vegetable oil

2 medium onions, thinly sliced

1 teaspoon brown sugar

⅝ teaspoon cinnamon, divided

1 teaspoon cornstarch

½ teaspoon ancho chile powder

¼ cup tomato paste

½ cup water

½ teaspoon kosher salt

1 teaspoon cayenne pepper

8 steamed buns

Spicy brown mustard

8 kosher hot dogs, simmered

Braised Sauerkraut (page 211)

1. In a small saucepan over medium heat, sauté the onions in the vegetable oil for 5 minutes, until soft and translucent.

2. Stir in the sugar, cinnamon, cayenne, and chili powder and cook for 1 minute.

3. Add the tomato paste, water, corn starch, and salt. Bring to a boil, reduce the heat to a simmer, and cook until the sauce thickens, about 15 minutes.

4. Stirring frequently, cook another 15 to 20 minutes, or until the water is reduced by about half.

5. Remove sauce from the heat and set aside.

6. Spread the spicy brown mustard on the bottom of your bun, add your hot dog and top with onion sauce and sauerkraut.

BEER PAIRING: ESB

DETROIT CONEY DOGS

Don't call it a chili dog within the city limits of Detroit. The things they'll call you are unprintable. Coney dogs are a really popular regional style championed by two adjacent restaurants (American Coney Island and Lafayette Coney Island) who *haaaate* each other, in the way you can usually only hate a family member who sold you on a shady "investment." They both serve natural-casing dogs covered in onions, cheese, and a mysterious Coney Sauce we're fairly sure has a beef heart component to it. We love beef heart, so we made our own delectable version.

If your butcher doesn't want to special-grind your meat, or you can't yourself, just place the beef in the food processor and pulse it 3 to 5 times after it's cooked.

½ pound finely ground chuck

½ pound finely ground short rib

½ pound finely ground beef heart

2 tablespoons kosher salt

1 teaspoon black pepper

2 tablespoons vegetable oil

1½ cups chopped white onion, plus more to serve

4 cloves garlic, minced

¾ cup tomato paste

1 teaspoon cayenne pepper

¼ teaspoon cumin

¼ teaspoon coriander

1 tablespoon white wine

1 cup tomato sauce

2 tablespoons Worcestershire sauce

1 tablespoon Marmite (optional)

2 tablespoons yellow mustard, plus more to serve

1 teaspoon corn flour (masa harina)

8 char-grilled beef-and-pork hot dogs

8 steamed hot dog buns

1. Season the ground meat with the salt and pepper, then brown in a large pot or Dutch oven. When the meat is cooked through, remove and set aside. Drain the fat.

2. Heat the vegetable oil over medium and sauté 1 cup of the onions for 5 minutes, until soft and translucent. Add the garlic and cook another minute, until fragrant.

3. Add the tomato paste, cayenne, cumin, and coriander. Mix with onions and garlic and cook another minute.

4. Deglaze pan with white wine, scraping up

the brown bits, and add the tomato sauce, Worcestershire, Marmite, and yellow mustard. Return the beef to the pot and stir to combine.

5. Mix the corn flour with a teaspoon of water to make a slurry. Add to the pot and stir through. Cook 15 minutes, then cover and reduce heat to low.

6. When your dogs are charred and buns steamed, serve with a ladle of chili, a handful of the remaining onions, and a generous slather of mustard.

BEER PAIRING: DUBBEL

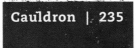

THE CRESCENT CITY REGRET DOG

New Orleans is America's leading exporter of bad decisions. It's very important to survive the gauntlet of jazz clubs, casinos, bar drinking, street drinking, and low-margin strip clubs with at least a few bucks left at the end of the night. This is because a small militia of vagrants, ruffians, and weirdos command a fleet of rolling metal hot dog stands that serve up hot dogs that are at the same time the best and the worst decision you'll make all night.

Owing to the proudly low-rent nature of this dish, you can feel free to use canned chili guilt-free. Otherwise, our Walking Taco Chili Filling (page 249) is really good with this.

8 jumbo bun-length pork-and-beef franks, steamed

Chili (from our Walking Tacos, your family recipe, or, most authentically, some really crappy canned stuff), to serve

8 hot dog buns, steamed

Ketchup, to serve

Yellow mustard, to serve

1. Remove the dog and bun from the steamer, and make sure you're authentically surly when you do it.

2. Add a ladle of chili, spreading it on both sides of the dog.

3. Top with a ridiculous amount of mustard and ketchup in dueling zig-zaggy lines, and serve to the drunkest person you can find. They'll be back for more. They always come back for more.

BEER PAIRING: BLACK LAGER

THE EMERALD CITY DOG

The rain in the Pacific Northwest, it gets to people. Slowly drives them mad, until they're throwing god knows what on a hot dog. But then you try one of these, maybe with a few beers in you, and you start to think that these people are on to something.

8 toasted hot dog buns

1 cup cream cheese, softened, to serve

8 char-grilled natural casing Polish sausages or hot dogs

2 cups chopped cabbage

2 jalapeños, sliced

8 green onions, sliced thin

1. Spread the toasted buns with cream cheese on both sides.

2. Add the Polish sausage or hot dogs and top with cabbage, jalapeños, and green onions.

BEER PAIRING: BROWN ALE

NORWAY FRANSKDOG

From the land of incredibly expensive hot dogs (and other foods, and alcohol, and basically everything) comes this dog served with onions so thin you can see through them and a sweet, creamy dressing.

½ cup mayo

2 teaspoons honey mustard

2 teaspoons Dijon mustard

1 teaspoon salt

½ teaspoon sugar

½ teaspoon mild curry powder

8 steamed hot dog buns

8 steamed natural casing hot dogs

2 thinly sliced and salted Persian cucumbers, to serve

Fried Shallots (page 274) or canned fried onions, to serve

1. Mix the mayo with the mustards, salt, sugar, and curry and set aside.

2. Lay the dog into the bun and top with cucumber, shallots or onions, and a generous squeeze of the sauce. Charge a price that hovers around nineteen dollars at current exchange rates.

BEER PAIRING: GOLDEN ALE

ICELANDIC DOG

Some claim that hot dog stands in Rekjavik are the best in the world, which speaks more to ice-induced madness than the global quality of hot dogs. Still, this tiny island nation isn't as villainous as *The Mighty Ducks 2* led us to believe, and they make a damn fine dog. Now you can too.

1 tablespoon chopped cornichons

2 teaspoons Dijon mustard

1 teaspoon chopped capers

½ teaspoon anchovy paste

½ teaspoon chopped chives

½ teaspoon chopped parsley

½ teaspoon chopped tarragon

1 cup mayo

8 steamed hot dog buns

8 steamed hot dogs (if you can find natural-casing lamb dogs, you're awesome)

Brown mustard, to serve

Ketchup, to serve

1 cup chopped white onion, to serve

1 cup pickled red cabbage, to serve (optional)

Fried Shallots (page 274) or canned fried onions, to serve

1. Fold the cornichons, Dijon, capers, anchovy paste, and herbs into the mayo and stir until combined, then spread on both sides of the steamed hot dog buns.

2. Lay the dog in the bun and top with mustard, ketchup, white onions, cabbage, and fried shallots.

BEER PAIRING: STOUT

THE RIO

How did it take us this long to crush up potato chips as a hot dog topping? Thank you, brave people of Brazil.

8 steamed hot dog buns

8 steamed hot dogs

Ketchup, to serve

Mustard, to serve

Mayo, to serve

1½ cups shredded cabbage tossed with 2 tablespoons cider vinegar

1 cup thinly-sliced red onion

1 3½-ounce bag potato chips, removed to a zip-top bag and crushed

Hot sauce, to serve

1. This is not a clean-eating hot dog. This is a messy celebration of life and food. Start by spreading way too much ketchup, mustard, and mayo on the dog.

2. Pile on the cabbage, onion, and potato chips. Squirt with hot sauce to taste and serve.

BEER PAIRING: BROWN ALE

THE COLUMBIAN

Similar to the Rio, but with more quail egg!

⅓ cup ketchup

⅓ cup mustard

⅓ cup mayo

2 tablespoons crushed pineapple

8 toasted hot dog buns

8 steamed hot dogs

Canned shoestring potatoes, to serve

4 boiled quail eggs, cut in half

1 lime, cut into 8 wedges

1. Mix the ketchup, mustard, and mayo in a bowl and stir in the crushed pineapple.

2. Lay the dogs into the buns and drizzle with the pineapple mayoketchupstard sauce. Top with matchstick potatoes and quail eggs and serve with a squeeze of lime.

BEER PAIRING: BERLINER WEISSE

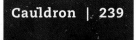

THE MOLOKA'I

This is John C.'s "whatever's in the fridge" recipe from his days as a young reporter working at a community newspaper in Kaunakakai, Hawaii. The original instructions read something like, "booze, booze, sneak over to the nice condos and use their grills, booze, booze, Maui onion chips, and watch reruns of *Magnum, PI* until you fall asleep on the couch." We've clarified this somewhat.

This is one of maybe six documented global cases where food invented under the influence of Jim Beam White Label and early-twenties poverty can't be improved upon.

4 tablespoons butter

4 tablespoons brown sugar

Splash of dark rum

1 cup fresh pineapple, cut into 1-inch cubes and threaded onto soaked wood or metal skewers

8 toasted hot dog buns

8 char-grilled hot dogs

1 cup crumbled blue cheese

MB(B)Q Sauce (page 273), to serve

1. Melt the butter and mix with the brown sugar and rum.

2. Grill the pineapple over medium-low heat, turning frequently and brushing with the butter mixture, for 12 to 15 minutes, until caramelized. Remove and dice.

3. Lay the hot dogs in the buns and top with the chopped grilled pineapple, blue cheese, and a generous squeeze of sweet barbecue sauce.

BEER PAIRING: DOUBLE IPA

UTOPENCI
(OR: VFW BAR SAUSAGE)

Two things we love: traveling the world and dive bars. Dive bars with food are where you get the feel of the regional flavors and one of our favorite cuisines is from Prague. Utopenci is a smoked skinless sausage (the actual translation is "drowned men") that's pickled with onions and in our case cucumbers and jalapeños. It's rumored to be a hangover cure.

MAKES 1 GALLON JAR

1 bay leaf

4 cups water

2½ cups white vinegar

1 teaspoon sugar

1 teaspoon salt

1½ teaspoons yellow mustard seed

½ teaspoon whole peppercorns

¼ teaspoon ground clove

3 14-ounce packages smoked kielbasa

3 white onions, sliced

1 jalapeño, sliced

32-ounce jar thick-sliced pickles

5 cloves garlic

1. Boil the bay leaf with water, vinegar, sugar salt, mustard, pepper corns, and clove for 5 minutes.

2. While liquid is cooling, cut the sausage into 4-inch lengths and then in half. In a gallon-sized pickling jar, layer 6 cut sausages, ½ onion, 2 slices jalapeño, 8 pickle slices. Top with garlic cloves and repeat to the top of the jar.

3. Pour the pickling liquid over to fill jar. Cover and refrigerate for 2 weeks. It's worth the wait.

4. Serve the sausage topped with onion and pickles.

BEER PAIRING: FLANDERS RED ALE

DORITOMALES

This is an easy, delicious snack that affects one's brain much in the manner of methamphetamine, fine whiskey, or a rare bit of praise from an emotionally distant father. Sure, it's not exactly health food, but if you're going to eat instant ramen and nacho chips, smashing them together into something amazing isn't going make it any worse for you.

Since instant ramen, bagged chips, and hot water are all items you can find in a bare-bones commissary, it illustrates the fact that we learned the art of Doritomales from those desperate, wild-eyed outcasts forced to the margins of society: graduate students.

(Later, we learned that prisoners pioneered the dish, which admittedly didn't change our descriptor much.)

MAKES 4 TAMALES

4 3½-ounce packets of Top Ramen (any flavor), flavor base packets removed

4 2⅛-ounce bags of cheese-flavored corn chips

Sriracha, to serve

1. Boil 4 cups of water in a kettle.

2. Remove flavor packets from ramen and crush that ramen up real good, son. Make sure to keep each block of noodle-bits separate, because we're making four of these glorious bastards. While you're crushing the noodles, crush the chips too. Maybe remove the chips from the bag to crush so it's not pierced by nacho shrapnel.

3. Place one of the crushed noodle portions in a chip bag along with one of the crushed chip portions. Shake it until everything's evenly distributed.

4. Place the bag on a small sheaf of newspaper and add half a cup of boiling water to the bag, then add the ramen flavor packet. Toss to distribute the seasoning.

5. Add the rest of the water, mix, and roll the bag from the bottom into a tube-like tamale shape. Wrap *that* with the newspaper, then place seam side down in a small pan that will corral any stray water. Let it sit for 15 minutes to become something new and amazing.

6. Unwrap, drizzle the tamale with Sriracha, and eat with a plastic fork. You can use whatever fork you like, but it's best with plastic.

BEER PAIRING: WEST COAST IPA

DIVE BAR PICKLED EGGS

MAKES 12 PICKLED EGGS

12 eggs

2 (15 ounce) cans whole pickled beets, juice reserved

½ cup chopped white onion

2½ cups white vinegar

¾ cup water

¾ cup sugar

1½ teaspoons salt

1½ teaspoons pickling spice

8 whole cloves

1 cinnamon stick

3 sliced habanero peppers

3 sliced jalapeño peppers

1. First off, keep your damn eggs in the damn refrigerator. Get a big pot of water to a rolling boil, then dunk the eggs straight from the fridge into the roiling waters. Cover the pot and reduce the heat to its very lowest setting.

2. Cook the eggs for 11 minutes while you prepare an ice bath for them. When they're done, shock them in the water and let them sit for 15 minutes. Remove and peel, or dry them and let them chill out overnight in the fridge.

3. When you're ready to get a-picklin', place the beets, onion, and peeled eggs in a non-reactive glass or plastic container and set aside.

4. In a medium-size, non-reactive saucepan, combine the vinegar, water, sugar, salt, pickling spice, 1 cup reserved beet juice, cloves, cinnamon stick, and peppers. Bring the mixture to a boil, stirring frequently, then lower the heat and simmer for 5 minutes.

5. Remove from the heat and pour the hot liquid mixture over beets, onions, and eggs. Cover and refrigerate at least 48 hours. For best results, refrigerate for 2 to 3 weeks. Use the time to cover your house in wood paneling and complain about the damn politicians and also kids these days.

BEER PAIRING: GUEZE

BAO
(STEAMED BUNS)

Steamed buns, or *baozi*, are a staple item in a lot of regional Chinese cooking. Soft, pillowy buns give way to . . . well, anything. Depending on where you're grabbing a snack, you can get barbecued char siu pork, bean paste, custard, or some scrambled eggs and hard sausage. Go nuts with it—Spam, bacon jam, a second smaller bao—the dough is your canvas.

MAKES 12 BUNS

3¼ cups (390 grams) unbleached all-purpose flour

¾ cup (185 grams) warm (120°F) water

2½ tablespoons (20 grams) fresh yeast

1 teaspoon (6 grams) salt

¾ pound chopped Yucatan Pork (page 185), Sesame Steak Manapua (page 183), Imperial Shortribs (page 251), or any meat of your choice, to fill

2 scallions, sliced thin

1. Add the flour and water to the bowl of a mixer fitted with the dough hook. Run on low until combined, then add the yeast and salt. Mix for 6 to 8 minutes, until smooth.

2. Remove the bowl, cover, and let rise in a warm place for one hour, until doubled.

3. Divide the dough into 8 to 10 equal balls, then roll out into circles.

4. Add a tablespoon of filling to each, add a pinch of sliced scallion, then lift around the edges and pinch closed at the top, twisting.

5. Line a bamboo steamer with cabbage leaves or parchment paper to avoid sticking and steam 12 to 15 minutes.

BEER PAIRING: APA

DUTCH OVEN KOREAN BBQ BEEF TACOS

RECIPE BY ED KOWALSKI

This is a simple, tasty dish that really brings out big, new flavors and requires minimal skill (and, more importantly, minimal clean up) to prepare.

SERVES 6

KOREAN BBQ SAUCE

¾ cup dark brown sugar

2 tablespoons minced garlic

1 tablespoon rice wine vinegar

1½ tablespoons Sriracha

1 teaspoon ginger, freshly grated

1 teaspoon toasted sesame oil

1½ teaspoons ground black pepper

1 tablespoon cornstarch

1 tablespoon water

MEAT

1 large red onion, thinly sliced

2⅓ pounds boneless beef chuck or flank steak, trimmed

TOPPINGS

½ head Napa cabbage, finely shredded

1 large carrot, peeled and shredded

8 scallions (white and green parts) thinly sliced on a bias (diagonal)

½ cup lightly packed cilantro sprigs

12 6-inch flour tortillas

1. To make the sauce, in a saucepan, combine all ingredients except cornstarch and water. Whisk to combine and bring to a boil.

2. In a small bowl, whisk cornstarch and water together until cornstarch dissolves; pour into boiling sauce mixture.

3. Reduce heat to medium-low and cook until thick, about 3 to 5 minutes.

4. To make the meat, preheat oven to 300°F, or set up your grill for indirect grilling at 300°F.

5. Place onions in the bottom of a Dutch oven (preferably cast-iron, but ceramic will work as well).

6. Add beef, then BBQ sauce. Cover tightly and cook until very tender, about 4 hours. Remove beef and shred, using two forks or BBQ claws.

7. Drain excess fat from the Dutch oven, then stir in ¼ cup water to the caramelized BBQ sauce. Place shredded beef back into crock pot, stir, and allow to cook for an additional 10 minutes. Drain beef, reserving sauce for later use.

8. To make the topping, combine all ingredients except tortillas.

9. For best results, grill tortillas for about 1 minute (30 seconds per side) before serving.

10. Add slaw to center of tortilla, then top with drained beef.

11. Top with reserved sauce and serve.

BEER PAIRING: RAUCHBIER

WALKING TACOS

Call it Frito Pie, Walking Tacos, Petros, or whatever, this is an American classic. It's our rich, spicy, beefy collective id all wrapped up on a colorful foil packet. Sure, it makes 12, but you'll eat 11 of them yourself.

MAKES 12 MOBILE TACOS

3 cloves garlic, skin-on

5 dried chiles de arbol, stems and seeds removed

2 dried mulato chiles, stems and seeds removed

2 dried pasilla chiles, stems and seeds removed

1½ tablespoon duck fat, bacon fat, or vegetable oil

1 large yellow onion, diced

3 cloves garlic, peeled and minced

2 cups chicken stock

1 pound beef brisket, coarse ground

1 pound boneless beef short rib, coarse ground

½ pound sirloin, coarse ground

1 tablespoon kosher salt

2 tablespoons brown sugar

20 grams (just under 1 ounce) bittersweet baking chocolate (70 percent cacao)

1 tablespoon soy sauce

2 tablespoons Worcestershire sauce

4 tablespoons tomato paste

1 teaspoon anchovy paste

1 teaspoon chili powder

½ teaspoon coriander seeds, toasted and ground

¼ teaspoon cumin seeds, toasted and ground

3 cloves, toasted and ground

1½ cups (12 ounces) brown ale or bock beer

¾ cup tomato sauce

1 cup Mexican crema (or sour cream)

1 medium avocado, sliced and tossed with lime juice

Juice of ½ lime

12 1-ounce bags of corn chips

Chopped white onion, to serve

Chopped jalapeños, to serve

Shredded extra-sharp cheddar, to serve

Hot sauce, to serve

RECIPE CONTINUES

1. Heat a heavy skillet over medium heat and toast the skin-on garlic until slightly blackened, about 3 to 5 minutes. Remove and set aside to cool.

2. Toast the chiles 2 to 3 minutes, flipping frequently and pressing down with a spatula, until just fragrant.

3. Remove the chiles to a bowl. Peel garlic and add to a heat-proof bowl with the chiles.

4. Bring the chicken stock to a boil and pour over the chiles and garlic. Cover with a heatproof sheet or foil for 20 minutes.

5. While the chiles steep, toss the beef together gently to evenly mix the ground cuts. Brown in a large pot in batches and remove, draining the excess fat. Set aside.

6. Carefully remove the chiles and garlic cloves to a blender carafe or food processor, taking care to reserve the steeping liquid. Pour over enough of the stock to cover and add the salt, sugar, and chocolate. Mix until thoroughly pulverized. Add additional soaking liquid if necessary. Strain and discard solids. Taste for seasoning and set aside.

7. Heat the fat or oil over medium heat and add onion. Sauté until onion softens slightly, about 5 minutes. Add the garlic and sauté another minute, until fragrant. Add the Worcestershire, soy sauce, tomato and anchovy pastes, and the ground spices. Mix and let cook 5 minutes.

8. Add the beer to the pot, scraping up any stuck-on bits. Add the meat and just under a cup of the chile puree, stirring to mix thoroughly. Add the tomato sauce. Check for consistency and add remaining stock as necessary, ¼ cup at a time. Bring to a boil and reduce to a simmer for 30 minutes.

9. Place the crema, avocado, and lime juice in a blender or food processor and process until completely smooth. Taste for seasoning and set aside.

10. Taste the chili and adjust with cayenne, salt, and/or lime juice.

11. Open the chip bags and scoop a couple ladelfuls of chili into them. Garnish with the onion, jalapeños, crema, cheddar, and hot sauce.

BEER PAIRING: BOCK

IMPERIAL SHORTRIBS

Imperial stouts create a solid buzz, what with the large volume of malt that's used to create a thick, sweet beer high in alcohol. This sweetness is also great for cooking. Take the bitterness of ancho and the sweetness of an imperial stout, throw in coffee for good measure and you're going to get a stellar braise.

MAKES 8 POTIONS

5 dried ancho chiles, stems, seeds, and ribs removed

1¼ cups fresh brewed coffee

3 cloves garlic, peeled

2 tablespoons honey

1 tablespoon oil

8 cross-cut beef short ribs (3 to 4 pounds total), excess fat trimmed

1¼ cups imperial stout

1 large yellow onion, quartered

1 teaspoon lime juice

½ teaspoon salt

½ teaspoon pepper

1. Preheat oven to 300°F.

2. Soak the chiles in bowl of water for 30 minutes until soft, then remove and combine chiles, coffee, garlic, and honey in food processor and puree.

3. On the stove, heat oil in a pot or Dutch oven over high heat and brown ribs. This should take about 5 minutes total but you may need to do it in batches depending on the size of your pan.

4. Remove ribs and oil, reserving 1 teaspoon for dripping.

5. Add chile puree and beer to pot, scrape the bottom, bring to a boil, and simmer for a few minutes.

6. Line bottom of braising pan with onions and top with short ribs. Spoon braising liquid over the top.

7. Cover and cook in the oven for 2½ hours, basting every hour, then uncover and cook for another hour.

8. Remove ribs and onions, skim fat, and the add the lime juice, salt, and pepper reduce the sauce until thickened, stirring constantly. Plate ribs and onions, then pour sauce over.

BEER PAIRING: GOSE

BACON SNICKER SNACK BARS

This comes in at more than twice the ingredients of our Doritomale (page 242), but you can still get everything you need at the closest convenience store. Remember, it still counts as street food if you've just stumbled in from the street.

This is another important building block in our dream to someday throw a seven-course, tasting menu dinner using entirely items from the Hudson News in Terminal 3 of O'Hare International Airport.

MAKES ONE 9 X 9-INCH PAN

5 strips of bacon, cut into ½-inch lardons

Bag of marshmallows

¼ cup butter

1 box of puffed rice cereal

2 king size snicker bars, cut into ½-inch chunks

1. Cook the bacon in a pot over medium until the fat renders and the pieces start to become crispy. Remove to a towel-lined plate.

2. Add the marshmallows to the pot, along with the butter, and stir until completely melted.

3. Drop the cereal in and remove the pot from the heat. Stir until everything is evenly mixed, then stir in the Snickers and bacon.

4. When everything's mixed nice and evenly, turn the mixture out into a greased 9 x 9-inch pan and pat down until everything's distributed evenly and the top is smooth.

5. Let cool for 30 minutes, then flip the pan over onto a cutting board. Cut into 2 x 2-inch squares and serve immediately.

BEER PAIRING: ENGLISH PALE ALE

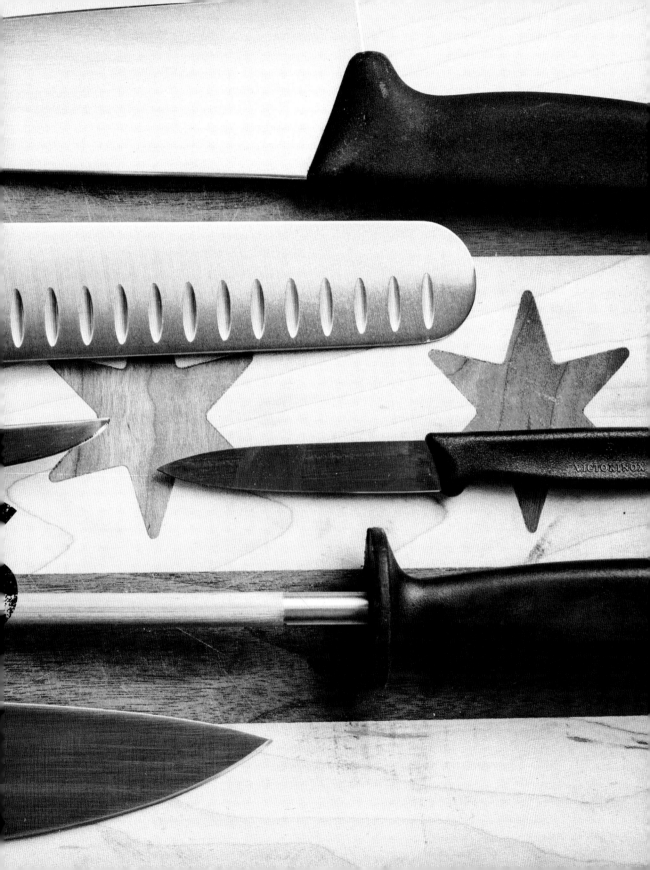

KNIVES AND STONES

In our brave new era of Science Cooking, it's important to remember that sometimes all it takes to make something delicious is something sharp to cut with or something heavy to smash the crap out of ingredients.

Let's give you the lowdown on buying a sharp knife and keeping it that way, then we'll make some delicious food with the aid of absolutely no cooking surface.

I WILL CUT YOU: Our Polite but Firm Suggestions for Using and Maintaining Knives

For all the fancy expensive-as-shit gadgetry that you can buy after watching other people cook on TV, The Knife stands alone in its usefulness. You can cook a steak on a hot rock if you want (they have entire restaurants for it!), but you can't fillet a fish with a prison shiv. A good knife is essential, and your ability to care for it is essential to its continued excellence.

If you've gone through the knife-buying process before, then you know that there's an endless selection of kitchen cutlery made of every imaginable material for supposedly every purpose. And just like any consumer product class, a lot of it is pure crap. Luckily, your Uncle ManBQue (who smells like whiskey but is generally a good sort) is here to help you sort through the bullshit and get what you need.

Buy what you need

It's really easy to step in front of a gleaming selection of knives and envision yourself as a badass lone Ronin on the culinary battlefields. But the entire expensive kitchen crap industry is based around these inflated expectations, because they want your money and they'll go overboard in stoking your fictional samurai ego to do so. So, much as it pains us to say, you probably don't need a Hattori Hanzo sushi sword, special kitchen shears, or something that can cut through soup cans.

In fact, if you're packing a culinary apocalypse kit, you really only need two knives—a chef's knife and a paring knife. The chef's knife should be between 6 and 10 inches long. There are various styles of chef's knives—French, santoku, cooks', drop point—and the real distinctions are comfort and personal choice. A paring knife is a paring knife, not a lot of options there.

Not that you need to keep things that ascetic. A good filet knife is important if you do a lot of whole fish. A dedicated boning knife means you're not beating up a good sharp edge on cartilage and bone. A serrated bread knife is good to have, and a thrift store knife will slice your brat bun just as well as a handcrafted full-tang cobalt with unicorn handle.

Skip the block sets

Generally speaking, big knife blocks are a gimmick to sell the other weird knives nobody normally buys. They waste counter space and are usually not worth the money. Buy the two or three you really need and skip the forty-two piece matching set your fiancée wants to register for.

"But," you say, "this one comes with steak knives!"

Those are silverware, not kitchen equipment, and they're usually poor quality throw-ins. Are you in the market for some new flatware? Great, get some steak knives that match and put them all in the drawer together.

Skip the space age polymers

You don't need poly-carbide-nanotube-cyborg knives. Robocop doesn't even need them, and he's...you know, a robot and stuff. Also, we don't think he eats. And he's fictional.

One popular alternate knife material is ceramic. It can be sharper than traditional knife materials, but ceramic knives are also prone to chipping. The catch there is that they can't be sharpened with typical equipment, if at all. Knives made of metal are more durable and easier to care for.

There are also countless "as seen on TV" knife products available. On that subject, don't. Just...don't.

The majority of quality kitchen knives are made of high carbon steel, stainless steel, or a blend of two called "high carbon stainless steel" (metallurgists aren't a very creative lot). High carbon steel sharpens easier, holds an edge longer, and is generally more durable than stainless. But it's more expensive and it rusts. Stainless is cheaper and won't rust, but it doesn't hold an edge nearly as well.

High carbon stainless, our creatively named hybrid, holds an edge longer than normal stainless steel, and it's still cheaper than carbon steel—it's really the best of both worlds. It's not a perfect balance, and there are definitely people who will argue at length that carbon steel is the only way to go. But for most cooks, high carbon stainless steel will offer the best performance for your money.

Shop in person

You don't necessarily need to buy in person, but get your actual physical hands on some knives before deciding. Unless you're on a TV show and someone is paying you gobs of money to shill their brand, comfort is the deciding factor. Stop into one of those high-end kitchen stores with French words or ampersands in their name and try out some options, see how they feel in your hand. Think of it like buying shoes. Really shiny, sharp shoes.

Don't fall for pretty knives

There are a lot of pretty knives out there. They tend to be expensive.

Some options on knives are cosmetic and will raise the price while offering little to the functionality of the blade. These include:

- **Hammered finish.** This uneven surface of the blade will break surface tension and keep foods from sticking to the blade. But a granton or scalloped edge will do the same without adding as much to the price tag.

- **Hollow ground.** The sharpened edge curves to the apex, which occurs when a blade is sharpened on a small wheel. It's common in straight razors, not so much with kitchen knives. This term is usually used (incorrectly) to describe a granton or scalloped edge.

- **Tropical wood handles.** Really pretty… and absolutely no function. Wood handles in general don't offer any additional benefit over composite. Wood vs plastic is a matter of personal choice as neither is "better" than the other.

- **Damascus steel.** Also known as wootz steel, originally an ancient material/method believed to have originated with the sword makers of the Middle East and India. Now applied to any metal that has cool swirls and patterns in it.

- **"Folded (insert number of) ___ times".** Reminiscent of samurai swords. The folding and hammering of metal doesn't actually add any benefit over modern forging methods. Sounds good, looks good, adds way too much money to the sticker.

It's not that pretty blades are bad. Actually, most of the brands that bother to make them pretty are good brands. But you can likely find something with similar functionality for a lot less. For our catering jobs, we'll use generic knives made by a dependable cutlery company—Forschner or Mundial knives are sharp enough that you'll want to use them every day, but if someone walks off with one, it's not Earth-shattering to replace a thirty-five dollar knife.

Easy with "The most dangerous knife is a dull one"

To begin with, that is probably the dumbest kitchen expression. A sharp knife will fuck you up the minute you start jacking around with it, just like a dull one. Kitchen knives are sharp, period. If it's not sharp, you'd have better luck deboning that leg of lamb with your teeth. You don't need a faux-sage catchphrase—just sharpen your damn knives.

Moreover, try to sharpen your own knives. It's not that hard, it'll save you money (providing you even take your knives in for sharpening as opposed to ignoring it), and there's something oddly satisfying about methodically polishing steel against a rock until it's sharp enough to shave with. There are as many choices of stone as there are knives, but here's the slow and skinny: Buy a two-sided, bonded abrasive stone, one side at 1,000 grit the other at 5,000. Pick up a two-dollar knife at Goodwill and practice. It's really that simple, provided you're asking us and not the guy at the expensive knife store.

So you've been watching a lot of food shows, taking notes and working on your best Bobby Flay impression. Suddenly the celebrity chef-of-the-week starts flipping the edge of his twelve-hundred dollar samurai chef knife back and forth across that metal sharpener thingy. It looks awesome. It *sounds* awesome. You need to learn how to sharpen your knife like that guy, right now. *SHICK SHICK SHICK.*

There are a few problems, but let's start at the beginning. It's TV, it's well edited, and it's not "real."

But almost as important, that's not a "sharpener" and that action doesn't sharpen a blade. That piece of equipment is honing steel, usually just called a steel. (Nobody calls it a "honer" . . .). They come in a wide variety of shapes, sizes, and materials; but they all serve the same purpose. They straighten the edge of the blade.

Using a knife will begin to fold the thinnest part of the edge to one side or the other; this is a normal occurrence and will happen with any blade under normal use. This fold, or burr, decreases the precision of the knife and if it becomes too severe will result in more of smushing action then actually cutting. A honing steel has either parallel ridges along its length or abrasive grit like sandpaper that is designed to remove a slight amount of material from the blade.

Using a honing steel is easy, but you have to take it slow and pay attention while you're getting the hang of it. Not enough of an angle and the motion does nothing effective. You'll continue to smash that tomato instead of slicing it. Too much angle and you will get immediate slicey results, but the steel can eventually dull the knife's edge. The angle between the blade and the steel should match the angle of the edge when sharpened. If you haven't sharpened the knife yourself, do that first. Generally speaking, most blades have thirty degree edges.

Ready? Sharp? Time to hone: Slide the knife down the length of the steel while simultaneously sliding the length of the blade away from the steel. Do the same to the reverse side of the blade and repeat a couple times. The direction of the blade in relation to the steel (push or drag) is mostly a matter of preference, but it's a good general rule to move the knife away from yourself.

Do this enough times, effectively enough, and maybe one day you can do the super-fancy TV *SHICK SHICK SHICK* motion and have a well-honed knife in four seconds. You'll look super cool. But until then, you'll have a really sharp, well-honed knife. And that's the biggest favor you can do for your cooking.

If you have an extra fancy ninja sword of a chef's knife, you should probably spend the money for the extra special honing steel that goes with it. Not only will the matching set go great with those shoes, but high end knives tend to be made of metal a lot harder than average kitchen implements—including steels. If you hone a knife on material softer than the knife, the knife will cut the steel, eventually smoothing out the steel instead of shaving off the burr.

PRETTY-DAMN-CLOSE MUFFULETTA SANDWICH

While it's not impossible to fool someone from New Orleans on an authentic dish from the Big Easy, it's damn well hard enough. We stopped trying years ago. Now we strive for a "pretty damn close," which is the regional equivalent of two Michelin stars. This gets you right to that almost-as-good-as-home line without the Catholic guilt kicking in.

MAKES 1 LOAF-SIZED SANDWICH

½ cup oil-packed black olives, chopped

½ cup oil-packed green olives, chopped

¼ cup chopped oil-packed artichoke hearts

¼ cup olive oil

2 tablespoons roasted red pepper, diced

2 tablespoons diced pimentos

1 tablespoon capers, rinsed and chopped

½ teaspoon garlic powder

½ cup diced Super 16-Bit Giardiniera (page 281), diced

1 round sesame loaf, split

½ pound provolone cheese, sliced

½ pound soppressata, sliced

¼ pound hot capicola, sliced

¼ pound mortadella, sliced

1. Mix the olives, artichoke hearts, oil, pepper, pimentos, capers, garlic powder, and giardiniera, and whisk to combine. If you're fond of the dark, muddy texture of a traditional olive salad, pulse it 2 to 3 times in a food processor. We like ours a little chunky.

2. Spread a protective layer of provolone along the bottom of the bread, then top with half of the olive salad.

3. Layer the meats in alternating geological shifts until you've exhausted the meats (we call that Dagwood-ing).

4. Spread the remaining olive salad over the top and press the top half of the loaf down firmly. Cut into quarters and find three other friends who miss the humidity and LSU football. Wrap leftovers in wax paper and foil.

BEER PAIRING: BOCK

BOURBON, BANANA, AND NUTELLA PALETAS

Paletas are the refreshing ice pop beloved of Mexico, Central America, and the Caribbean. You can flavor them any way you want (the Kentucky whiskey and Italian hazelnut spread are … not traditional). Plus, in countries where paleta carts crawl up and down the street during hot August afternoons, you never ever have to hear the eerie Lynchian droning of an ice cream truck speaker.

MAKES 6 PALETAS

1 very ripe banana, sliced

1 cup of bourbon

2 cups coconut milk

4 tablespoons Nutella

1 tablespoon crushed walnuts

1. Soak banana slices in bourbon for up to two weeks.

2. Whisk together the coconut milk and Nutella until all of the clumps have been smoothed out.

3. Transfer the coconut/Nutella mixture into a blender or food processor, add the bananas, and mix until very smooth.

4. In a separate bowl, add the crushed walnuts and mix evenly.

5. Pour into 4 to 6 molds and freeze at least 4 hours or overnight.

6. Unmold by first running a little cold water over outside of molds, then gently pulling the sticks.

CHIPOTLE COCTEL DE CAMARONES

The best part about Mexico beach vacations has always been the seafood. There was always chilled shrimp cocktail from a beach-side shack. We've tried and made many iterations of shrimp cocktail, trying to get that exact taste just right. You can get as complicated as you want with shrimp cocktails but this recipe should be the baseline for whatever creation your mind will come up with.

SERVES 4

1 pound medium shrimp, raw

1 cup chopped red onion

1 cup peeled, diced cucumber

½ cup chopped celery

1 jalapeño, minced

1½ cups freshly chopped tomatoes, with their juices

½ cup tomato sauce

½ cup adobo sauce

¼ cup chopped cilantro

2 tablespoons fresh lime juice

1 avocado, chopped

Sea salt, to taste

Saltines, to serve

1. Bring a large sauce pan filled with salted water to a boil (a tablespoon of salt for every 2 quarts of water, feel free to add other seasonings). Add the shrimp, and cook for 2 to 3 minutes, until just cooked through. The shrimp should be pink and opaque.

2. Add chopped onions, cucumber, celery, jalapeño, tomatoes, tomato and chipotle sauces, cilantro, lime juice, and avocado into a large bowl.

3. Cut ¾ of the shrimp into large chunks, leaving the other ¼ whole and add to the bowl with the other ingredients. Combine all the ingredients, gently stirring together.

4. Chill for at least 15 minutes before serving.

5. To serve, add salt to taste and serve with saltines.

BEER PAIRING: PILSNER

GUACAMOLE
("IT'S EXTRA, YOU KNOW THAT, RIGHT?")

Guacamole is beautiful in its simplicity, right up to the point where you screw it all up by trying to get fancy. Stick to this, friend. It will never steer you wrong.

Also, someone may have told you at one point that keeping the avocado pit in the guac is going to keep it from going brown. That's not even remotely true or effective, but it does indicate who among your friends makes guacamole and doesn't look into the explanations of things. Anything you do to preserve the life of the guac is going to involve keeping air and oxidation out. Your best bet is a layer of lime juice on top, a layer of plastic wrap directly on that, and then covering the whole shebang in an airtight container. Or just eat it all now, while it's at its very peak. Live for today, man.

MAKES ABOUT 3 CUPS

2 teaspoons sea salt

1 teaspoon lime juice

2 ripe avocados, pitted and diced

½ cup diced red onion

3 cloves garlic, minced

1. Sprinkle salt and lime juice on the avocados.

2. Fold in onion and garlic, mashing slightly with a wooden spoon if that's your thing.

3. Serve immediately—each moment is the very best that guac is going to ever be.

BEER PAIRING: LAGER

SMØRREBRØD

Smørrebrød are delicious, tiny open-faced sandwiches served on rye bread with the approximate density of a dying, faraway sun. The key is using good bread (any bakery-fresh dark rye will do) and a healthy smear of some good, fresh butter. If you've ever scoffed at the price of farm-fresh butter at the farmer's market, let this be the moment of your awakening.

You can make Smørrebrød with almost anything you want and that will fit on a 2 x 2 inch square of bread, but these are our favorites.

**MAKES 12 TINY OPEN-FACED SANDWICHES THAT
WILL MAKE YOU WISTFUL FOR SCANDINAVIA**

4 slices Danish rye (rugbrod), toasted and cut
   into 4 equal squares

Whipped butter, to spread

1. Spread the bread with the butter, then pile on:

OPTION 1: BEEFY

1 pound thinly sliced roast beef

Prepared horseradish

Thinly sliced red onion

Pickles or chopped cornichons

Dill

OPTION 2: CRAB-TASTIC

1 thinly-sliced Persian cucumber, salted

Crab salad

Remoulade (the Icelandic Hot Dog remoulade
   on page 238 and even a squirt of Harissa
   (page 286) works well)

Chopped fresh chives

OPTION 3: TEN MILLION TINY SHRIMP

½ pound rock shrimp, poached in olive oil

Pickled sliced radish

Chives

OPTION 4: SMOKY

½ pound smoked salmon

½ cup matchstick-cut radish

Crème fraiche

Chopped fresh chives

BEER PAIRING: HEFEWEIZEN

SWORDFISH & SCALLOP MANGO CEVICHE TOSTADAS

Jesse has an uncle that lives in Manzanillo, Mexico. He was a very accomplished sport fisherman. The guy has a huge sailfish mounted in his living room. He would have some great cookouts on the beach and he always made this amazing ceviche. Jesse once asked for his recipe and the guy laughed him away. In response, we came up with our own and it's better than his. Plus his kid is an asshole. So Jesse wins. But thanks to him all the same for inspiring this recipe.

MAKES 4 TOSTADAS

¾ pound swordfish, skinned and diced into ¼-inch pieces

¼ cup bay scallops

1 cup fresh mango, diced

½ cup finely chopped red onion

¾ cup cilantro

1 cup lime juice

½ cup jalapeño

1 finely chopped serrano pepper

3 tablespoons mezcal

2 tablespoons virgin olive oil

3 teaspoons sea salt

1 teaspoon black pepper

4 tostadas

1. In a large bowl, mix the swordfish, scallops, mango, onion, and cilantro.

2. Stir in the lime juice, jalapeño, serrano pepper, mezcal, and olive oil.

3. Season with sea salt and pepper and mix well. Cover tightly with plastic wrap and refrigerate for 4 to 5 hours.

4. Serve on tostadas, add some avocado/tomatillo salsa between the ceviche and tostada.

BEER PAIRING: FARMHOUSE SAISON

TRAMEZZINO

Tramezzino is the Italian's take on a British tea sandwich. This is our take on the Italian's sandwich. Where will it stop? We don't drink much tea either, so pair it with a beer. The sandwich is a crustless square bread sliced in half. It takes minutes to make and is an on-the-go dish in Italy. You can eat each sandwich in four bites!

MAKES 8 SANDWICHES

½ pound soft fresh goat cheese

⅓ cup forelle pear, chopped

½ tablespoon chopped walnuts

1 loaf Italian bread, sliced

8 slices Prosciutto, cut into strips

Baby arugula

1. In a food processor, combine goat cheese and pears, then process until smooth. Mix in chopped walnuts.

2. Slice bread and cut off crusts so slices are square.

3. Layer prosciutto, arugula, and the goat cheese spread on sandwich. Slice sandwich into triangles and serve.

BEER PAIRING: BERLINER WEISSE

PIGWICH

If you had to choose one sandwich to eat for the rest of your life, this should be it. You can make a full Smoked Porchetta from scratch (page 164), use leftovers, or purchase some fine cured meats from a ruddy butcher with a heart of gold.

MAKES 12 SANDWICHES

¾ cup mayonnaise

1 tablespoon capers, chopped

3 cloves garlic, minced

2 tablespoons lemon juice

½ teaspoon kosher salt

½ teaspoon freshly ground black pepper

12 ciabatta rolls, split

6 pounds porchetta, chopped

3 cups baby arugula

1. To make the aioli, mix the mayonnaise, capers, garlic, lemon juice, salt, and pepper with a whisk or in a food processor until blended. Refrigerate for 30 minutes.

2. Open ciabatta roll and layer porchetta and arugula on the bottom half. Spread the aioli on the inside top half of ciabatta and place onto the pork and arugula to make the finest pork sandwich ever.

BEER PAIRING: SAISON

DRUNK GUY NACHOS!

RECIPE BY LUKE GELMAN

If you're like us, you love to drink, enjoy life, and eat some nachos. This simple recipe takes five minutes and requires minimal motor skills. We call them pay-it-forward nachos because you can prep the nachos before you go out to the bars and you can quickly make them. Plus if you decide to go to bed without eating . . . BOOM! Breakfast nachos.

Note: This is a 5-minute recipe. You can substitute everything here for store bought and pre-prepared. The first time we tried this it was with leftovers from a local Tex-Mex.

MAKES 1 GIANT PLATE OF NACHOS

2 strips bacon

1 egg

Tortilla chips

½ cup shredded cheese

¼ cup Grilled Fruit and Sweet Corn Salsa (page 296)

¼ cup Guacamole (page 263)

Hot sauce, to taste

1. First up, get a plate and 2 sheets of paper towels. Lay your bacon on one paper towel and cover with the other paper towel. Put it in the microwave for 1½ to 2 minutes, until they are just about crispy. Watch out, it will be hot.

2. While your bacon is in the microwave, fill a small coffee mug halfway with water and drop your egg in. When the bacon comes out, microwave your egg for 45 seconds to 1 minute and check to see if the water is getting cloudy. If so, you are good.

3. Place one layer of chips on your plate and cover with the shredded cheese. Then add another layer of chips and more cheese. Almost like a lasagna. Go 3 layers and put it in the microwave for 1 minute. While this is going, shred your bacon into chunks.

4. When the cheese is melted, plate your cooked egg, bacon, salsa, and guacamole, and pour your hot sauce all over. You're done. 5 minutes, amazing nachos.

BEER PAIRING: PILSNER TONIGHT AND AN INTERVENTION TOMORROW.

PIMENTO CHEESE

This is caviar of the South, according to people who don't seem to know what caviar is or tastes like. Nonetheless, it is a delicious burger topping, anytime snack, or spectacularly ineffective toothpaste.

MAKES 2 CUPS

1 pound extra-sharp cheddar, grated

½ cup mayonnaise

½ cup diced pimentos

2 cloves garlic, minced

1 teaspoon cayenne pepper

1 teaspoon Worcestershire

½ teaspoon Marmite (optional)

1 jalapeño, seeded and diced

1. Place the shredded cheddar in a large, chilled mixing bowl and gently stir in the mayonnaise. You're not making a beer cheese here—it should just loosely come together.

2. Fold in the pimentos, garlic, cayenne, Worcestershire, Marmite, and jalapeño. Serve immediately with crackers and hot sauce.

BEER PAIRING: PALE LAGER

THE PANTRY

We know better than anyone that there's not always enough time to cook something, but there's always time to open a jar. Or a beer and a jar, in whatever order you like. These are the stockpilable (yes, it's a word) and time-tested recipes for our favorite condiments and pantry staples. Throw these on some leftovers or something ready-made and you've got a more interesting dish. We got the idea from that lady on TV who makes Kwanzaa cake with Entenmann's and asks riddles under the bridge.

MB(B)Q SAUCE

Just taking the time to make an easy barbecue sauce will do wonders for your cooking reputation among your friends. Take it from us—there's no store-brought sauce that comes close to the fresh, tangy taste of the quick homemade version. Send that gloppy vat-birthed ketchup back to Hell where it belongs.

MAKES 4 CUPS

2 cups tomato sauce

⅓ cup cider vinegar

2 tablespoons peanut oil

4 tablespoons yellow mustard

¼ cup molasses

¼ cup raw sugar

1 cup dark brown sugar

1 tablespoons kosher salt

2 teaspoons hot sauce

1 teaspoon smoked sweet paprika

1. Mix everything in a medium saucepan. Bring to a boil, reduce the heat to a simmer, and cook for 25 to 30 minutes, stirring often.

2. Blend, strain, and store in an airtight glass container for up to a few weeks. You'll probably use it all before then.

FRIED SHALLOTS

MAKES 4 CUPS

4 shallots, sliced thin on a mandoline

2 cups flour

1 tablespoon salt, plus more to season

2 teaspoons black pepper

Peanut oil, to fry

1. Heat oil to 325°F.

2. Pat shallots dry and dredge in flour.

3. Fry in batches for 1 to 2 minutes, until crisp and browned.

4. Remove to drain on paper towels, newspaper, or a paper bag. Season with salt immediately.

5. Let cool and store at room temperature in a covered container for up to 1 week.

KATSU SAUCE

This is a great sauce for anything fried, but especially our Katsu Pork (page 93)

MAKES 2 CUPS

1 cup ketchup

½ cup Worcestershire sauce

¼ cup demi-glace

¼ cup sugar

3 tablespoons soy sauce

2 tablespoons mirin

2 tablespoons mustard

½ teaspoon garlic powder

1. Combine all ingredients in a small saucepan. Heat over low, stirring, until the sugars dissolve and the mixture achieves consistency. Use immediately.

SPICY PICKLED WATERMELON

If you can pickle watermelon rind, truly the armadillo of fruits, then you can officially pickle anything to make it delicious.

You'll need to plan on an overnight soak to carry this recipe through completion, so we hope this isn't a watermelon rind emergency.

MAKES 3 PINTS

Rind from half of a medium-sized (5 to 10 pound) watermelon

1½ cups cane sugar, divided

¼ cup sea salt

2 sticks cinnamon

¾ tablespoon whole cloves, divided

1 large orange, thinly sliced

2 limes, thinly sliced

½ cup apple cider vinegar

½ cup distilled white vinegar

1 tablespoon coarsely chopped Thai chiles

1. Prepare the watermelon rinds by removing the green skin with a peeler or utility knife. Cut away most of the red flesh with a knife, but leave a thin coat. Cut as much of the rind as possible into ½-inch cubes (though much like people, many of the pieces will be oddly shaped) until you have 10 cups of rind. Set aside.

2. In a large stockpot over medium-low heat, combine 3 quarts of water with ¼ cup sugar, the salt, 2 cinnamon sticks, and 1 tablespoon cloves. Stir until the sugar and salt are completely dissolved, then remove from heat and let cool.

3. Transfer the watermelon rind into the brine. Weigh down the rind with a plate so they stay completely covered. Soak overnight.

4. Did you stay up all night because you were so excited about rinds? No? You say that's what a weird person would do? Fine. Drain the rind and rinse several times with cold water. Ass.

5. Place the rinds in a large stockpot and cover with cold water. Bring to a boil, lower heat to a simmer, and cook 10 minutes, until the pieces are tender but still crisp. Remove from heat, drain, and set aside.

6. Place the orange and lime slices, vinegars, remaining sugar, cinnamon sticks, Thai chiles, and remaining cloves in stockpot with 3 cups of water. Bring to a boil over high heat.

7. Add the rinds, bring back to a boil, reduce heat to low, cover, and simmer for 10 minutes.

8. Drain the rinds, catching the liquid in a bowl, and set them aside. Add the liquid back to the stockpot, bring to a boil over high heat, and reduce until it thickens slightly, 12 to 15 minutes. Transfer the syrup to a metal bowl and let it cool.

8. Pack the rinds into three glass pint jars. Divide the syrup evenly between jars, cover, and they're ready to eat. It keeps in the refrigerator for up to 2 weeks.

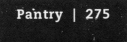

UK BROWN SAUCE

This is our own version of the United Kingdom's beloved HP sauce, which is what it would be like if the English had invented Heinz 57. Weirdly enough considering the subject matter, the Latin market is probably your best bet for finding tamarind pulp.

Yes, this is a lot of ingredients. Offer it up for the Queen.

MAKES ABOUT 4 CUPS OF FINISHED SAUCE

2 cups chopped apple

1 cup chopped yellow onion

⅓ cup water

½ cup white wine vinegar

½ cup cider vinegar

¾ cup tomato paste

½ cup apple juice

½ cup orange juice

½ cup tamarind pulp

¼ cup molasses

3 dates, pitted and chopped

3 prunes, chopped

1½ teaspoons kosher salt

½ teaspoon onion powder

½ teaspoon crushed black peppercorns

½ teaspoon cracked mustard seed

½ teaspoon allspice berries

¼ teaspoon whole cloves

¼ teaspoon garlic powder

⅛ teaspoon cinnamon

1. Add everything from the apples to prunes to a large saucepan. Bring to a boil, reduce heat to a simmer, and let cook 45 minutes.

2. Add the salt and spices, stir to combine, and simmer another 30 minutes to thicken.

3. Puree then push through a mesh strainer.

4. Taste and adjust seasoning with additional cider vinegar and/or salt. Store in glass jars.

CALIENTE CHOCOLATE SAUCE

This is a great dipping sauce for Churros (page 69) or fried sweet anything. It adds depth to grilled fruits like pineapple.

MAKES ABOUT 1½ CUPS

½ cup heavy cream

¾ cup chopped Mexican chocolate

½ teaspoon arbol chili powder

½ teaspoon vanilla extract

¼ teaspoon ground cinnamon

1. Heat the heavy cream in a medium saucepan over medium-low heat until it begins to simmer.

2. In a separate bowl, combine the chocolate, chili powder, vanilla, and cinnamon.

3. Pour the hot cream over the combined ingredients and whisk until smooth—pick one direction, clockwise or counter-clockwise, and stick with it for a more attractive result.

VANILLA CAJETA

MAKES ABOUT 5 CUPS

4 cups goat's milk

4 cups whole milk

2 cups sugar

1 tablespoon ground cinnamon

½ teaspoon baking soda

1 teaspoon water

2 tablespoons vanilla extract

1. In a large pot, whisk together the milk, sugar, and cinnamon and set over medium-high heat. Bring to a simmer, whisking periodically.

2. In a small bowl, mix together baking soda and water until combined. Remove pot from heat and slowly whisk in baking soda. The mixture will bubble up, so be careful to not let it spill over. Huge mess—we'd know.

3. When the bubbles subside, place the pot back over medium-high heat. Bring back to a simmer, stirring frequently. Keep an eye on the heat.

4. Cook for 2 hours, stirring frequently so the cajeta doesn't burn at the bottom.

5. When it's reduced by half, remove from heat and stir in the vanilla. Serve warm.

99 LUFTBALONS CURRY SAUCE

This is our very best version of the beloved German street food ketchup.

MAKES ABOUT 2½ CUPS

2 tablespoons vegetable oil

¾ pound chopped yellow onion

2 tablespoons curry powder

1 tablespoon smoked hot paprika

2 cups peeled canned tomatoes, crushed (along with the juices)

½ cup sugar

½ cup cider vinegar

1. Heat the oil over medium heat in a large skillet. Sauté the onion until translucent, then add the curry and paprika and cook another minute.

2. Add the tomatoes, sugar, and vinegar. Bring to a boil, reduce heat to a simmer, and cook 15 to 20 minutes, until thickened.

3. Puree in a blender or food processor and strain before serving.

DINER SAUCE
RECIPE BY LUKE GELMAN

Are you griddling a slab of meat? Cooking onions until they're held together only by sugar and hope? Do you just need something to taste like a kickass short-order cook had a hand in it? Then this is the sauce you need.

MAKES ABOUT 1½ CUPS

4 egg yolks

2 tablespoons cider vinegar

¾ cup grape-seed oil

4 tablespoons yellow mustard

1 teaspoon kosher salt

¼ teaspoon black pepper

¼ cup grated onion

½ teaspoon hot paprika

1. Whisk the eggs and vinegar, slowly adding the oil, until it thickens. Does this seem familiar? That's because you're making mayo.

2. When the mayo forms, stir in the mustard, salt, pepper, onion, and paprika.

3. Taste for seasoning, adjust with salt or vinegar, and enjoy this beloved bastardized sauce you've made. Well done.

ISLAND PEANUT SAUCE

MAKES ABOUT 2 CUPS

1½ cups coconut milk

¼ cup smooth peanut butter

⅓ cup dark brown sugar

1½ tablespoons soy sauce

1 tablespoon red curry paste

3 tablespoons fresh lime juice

1. Whisk the coconut milk, peanut butter, brown sugar, soy sauce, and red curry paste in a saucepan. Bring to a boil, reduce heat to a simmer, and let cook for 3 minutes.

2. Remove from heat and whisk in the lime juice.

PINEAPPLE BOURBON SAUCE

MAKES ¾ CUPS

¾ cup pineapple juice

½ cup water

¼ cup bourbon

1 tablespoon packed brown sugar

1 teaspoon vanilla

1. In a small bowl, mix all ingredients well.

2. In small pan over medium-high, reduce sauce mixture for 4 minutes; should reduce down to half.

3. Let sauce cool to room temperature before using as a dipping sauce for your Scotch Egg (page 65).

CAJUN REMOULADE

MAKES 1¾ CUPS

1¼ cups mayonnaise

¼ cup stone-ground mustard

1 clove garlic, smashed

1 tablespoon pickle juice

1 tablespoon capers

1 teaspoon prepared horseradish

¼ teaspoon ground cayenne pepper

¼ teaspoon hot paprika

½ teaspoon tabasco sauce

1. Place all ingredients into a food processor and blend until smooth. If you lack such Jetsons-era technology, then whisk the holy hell out of it. Chill until ready to serve.

DUCK SAUCE

Duck (or orange) sauce is a bit of a conundrum: It contains neither duck nor orange and, despite being featured prominently in most Chinese restaurants in the good ol' U.S. of A., it is not of Chinese origin. An American creation (in keeping with our society's love of dipping fried chunks of meat in a sauce of some kind or another), it gets the name "orange sauce" from the orange color imparted by its ingredients.

There are duck sauce recipes on the ol' interweb that basically call for dumping fruit preserves in a bowl and mashing them up, but we prefer this method, in which real fruit is cooked down to release all of their respective flavors and then pureed into a smooth, rich sauce suitable for dipping. It also makes a fantastic glaze for chicken wings or pork.

MAKES ABOUT 2 CUPS

½ pound fresh plums, pitted and roughly chopped

6 ounces dried apricots, roughly chopped

1 cup apple juice

¼ cup unseasoned rice wine vinegar

3 tablespoons light brown sugar, packed

2 teaspoons soy sauce

1 teaspoon fresh ginger, grated

¼ teaspoon mustard powder

¼ teaspoon crushed red pepper

1. Place all ingredients in a medium saucepan and bring to a boil over medium heat.

2. Reduce to a simmer and let cook until fruit is completely soft and sauce is thickened, approximately 30 minutes, stirring occasionally.

3. Puree until smooth with an immersion blender or in a regular blender. Serve immediately, or put it in an airtight container, where you can keep it refrigerated for up to 3 weeks.

SUPER 16-BIT GIARDINIERA

Giardiniera is absolutely essential to a delicious Italian beef. Equally essential, most everywhere outside of Chicago, is making it yourself. But don't worry, it's some chopping, some mixing, and then just letting stuff chill in a jar.

One traditional thing that we completely eliminate from the recipe is cauliflower. Ever get an about-to-go-bad cauliflower from the grocery? Horrific. If you're ever at an office party with crappy hors d'oeuvre and you're wondering what's dead, it's because the caterer didn't double-check their product. Best to avoid that possibility altogether.

In the interest of not repeating anything from our last book, we've created a new version of this classic condiment. And we appended "Super" and "16-Bit" to it, because our childhoods taught us that it's what you do when you upgrade things.

MAKES 1 QUART

1 cup carrots, cut into matchsticks

¾ cup sliced celery

½ cup sliced red bell pepper

½ cup quartered and diced jalapeños

½ cup sliced serranos

¼ cup oil-packed sport peppers, chopped

¼ cup kosher salt

2 teaspoons dried Mexican oregano

1 tablespoon crushed red pepper flake

1 teaspoon coarse-ground black pepper

½ teaspoon celery salt

1 cup white vinegar

1 cup grape-seed oil

1. Mix the carrots, celery, and peppers with the salt in a large bowl. Refrigerate overnight.

2. Rinse under running water, shake off excess water, and mix vegetables well.

3. Add the oregano, red pepper, black pepper, and celery salt to the vegetables and toss to coat.

4. Add the vinegar to the bowl and stir.

5. Whisk in the oil, and pour everything into a quart jar. Serve immediately or refrigerate.

OH WAIT, THIS ONE IS MY (BACON) JAM

MAKES 2 CUPS

1⅔ pounds smoked, cured bacon, diced

1 cup diced white onion

2 tablespoons dark brown sugar

⅓ cup cider vinegar

⅓ cup grade B maple syrup

4 cloves minced garlic

½ teaspoon chipotle powder

1. Over medium heat, cook the bacon in a Dutch oven until the fat is rendered.

2. Add the onion and cook 5 minutes, until soft and translucent.

3. Add the remaining ingredients and simmer, partially covered, until thick and reduced. Blend to a chunky consistency and serve with almost anything.

BAVARIAN SWEET MUSTARD

This mustard from southern Germany hasn't yet caught on as much as its more-popular Bavarian brothers—yet. Be a trailblazer and slather your brats with this to spread the word. HA! SPREAD! Dad jokes!

MAKES 2 CUPS

⅔ cup yellow mustard seed

⅓ cup brown mustard seed

⅔ cup dark brown sugar

½ cup water

½ cup dark German lager

1 cup cider vinegar

2 tablespoons honey

½ teaspoon ground cloves

1. Finely grind yellow mustard in a spice grinder, and then coarsely grind brown mustard.

2. In a saucepan, dissolve sugar in water, beer, and vinegar. Boil over medium-high for 8 minutes to reduce.

3. Remove from heat and mix in honey, cloves, and ground mustard. Pour mustard into a jar and refrigerate for 1 week before serving.

BAYRISCH KRAUT

RECIPE BY DANIEL SISTO

MAKES ABOUT 4 CUPS

¼ pound bacon, cut into small cubes

2 sweet onions, sliced

1 apple, julienned

½ tablespoon cumin seeds

1 cup light brown sugar

⅜ cup apple cider vinegar

1 small cabbage, cored and chopped

1 cup chicken broth

½ tablespoon honey

¼ teaspoon salt

¼ teaspoon pepper

1. Heat a large pan or pot over medium heat and fry the bacon.

2. Add onions and apple and cook in the grease for 3 minutes, then add cumin seeds.

3. Pour in the sugar and as soon it's caramelized, add vinegar.

4. Let the vinegar reduce by 50 percent and add the cabbage.

5. Add broth ¼ cup at a time over cabbage. Let reduce, then add another ¼ cup. Repeat until the cabbage is cooked but still has some bite.

6. Remove from heat and add honey, salt, and pepper.

BLUE CHEESE ALE SAUCE

½ cup cream

½ cup beer

½ pound blue cheese

1 teaspoon Worcestershire sauce

1 teaspoon arrowroot powder

1. In a saucepan, bring cream and beer to a simmer. Mix in blue cheese and Worcestershire sauce.

2. While cheese is heating, mix arrowroot with 1½ tablespoons of water in a bowl.

3. When cheese is fully melted, remove from heat and mix in arrowroot slurry. Stir until thickened. Pour into a squeeze bottle and keep cold until you need it.

CHIMICHURRI

Argentina knows meat and chimichurri goes so damn well with flank steak. It's also versatile as a dipping sauce for empanadas, pasta sauce, or in a salad. But mostly meat. Pour it over your meat.

MAKES ABOUT 1½ CUPS

1 cup cilantro leaves, tightly packed

½ cup fresh flat-leaf parsley

1 teaspoon shallot

5 garlic cloves

½ teaspoon dried oregano

1 red jalapeño, quartered

2 tablespoons red wine vinegar

⅓ cup extra virgin olive oil

½ teaspoon salt

1. In a food processor, mix cilantro, parsley, shallot, garlic, oregano, jalapeño, and red wine vinegar then process until smooth. Add olive oil and salt and pulse until well blended.

GUASACACA

2 ripe avocados, chopped

1 small red onion, chopped (about 1 cup)

1 medium green pepper, chopped (about 1 cup)

2 cups chopped steamed cauliflower

2 cloves garlic

½ bunch cilantro

½ bunch curly parsley

¼ cup cider vinegar

1 teaspoon black pepper

1 tablespoon kosher salt

½ cup olive oil

1. Combine all the ingredients except the olive oil in a blender or food processor.

2. Pulse the ingredients until they're well mixed, but still chunky.

3. Slowly add the olive oil while pulsing until a smooth sauce starts to form, then store in a bowl or glass jar and refrigerate until it's time to serve.

HONEY SRIRACHA MAYO

MAKES ½ CUP

⅓ cup mayonnaise

½ teaspoon lime juice

3 teaspoons Sriracha

3 teaspoons honey

1. Whisk ingredients together in a bowl and refrigerate at least 30 minutes before serving.

ANCHO CHILE BBQ SAUCE

MAKES 3½ CUPS

2 dried ancho chiles, seeded, chopped

1 tablespoon olive oil

1 cup chopped onions

2 garlic cloves, minced

1½ cups chili sauce

1 cup apple juice

⅓ cup Worcestershire sauce

¼ cup apple cider vinegar

1 (8-ounce) can tomato sauce

1 teaspoon cumin

1 teaspoon dry mustard

¼ teaspoon salt

⅔ cup brown sugar

1. Soak the ancho chiles in hot water for 30 minutes.

2. Heat oil in medium saucepan over medium-high heat until hot. Add onions and garlic. Cook and stir until crisp-tender, about 3 to 4 minutes

3. Add all remaining ingredients. Mix well. Bring to a boil. Reduce heat to low. Simmer 1 hour. Strain and serve.

HARISSA

RECIPE BY JASON GILMORE

Harissa is the unofficial national condiment of Tunisia and is a well-known flavor of northern Africa. This hot pepper paste is used for flavoring stews, meat rubs, and to liven up vegetables.

MAKES 2 CUPS

2 red bell peppers

5 red jalapeño peppers

40 dried arbol chiles

8 garlic cloves

1 teaspoon coriander

1 teaspoon cumin

1 teaspoon caraway seeds

½ teaspoon salt

1 lemon, juiced

½ cup extra virgin olive oil

1. Roast the peppers over an open fame. Place in bowl and cover to cool. When cooled, remove skin and seeds.

2. Deseed the arbol chiles and toast quickly in a pan until fragrant, about 1 minute.

3. Soak the arbol chiles in hot water for about 20 minutes until they are rehydrated. Meanwhile, toast the spices in a dry pan until fragrant, about 3 minutes.

4. Drain the arbol chiles and add all the ingredients to a food processor. Then blend until smooth.

HAWAIIAN MILK BREAD

MAKES 2 LOAVES

⅔ cup room temperature heavy cream

1 cup room temperature whole milk, plus 1 tablespoon

2 eggs, room temperature, divided

⅓ cup sugar

4 cups all-purpose flour

1 tablespoon cornstarch

1 package (¼ oz) active dry yeast

1½ teaspoons salt

2 teaspoons pineapple juice

1. Combine the cream, 1 cup of the milk, 1 egg, sugar, flour, cornstarch, yeast, salt, and pineapple juice in the bowl of a stand mixer with a dough hook attachment.

2. Mix the dough on low speed for 15 minutes.

3. Turn off the mixer, move the mixing bowl to a warm place, and cover with a damp towel to proof for 1 hour. (If you're using this for the Manapua, you're good to go from here. If you want to make bread or rolls, by all means keep reading.)

4. Return to the stand mixer and stir with a bread hook for 5 minutes to remove any air bubbles.

5. Cut the dough in half and place in 2 buttered loaf pans. Cover with a damp cloth and let them rise for another hour.

6. Preheat oven to 350°F.

7. Make an egg wash by mixing the remaining egg and tablespoon of milk, then brush over the top of the loaves.

8. Bake until golden brown, 20 to 25 minutes.

HONEY BUTTER

MAKES 1½ CUPS

8 ounces salted butter, room temperature

½ cup honey

¼ tablespoon cayenne pepper

1. Place the butter into a small mixing bowl. Whip with a fork or hand mixer while adding the honey and cayenne.

2. When all ingredients are incorporated, spoon the butter onto a sheet of wax paper. Roll the paper, forming the butter into a log, and tie off the ends. Refrigerate for at least 48 hours to let the flavors marry.

CUBAN MOJO SAUCE

This classic marinade, pronounced "MOE-hoe," is the secret ingredient for the pork we layer into our Cuban Sandwiches (page 28). Sour oranges are sadly unavailable most everywhere, so we've accounted for that. If you're one of the lucky ones, substitute the orange and lime juices for ⅔ cup sour orange juice.

MAKES 1 CUP

12 cloves garlic, minced

⅓ cup orange juice

⅓ cup of fresh lime juice

2 tablespoons grape-seed oil

2 tablespoons dried Mexican oregano

1 tablespoon kosher salt

1 teaspoon black pepper

1. Mix everything together in a jar, seal, and shake furiously, *con pasión*. Use to marinade pork, chicken, and anything else that needs a citrus kick.

HOPS BUTTER

This four-ounce slice of hop heaven is the result of many, many failures. We attempted various hop-flavored permutations in advance of our first book and whiffed on all of them. At best, they were flat and one-note. At worst, we dubbed them Aspirin Wings. But we've finally killed this particular white whale, and there's no heavily symbolic price for our single-minded obsession. Just delicious beer-butter.

We take a technique from beer brewing to extract flavor from the hops and magically put it into butter. Brewing requires adding hops at precise times to give certain characteristics. Typically adding hops to wort and boiling for sixty minutes adds bitterness to beer, thirty minutes flavor, and ten minutes aroma. Since we're cooking with hops, we want the flavor. Be warned, this recipe calls for low alpha hops (Saaz), and trust us, you want to use low alpha hops. You may be a "hop head" and think you can handle a 10 percent alpha hop butter, but high-alpha will ruin everything you put it in.

MAKES 4 OUNCES

½ cup water

4 ounces (1 stick) unsalted butter

3 hops pellets (use a less than 5% alpha hop varietal)

1. On the stove, combine water and butter into saucepan and bring to a boil, then lower heat to heavy simmer.

2. Drop 3 hops pellets into the water and simmer for 30 minutes. For fucks sake, don't put the entire 1 ounce package of hops into the boil. Maybe a little perspective will help—1 ounce will flavor 5 gallons of beer; you're making 0.03125 gallons of butter.

3. After 30 minutes, remove from stove and cool until you can handle it. Pour mixture through a cheesecloth. It's recommended you strain through twice. Place in a container with a lid and put into the refrigerator overnight.

4. The next day the butter and water will have separated. Poke a small hole on the butter layer and pour the water out. Voila, you have hops butter.

PICKLED HOP SHOOTS

You see fields of hops in beer commercials, usually followed by a brewer rubbing their nose in a huge hop cone pile. Bavarian fields filled with the vine conjure the idea that hops are hard to grow. Sure, if you're going to harvest them for large breweries, then yes, they need to be specialized, but backyard hops are almost effortless to grow. They will make you and your yard look really cool and keep you company while you drink beer outside. We first started with hops in the city primarily to cover up an ugly chain link fence. It cost four bucks and it looked manlier than some purple morning glory.

If you're a homebrewer or beer lover, the first step into making your yard into a beer haven is to buy the hop rhizome. You can buy specific hop varieties, so pick your favorite one. If you plan to use these for brewing then choose a lower alpha hop since you can't actually measure the alpha acids and they tend to be higher than commercial ones. A rhizome costs less than ten bucks and will arrive in late March for planting. It'll be a four-inch thing that looks like a root that should be planted in the ground, not a pot. We've never seen hops thrive potted, plus they come back year after year. Plant once and be done with it.

Hops are easy to grow. Seriously, they can grow over a foot a day so you better have a plan. Wind them through a chain link fence, have them climb a pergola, or have them climb a rope. The first year you can expect a decent size plant that consists of a few shoots and grows to ten feet. You can harvest the hops or wet hop your beer that's in your hand around September. Our test to tell if hops are ready to harvest is if the cones fall off when you flick them. It's wise to cut your plant all the way down at the end of the growing season.

The root system becomes larger every year so the second year you'll see shoots coming up in a greater radius around your initial rhizome. We would suggest trimming these back and have the strongest part of the hop plant grow. This year the plant will take off and grow up to twenty feet and fill out. You'll need to spend time pruning it and training it to go where you want it to grow.

After three years of growth, the root system has expanded and there will be purple shoots in a large radius around you the first planting. They'll look somewhat similar to thin asparagus. Since first growth should be cut down, it seems a waste not to use them. Pickling hops never occurred to us in previous years until a friendly neighbor asked if we ever ate hops. With a puzzled look we thought the neighbor was referring to eating hop cones so we dug a little further. As a native of upper Wisconsin, he informed us that pickled hop shoots were served at many bars. This being new to us, we were immediately intrigued and started conceptualizing a recipe for next spring. The best time to pick is in late April.

MAKES ONE 16 OUNCE JAR

1 hop cone

½ teaspoon whole coriander

1 garlic clove

3 juniper berries

1 bunch of freshly cut hop shoots, leaves
   removed and washed

1½ cups champagne vinegar

½ cup water

1 cup sugar

1 tablespoon non-iodized salt (like sea salt)

1. Place a sealed jar in a large pot and fill with water to cover by a ½ inch. Remove and dry the jar. Bring the water to a boil while you prepare your pickling liquid.

2. Add the hop cone, coriander, garlic, juniper, and hop shoots to a jar.

3. Combine the vinegar, water, sugar, and salt in a saucepan and bring to a boil, stirring, until the salt and sugar dissolve.

4. Remove from the heat and pour the liquid over the hop shoots to the fill line in the jar, then tightly screw on the lid.

5. Carefully place the closed jar into the boiling pot and process in a water bath for 10 minutes. Cool at room temperature to seal the jar. Refrigerate for 3 weeks before opening.

PESTO

Worried about what you're going to do with all the basil in your yard before the first frost kills it? You can never go wrong with pesto, which tastes good with any pasta and freezes like a champ.

MAKES 2 CUPS

3 tablespoons toasted pine nuts

2 cups basil leaves, packed

2 cloves garlic

½ cup olive oil

¼ cup grated Parmesan

½ teaspoon kosher salt

1. Mix everything except the olive oil in a blender or food processor. If you're feeling old school, mash it up in a mortar and pestle and learn what it's like to truly hate ingredients.

2. Transfer to a glass container, drizzle with a layer of olive oil over the surface, then place a square of plastic wrap over the top before covering. Freeze any unused pesto after 2 weeks.

PEAR CHUTNEY

Chutney is one of those rare condiments that you can eat by itself with a spoon without looking like a psycho. This is a pretty classic culinary school version of chutney, so you can sub in equal amounts of your favorite fruit to make the condiment of your dreams.

MAKES 4 CUPS

1 tablespoon vegetable oil

1 tablespoon grated ginger

1 tablespoon garam masala

3 jalapeño, diced

½ cup white vinegar

¼ cup apple cider vinegar, divided

¼ cup sugar

3 pounds ripe pears, diced

Salt, to taste

1. Heat the vegetable oil in a large saucepan over medium heat. Add the ginger, masala, and jalapeños and cook one minute, until fragrant.

2. Add the vinegars and the sugar. Heat, stirring, until the sugar dissolves.

3. Add the pears. Bring to a boil, reduce heat to a simmer, and cook 30 minutes, until the liquid thickens.

4. Season to taste with salt and cider vinegar.

PICKLED MUSTARD SEEDS

MAKES 2 CUPS

1 cup yellow mustard seed

1 cup water

½ cup sugar

2 tablespoons salt

1 cup champagne vinegar

1. Cover your mustard seeds with hot water in a large saucepan. Boil them, rinse them with a fine mesh strainer, return to the pot, and repeat the process 4 more times. This helps remove the natural bitterness of mustard seed. Remove seeds to a clean glass gar with a tight-fitting lid when they're finished.

2. Mix the water, sugar, salt, and vinegar in a saucepan and bring to a boil, stirring to dissolve salt and sugar. Remove from heat, pour over mustard seeds, and cover. They're good to go now, and they last weeks.

PICKLED PINEAPPLE RELISH

RECIPE BY KEN HAYNES

MAKES 2 CUPS

1½ cups rice vinegar

1 teaspoon cup sugar

1 jalapeño, sliced into rings

½ tablespoon kosher salt

Juice of two limes

1 fresh pineapple

¼ cup roughly chopped cilantro

1. Place the vinegar, sugar, jalapeño, salt and lime juice in a small sauce pot. Bring to a simmer and stir until the sugar is completely dissolved. Remove from the heat and let cool to room temperature.

2. Divide the pineapple in half and slice one half into rings. Dice the other half and return to the fridge in a sealed container for later.

3. Place the pineapple rings and cilantro into a large jar and pour the vinegar mixture over, making sure all the fruit is covered.

4. Seal and refrigerate for at least one day.

5. Remove pineapple slices from the jar and dice both the pickled and fresh pineapple then combine.

PORTER BEER MUSTARD

RECIPE BY JASON GILMORE

6 ounces porter

1 cup yellow mustard seeds

½ cup rice wine vinegar

½ tablespoon kosher salt

½ teaspoon fresh ground pepper

⅛ teaspoon ground cinnamon

⅛ teaspoon ground cloves

⅛ teaspoon ground nutmeg

⅛ teaspoon ground allspice

½ teaspoon whiskey

1. Combine all ingredients, cover, and soak overnight.

2. After the mustard seeds have absorbed most of the liquid, transfer everything to a food processor and blend to desired consistency.

RAS EL HANOUT

Arabic for "head of the shop," this spice blend can be found as a specialty in many North African spice shops. The fragrant blend adds bitter warmth with sweet finish to dishes and works great as a marinade, rub, or mixed with butter, yogurt, or sour cream as a topping.

MAKES ⅓ CUP

2 teaspoons ground cumin

2 teaspoons ground ginger

2 teaspoons ground nutmeg

2 teaspoons ground coriander

2 teaspoons turmeric

1½ teaspoons cinnamon

1½ teaspoons smoked paprika

1½ teaspoons cardamom powder

1 teaspoon ground black pepper

1 teaspoon cayenne pepper

½ teaspoon ground allspice

½ teaspoon ground cloves

¼ teaspoon ground mace

1. Mix all ingredients together. Store in an airtight jar.

ROASTED PEAR AND PINEAPPLE SALSA

RECIPE BY DAVE HANLEY

1 cup pineapple, diced

3 cloves garlic

2 green Anjou pears, diced

⅓ cup silver tequila

3 tablespoons light brown sugar

½ white onion, diced

1 cup cilantro, chopped

1 red pepper, diced

½ teaspoon salt

Juice of 3 limes

1. Preheat oven to 350°F.

2. In a roasting pan, add pineapple, garlic, and pears, coat with tequila and brown sugar, cover and roast 15 minutes till soft and slightly browned. During the last 5 minutes of cooking, remove cover to reduce juices.

3. After pineapple and pears have cooled, mix in a bowl with the rest of the ingredients.

DILL TZATZIKI

MAKES 2½ TO 3 CUPS

1 cucumber, peeled and grated

2 teaspoons kosher salt, plus more to taste

8 ounces Greek yogurt

3 cloves garlic, chopped

1½ tablespoons fresh dill, chopped

1 teaspoon lemon juice, plus more to taste

1. Toss the grated cucumber with the salt and place in a colander over a sink or a bowl.

2. Weigh down the cucumber with a heavy plate or water-filled bowl. Let sit 30 minutes to drain.

3. Remove the bowl and squeeze any remaining water out.

4. Place the cucumber in a food processor or blender, along with the yogurt, garlic, dill, and lemon juice. Process until smooth.

5. Taste for seasoning and adjust with salt and/or additional lemon juice.

GRILLED FRUIT AND SWEET CORN SALSA

MAKES 3 CUPS

2 ears sweet corn, husked, kernels removed

2 tablespoons olive oil

¼ cantaloupe, peeled, seeded, and sliced

¼ honeydew melon, peeled, seeded, and sliced

1 large red bell pepper, finely chopped

1 small red onion, finely chopped

Juice of 2 lemons

2 tablespoons fresh mint, chopped

2 tablespoons fresh cilantro, chopped

¼ teaspoon kosher salt

1. Preheat the oven to 350°F.

2. Toss the corn kernels with olive oil to coat and spread evenly on a baking sheet. Place the sheet on center rack of the oven and cook 10 to 15 minutes until kernels begin to brown, then remove from heat and allow to cool.

3. Set up grill for direct medium-high heat. Place the slices of fruit on the grill and cook for 30 seconds per side, then remove from heat.

4. Dice the fruit into ¼-inch pieces, place in a bowl with all other ingredients, toss to combine, cover, and refrigerate.

NEW MEXICO GREEN CHILE SAUCE

RECIPE BY ADAM PALMER

Green chiles are to New Mexicans as wine is to Italians—they go with everything. New Mexico is known for a lot of great things including the skiing and art in Santa Fe, the Native culture of the pueblos, and the meth cooking of Albuquerque, but the pride of New Mexico will always be the Hatch Green Chile. A little known fact—the Hatch Chile is actually a fruit, but is cooked and eaten as a vegetable. Traditionally, green chile sauces were simple, with no more than two ingredients. However, everyone has their own way of creating this beautiful dish. Please note: It is meant to be chunky, not blended.

MAKES 1½ CUPS

7 ounces green chile

¼ cup vegetable oil

¼ white onion, diced

⅛ cup chicken broth

1. If using whole chiles, place in aluminum foil and on the grill over indirect heat for 10 minutes to roast.

2. Once roasted, de-stem and deseed green chiles before dicing.

3. Over medium heat, add oil to a non-stick pan.

4. Add the onion to hot oil and let simmer for 2 minutes.

5. Add diced chiles to pan and let reduce. If using canned chiles (I don't know why you would), drain before adding.

6. Stir constantly so the chiles don't burn.

7. Once reduced, add chicken broth, cover pan and let reduce for 2 minutes.

8. Add pinch of salt and stir.

9. Turn off burner and let cool for 5 minutes.

10. Add to blender and pulse twice, making sure you don't puree it.

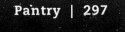

NEW MEXICO RED CHILI SAUCE

RECIPE BY ADAM PALMER

It's like the Green Chile Sauce, but red. If you're looking for less heat, remove the seeds from the chile pods.

MAKES 1½ CUPS

12 New Mexico red chile pods

½ tablespoon cumin

1 tablespoon flour

1 tablespoon minced garlic

Salt, to taste

1. Roast the chiles using your broiler, a heavy skillet, or by laying the chiles directly over your stove burners, until charred.

2. Remove the stems from the chiles. Retain or remove the seeds depending on your tolerance for heat. Place in a heatproof bowl.

3. Boil a kettle or pot of water and pour over chiles. Cover and let sit for 20 minutes.

4. Take the chiles out of the bowl and remove skins when cool enough to handle.

5. Place the chiles into a blender or food processor with cumin, flour, garlic, and salt, and puree until smooth.

6. Taste for seasoning and store in a glass jar.

BBQ RUB

MAKES ABOUT ¾ CUP

¼ cup brown sugar

2 tablespoons kosher salt

1 tablespoon ancho chili powder

2 teaspoons black pepper

1 teaspoon sage

¾ teaspoon onion powder

½ teaspoon cayenne powder

½ teaspoon sweet paprika

½ teaspoon mustard powder

¼ teaspoon garlic powder

¼ teaspoon celery salt

1. Mix all ingredients together.

RED GRAVY

Marinara, tomato sauce, gravy. It's all the same thing, and the name you call it typically depends on what the main characters in your favorite Italian-American piece of pop culture refer to it as. Everyone thinks theirs is time-honed and the best, but we've found that the real secret is just taking the time to watch and simmer it. It's also easy to double or triple the batch and store in tightly-covered glass jars for a quick dinner or lunch option. You can use it for pasta, The South Sider steak sandwich (page 98), or to dip calamari or other fried delights. Canned San Marzano tomatoes are great for this if you want to buy the slightly more expensive kind.

MAKES ABOUT 3 CUPS

28 ounce can whole peeled tomatoes with juices

5 tablespoons unsalted butter

1 white onion, peeled and cut in half through the root

1 teaspoon salt, plus more to season

2 cloves garlic, peeled and halved

3 large fresh basil leaves

1. Make sure your hands are clean and crush the tomatoes directly into a pot or saucepan. Dump in any extra juices from the can, then add the remaining ingredients. Stir to combine.

2. Heat sauce over medium heat until it begins to boil, then reduce the heat so it cooks at a slow, lazy simmer.

3. Simmer that fucker for 45 minutes, stirring frequently. Chat with guests during this time. Tell them never to ask about your business.

4. Discard the onion and blend to a smooth texture. Check seasoning and add salt if necessary.

VODKA SAUCE

RECIPES BY CATHY BRANDT

This is a recipe from a friend of ManBQue who grew up in the restaurant industry. Through decades of dining preferences, years of excellent and shitty customers, and the changing palate of the American diner, this simple recipe has remained a steadfast favorite. It's the richest of all possible sauces, and for that we love it.

MAKES 2 CUPS

8 tablespoons (½ cup) unsalted butter

¾ cup (6 ounces) tomato paste

1 tablespoon crushed red pepper

1 teaspoon kosher salt

½ teaspoon black pepper

1 cup heavy cream

3 ounces vodka

1 cup freshly grated Parmesan

1. Melt the butter over medium-low heat and add tomoto paste. Add the red pepper, salt, pepper, and cream. Stir to combine and simmer for 5 minutes.

2. Add the vodka and Parmesan. Bring to a simmer and cook for 20 minutes.

3. Remove from heat, stir, and serve immediately. The sauce won't hold, so consume all of it now—an entire loaf of garlic bread works really well. Bathe in the rich, buttery joy of the sauce and know that you are truly living.

TEQUILA LIME CREMA

MAKES 1½ CUPS

1 cup Mexican crema or sour cream

3 tablespoons silver tequila

Juice of 2 limes

2 tablespoons whole milk

1 clove garlic, minced

¼ teaspoon ground cumin

3 tablespoons chopped cilantro

½ jalapeño, seeded and minced

¼ teaspoon salt

1. Mix all ingredients using a food processor or blender until smooth. Store in an airtight container and refrigerate overnight.

SUPPER CLUB BEER CHEESE

RECIPE BY JAYME ADKINS-IRONSIDE

In the delicate Middle American ecosystem of things, cheese treats from Wisconsin are *way* different than cheese treats from Kentucky. It's part of what makes this country so great, and our bones so strong. This particular expression of the dairy art form is rooted in the closest thing that unincorporated Wisconsin towns have to white tablecloth places. Supper clubs are beloved of natives and vacationers alike, serving the usual prime rib, Great Lakes whitefish, and loads of domestic beer. The pub cheese that this recipe comes from is the first item to arrive at the table of all reputable clubs. It's usually served on a tray with celery, carrots, summer sausage, and crackers. Two of those things usually remain untouched. It's got a more airy, spreadable texture than the Kentucky bar cheeses, and a milder buttery flavor. That may be because of the butter, but the scientists haven't yet confirmed.

MAKES 16 OUNCES OF PUB CHEESE

8 ounces sharp cheddar, grated

8 ounces mild cheddar, grated

4 ounces brown ale

2 tablespoons butter, at room temperature

Sriracha, to taste

Ritzy-ass crackers, to serve

Sliced summer sausage, to serve

Hot sauce, to serve

1. Add the cheeses, ale, butter, and Sriracha to the bowl of a blender or mixer. Use that setting you've always been afraid of and let it run until you have a perfectly blended lake house appetizer.

2. Serve immediately for the best textural results. If you store and serve later, take it out of the fridge 30 minutes so before to let come to room temperature.

Nothing complements a great meal the way that a well-picked beer does. The interplay of the flavors in the food and the beer can combine to take your meal to the next level. Understanding the components and styles of beer will ensure you always experience the joys of a perfectly paired combination.

There are dozens and dozens of beer styles—classifications that brewers, authors, and drinkers use to understand what's in the glass in front of them. These styles are rooted in the brewing traditions of Germany, England, and Belgium. But they are also living, breathing guidelines that are evolving in response to the ever restless American craft brewers who are constantly pushing the envelope of flavors and the parameters of the beers they brew.

Everyone has their favorite styles of beer—from a traditional Bohemian pilsner to an American wheat ale to the malty wee heavy to the ubiquitous American hopbomb of a double IPA. Each of these and the dozens of other styles has a place at the table and can work with many of your favorite foods if you understand some of the style basics and pairing principles.

1. Intensity. The intensity and complexity of a dish should be matched by that of the beer

2. Flavor. The flavor components of the beer should complement and play off those of the meal

3. Tradition. Heed the centuries of cultural wisdom that has grown up around regional cuisine and brewing traditions

4. Creativity. Don't be beholden to any of these rules . . . your palate and preferences and those of your guests are all complex and ever changing . . . play to them.

Finally, don't be overwhelmed! The world of beer is complex and convoluted but ultimately a wonderful friendly place. Seek help from your local brewer, the beer buyer at your local craft beer store, the bartender at your local watering hole, and even that beer nerd friend you have. All should be happy to field questions on style and food pairing.

Understanding the Flavors of Beer

Beer begins its life when the brewer combines water, grain, and hops under the influence of heat to make a sweet liquid called wort. The wort is then cooled and a carefully chosen yeast strain is pitched into the wort to begin its job of fermentation. The end result is the beverage we know as beer. It is a surprisingly complex drink of low to moderate alcohol containing hundreds of flavor and aroma compounds that delight our senses. Each of the component ingredients provide their own unique flavors that help to pair the resulting beer with a wide range of foods.

Matching Intensity

When we sit down to a meal there is often a progression of dishes . . . from a simple salad to a tempting appetizer through to the main course and ending at dessert. Each item on the menu has a certain intensity of flavor and ingredients that we can recognize as light and enticing or rich and fulfilling. Your beer pairings should match this level of intensity.

Intensity in beer comes from a variety of sources including strength, hopping levels, carbonation, amount of residual sweetness, and even color. All of these factors combine in a single beer and we can perceive this intensity when we imbibe. Anyone that has had a macro lager knows its intensity is much lower than a German pils. Going up on the intensity scale from there we arrive at saisons and English pale ales with medium intensity. Finally, at the top end of the spectrum, we have the double IPA and huge barrel aged stouts, both of which pack their own unique and pleasant wallops to the palate.

The Flavors of Malt

The basis of the brewer's recipe is malted grain, most often barley or wheat. Malt primarily contributes fermentable sugars to the wort that the yeast will convert into alcohol. Secondarily though, the malt provides nonfermentable sugars and a wide array of flavor compounds. The brewer carefully selects and combines malts which range in flavor from bready and toasty to caramelly, toffeelike, and nutty, all the way through to chocolatey and roasty. You can taste the results in everything from a bready German lager to a roasty Irish stout.

The Flavors of Hops

Hops have a dual use in brewing. First, they provide bitter alpha acids to the wort which balance the sticky sweetness derived from the malt sugars. Second, they provide the beer with flavor and aroma compounds through their essential oils. The brewer carefully considers how much bitterness to impart to the finished beer as well as the flavor profiles of the hops being used.

Hops come in hundreds of varieties which can add spicy, herbal, floral, citrusy, piney, or even fruity notes. Brewers are chasing new hop varieties every year, continually increasing the flavor profiles available in beer.

Yeast-Derived Flavors

Yeast is the living organism that is the workhorse at the heart of the beer-making process. In the process of converting sugars to alcohol, yeast also generates hundreds of byproducts.

These lend unique flavors and aromas to beer including notes of spices, pepper, banana, clove, and fruitiness. While many beers are filtered, some styles retain the yeast in the bottle, which adds even more complexity to the flavor of the beer.

Additional Flavor Sources

The ingredients mentioned so far meet the Reinheitsgebot, a sixtenth century brewing purity law. Many other brewing traditions use additional ingredients to impart flavor according to the brewer's vision. Traditional Belgian brewers routinely brew with spices, citrus peel, and cherries or other fruit. Modern American craft brewers also push the envelope by adding just about any food ingredient you can think of—from pumpkin to juniper to PB&J to beef heart. Some of these can create sublime pairings with food, such as a Belgian wit (brewed with coriander and Curacao orange peel) with steamed mussels. But certainly some of the weirder flavors may be too obtuse to marry well with a dish you've created, so be judicious.

Many beers are also aged in wooden barrels which have previously aged alcoholic spirits. Most commonly these are bourbon barrels, but can also be from wine, rum, gin, and so on, each imparting unique flavors to the beer. Beers often pick up hints of vanilla, tobacco, oak, and of course the underlying spirit.

Some beer styles like lambic, geuze, Flemish ales, gose, Berliner weisse, American wild ales, and more are brewed with additional yeasts and bacteria that can add an amazing array complexity including tartness, sourness, and funkiness. These beers often have a high level of acidity which can help cleanse fatty foods from the eater's palate.

The alcohol in your beer also affects its flavor perception and pairing ability. Anyone who has ever taken a shot of hard liquor knows just how potent alcohol can be on the palate and down the pipes. Beers high in alcohol content, like Russian imperial stouts and barleywines can have increased alcohol heat.

Finally, the carbonation in beer helps to lift fatty and oily food residues from the tongue and refresh the palate so that you want to go back for another bite. This is a great advantage that beer has at the dinner table that other beverages often lack.

FRENCH PRESSED BEER

This will probably make the face of every craft brewer cringe, but we've been infusing beer using a French press. Restaurants and breweries use custom equipment to infuse flavors, but who has that kind of setup? The tried and true coffee infused beer is a great starting place to begin experimenting.

3 tablespoons high quality coffee, coarsely
  ground

12 ounces stout beer

1. Spoon coffee into the bottom of the French Press.

2. Pour beer over coffee and put the top onto the French press. Press the filter down to just below to top of the beer.

3. Steep for 5 minutes, pour into glass and enjoy.

Get the idea? Now do something crazy. Jalapeños!

SUMMER RADLER

Stiegl brought the radler to the beer aficionados; Leinenkugel brought the shandy to the mass market. We preferred to make our radlers with Hacker Pschorr and Italian soda.

MAKES 2 DRINKS

16 ounces German wheat beer

8 ounces Italian soda

1. Pour beer into a glass (which you should be doing anyway).

2. Pay. Close. Attention.

3. Pour soda into the same glass as the beer. Commence day drinking.

SAISON GIN FIZZ

RECIPE BY CHRISTINA PEROZZI

MAKES 2 DRINKS

2 egg whites

3 ounces Plymouth Gin

¾ ounce simple syrup

1 ounce lemon juice

Splash of cream

12 ounces Belgian farmhouse ale

1. Place the egg whites, gin, simple syrup, and lemon juice in a cocktail shaker and shake it for 1 minute.

2. Add the ice and cream to shaker and shake like you mean it until you get tired.

3. Double strain (i.e. pour through a cocktail strainer *and* a tea strainer) into two cocktail glasses and top with the farmhouse ale.

WEISSEN SOUR

It's a compact cocktail that packs a punch. Whiskey. Beer. Be sure to play some rock and roll when drinking this.

MAKES 2 DRINKS

4 ounces bourbon

½ ounce simple syrup

1½ ounces fresh lemon juice

6 dashes of orange bitters

2 tablespoons orange marmalade

8 ounces Weissbier or Witbier

1. In a shaker, mix bourbon, syrup, lemon juice, bitters, and marmalade and stir to break up marmalade. Pour in beer, add ice, then shake, strain, and serve in a bell taster beer glass.

CRAFT-AND-TAN

You don't need to use Irish beer to make a black and tan. In fact, owing to the brutal British police auxiliary of the same name, you probably shouldn't use that name around Irish anything. But we're using American craft beers anyway. An imperial stout and IPA layered on top of one another, in fact, tastes a hell of a lot better than the ye olde version, with none of the Loyalist baggage coming along for the ride.

If you're into black IPAs, this is the drink for you. This may be one of the recipes where you need a couple tries to master, even though it only has two ingredients. Pour too hard and mix them and you'll stop, drink your failure, and start over. You'll get better at it, but it's up to you how much failure-beer you drink in the quest.

6 ounces Imperial Stout

6 ounces IPA

1. Pour the stout into the glass, allowing the head to form.

2. Place a spoon back side up over the stout, then slowly pour the IPA over the back of the spoon, so it runs down the side of the glass. If you do it correctly, the stout will stay on the bottom and the IPA on top. If not, fuck it and drink it anyway because it tastes great.

FANCY GUINNESS

Here's another variation, this time on the classic Black Velvet. We just love our name more.

MAKES 4 FANCY-PANTS DRINKS

16 ounces stout

16 ounces Champagne

1. Pour 4 ounces of stout into each of four champagne flutes, allowing the head to foam and subside.

2. Carefully pour the champagne over the back of a spoon rested against the side of the glass, so the champagne runs down the sides and stays atop the stout.

3. Wait until someone says something especially gauche or shocking, then drop your monocle in. Drink and have your manservant Carlsworth bring you another. And a third, even!

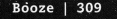

THUG PASSION

Last year, we found a thing we really like (seasonal summer ale and orange juice for breakfast) with a name we really didn't (BeerMosa). It sounded diminutive, cutesy, and weak. So we renamed it using the toughest-yet-softest name we can think of. Can't take yourself too seriously when you're orange-juicing your beer at 8:30 on a Sunday morning.

There are plenty of hibiscus-related choices on the beer store shelves during the summer, but feel free to substitute your choice of seasonal craft ale or lager.

MAKES 2 DRINKS

24 ounces hibiscus ale

8 ounces fresh orange juice

1. Fill two pint glasses with 12 ounces of ale and 4 ounces of juice.

There's Also Wine, You Know . . .

But what if your guests aren't all beer drinkers? No worries. Many of our friends drink wine, and two of us are Catholic, so we can offer you some measure of guidance on this particular topic. Here are the (very) basics, and some recipes to play around with.

If you'd like more information on wine, your local librarian can point you to roughly nine million staggeringly lengthy examinations on the subject.

What's It Called?	What Color is It?	How Does it Taste?	Drink it With:
Chardonnay	White	Anywhere from disgustingly sweet to bracing and mineral.	Shellfish, salad
Riesling	White	Crisp, sweet, and efficiently German.	Fish, dessert
Pinot Grigio	White	Spicy	Pasta, poultry
Sauvignon Blanc	White	Crisp, aromatic, New Zealand-y	Vegetables, seafood, poultry
Merlot	Red	Sweet, fruity—the bane of Paul Giamatti	Lamb, beef
Cabernet Sauvignon	Red	Dry, ripe fruit	Lamb, beef
Pinot Noir	Red	Earthy, dry. Wine people tend to pull out weird shit like "dying vegetation" and "the single tear of a lonely child" for this one.	Braised vegetables and meats, game, poultry

And Now We Booze

We've also got some tasty cocktails, none of which have that accursed "make one at a time, four minutes at a time" preparation that our nation's finest and fartiest cocktail lounges hold so dear. Grab a pitcher, get the mismatched freebie glasses, and let's get *DRANKIN*.

"NO, THE HAYRIDE WILL BE FUN THIS YEAR" MULLED CIDER

We drink during fall to deal with the impending doom of winter. It's a Midwestern thing. And nothing delivers the warm fuzzies like a bubbling pot of cider chockablock with an irresponsible amount of spiced rum. This is how you convince someone that sitting on sharp hay and bouncing around a pockmarked moonscape of a field in the 40 degree air is a beloved seasonal tradition. Thanks, alcohol! In addition, this recipe is great to leave over low heat on the stove in a big pot with a ladle to the side. Your house will smell great, which is a fair tradeoff considering your oven will never be clean again after two hours of guests drizzling apple, sugar, and rum near the burner.

Use a quality cider for this, spend a couple extra bucks—that's the line between "oh, how quaint" and "oh my—she's using apple juice to get drunk like a railyard hobo." Obviously you can adjust the rum content in this, but don't drive. In fact, throw your keys down a well.

MAKES 2 QUARTS OF CIDER

Zest of 1 orange

1 whole nutmeg, crushed, divided

3 cinnamon sticks

10 allspice berries

15 cloves

1 star anise

1 cardamom pod

½ gallon apple cider

8 ounces dark rum

1. Spread the orange zest out on a sheet of parchment paper and allow to dry in the oven over a pilot light overnight. If you're anything like us, you'll forget this and just throw the orange zest in anyway. At least we both tried.

2. Crush the whole spices, picking out half of the nutmeg and reserving for later use. Slide it all into a cheesecloth bag or spice sachet. Alternately, just have a strainer for people to pour their drinks through.

3. Place the spice bag in a large pot or Dutch oven. Cover it with the cider and heat over medium until the liquid just beings to steam. Then cover and reduce the heat to low until you're ready to serve. At that point, stir in the booze and dish it out.

SINTERKLAUS VODKADRANK

You've almost made it through the year. What lies between you and a new tomorrow is one final gauntlet of family and in-laws. This is how the Swedish deal with that.

You'll notice there's 100 milliliters gone from the bottle of vodka we call for. We're sure you'll figure something out.

MAKES 15 COCKTAILS

2 tablespoon turbinado sugar

2 sticks Ceylon cinnamon

10 cloves

10 cardamom seeds

650 ml vodka

3 inch x ¼ inch strip orange zest

Ginger ale and remaining orange zest, to serve

1. Place the sugar, cinnamon, cloves, and cardamom in the vodka bottle and shake it. Shake it real good. Yes, like that.

2. NO NOT LIKE THAT YOU'LL RUIN EVERYTHING.

3. No, just kidding. Keep shaking.

4. Forget about it in the fridge for at least two days, or up to a week. It'll probably keep until next Christmas. It's alcohol, after all.

5. A day before you're in the mood for holiday-themed vodka, throw the zest in the bottle, shake, and return to the fridge.

6. Serve the vodka at a 1:1½ ratio with some good ginger ale and garnish with orange zest. Or just drink it straight and eat with rye bread and sardines. The winter darkness of Scandinavia can do odd things to a person's preferences.

RIOT PUNCH

This is our once-a-year Christmas Party concoction. It puts the RAGE in beverage. Just make one of these pitchers for your party, because even one drop above a pitcher is going to turn your home into a *Road House* scene.

750 ml Hpnotiq liqueur

750 ml champagne

50 ml limoncello

1 lime, cut into wedges

1. Mix the liquor, champagne, and limoncello. Serve over ice with a wedge of lime. Watch the fuck out. Things are about to get serious.

TELENOVELA HOT CHOCOLATE

2 cups milk and/or water

3 cinnamon sticks

¼ cup semi-sweet chocolate

1 teaspoon vanilla extract

4 tablespoons almond meal or finely ground almonds

½ teaspoon arbol chile, finely ground

4 tablespoons sugar, or to taste

Ground cinnamon, to garnish

1. In a saucepan, add the milk, 1 cinnamon stick, and the rest of the ingredients. Bring to a simmer over medium heat.

2. Remove from heat and whip with a whisk until you get a frothy head.

3. Serve in two mugs, sprinkle cinnamon over froth and add cinnamon stick to each drink for garnish.

As we've packed in the food researching, cooking for, and writing this book, we came to realize that some of our best street food memories come with a soundtrack built in. That's the fun of food as a social experience—you'll never hear Huey Lewis and the News at a three-star Michelin place. And that, friends, is a damn shame. So here, for your playlist-ing pleasure, is our perfect soundtrack for this book.

We almost called this chapter "Whistle While You Eat" before we realized that's the most disgusting possible thing you can do. So kick some jams. KICK THEM.

Hungover at Waffle House on a cool fall Sunday morning (or is the hangover a given?).
"Rusty Cage"—Johnny Cash

Buying ice and beer... and maybe we need more ice ... and some chips ... and pops for the non-drinkers. What time are people coming over again?
"Dennehy"—Serengeti

Drunk at karaoke, needing the ultimate 80s jam to be recognized as the performance god you are. Tequila courage!
"Romancing the Stone"—Eddy Grant

Sweating your ass off in the middle of July on a park district field. If your shitty pitcher can get one more out, you can grab a High Life in the dugout. Softball season is the best.
"Slip Slide"—Donnie Trumpet & the Social Experiment

Getting invited to a boat party and demolishing the plate of fancy meats and cheeses solo.
"Portable Radio"—Hall & Oates

Tracking down something, anything, other than a chain restaurant while visiting a strange city. Also, it has to have a bar.
"Outside Inside"—The Streets

Frying an absolute shitload of chicken.
"Whole Bunch of Chicken"—Snakes

Waiting in line at the all-night taqueria.
"Jealous (I Ain't Wit It)"—Chromeo

Convincing yourself that a scorpion pepper hot wing challenge is not only doable, but a good idea.
"Psalm 82"—Cannibal Ox

The neighbor's kids were loud last night, so the stereo's getting a workout this morning.
"Turn Down for What"—DJ Snake and Lil Jon

Taking two bags of bottles to the recycling bin after one hell of a Saturday cookout.
"Love Jones"—J Dilla

Up at 6:00 a.m. to get in line for Texas brisket.
"18 Wheels of Love"—Drive-By Truckers

Getting a counter seat at your favorite hot dog stand.
"Glory Days"—Just Jack

That moment at the cookout when the song changes over and someone asks if this is your song and you meant to play it. Own it, man. Double down.
"Pop It"—Anamanaguchi

Riding with four people in a back seat of a car in Nashville hitting up hot chicken joints and dive bars.
"Wagon Wheel"—Old Crow Medicine Show

Walking slightly hungover and in need of two more hours of sleep to get tamales from the lady who sells them in the gas station parking lot.
"If I Had A Heart"—Fever Ray

Ribfest. Any ribfest.
"I Want to Conquer the World"—Bad Religion

Stopping at a truck stop while traveling alone at night.
"Live Oak"—Jason Isbell

Standing in line at the Maxwell Street Polish sausage stand after attending a beer festival.
"Blood-Red, White & Blue"—Rise Against

Walking through a farmers' market on a hot summer day and discovering an amazing stand.
"Fitzpleasure"—alt-J

Walking into a bar while wearing a white blazer.
"Robot Rock"—Daft Punk

Visiting a hog roast in your hometown after moving to the city.
"A Country Boy Can Survive"—Hank Williams, Jr.

Running after the elote lady's cart after hearing her go honking down the street. You know, the one with the umbrella on top.
"Waiting Room"—Fugazi

Hitting up a childhood friend's cookout who has teenage kids and is using lighter fluid to fire up the grill but still somehow seems happy.
"Stressed Out"—Twenty One Pilots

Eating split-roasted lamb in a desert.
"Burn After Writing"—The Menzingers

Buying a doner from a food truck and discovering that it has red cabbage on it by depositing some on your shirt.
"Start Wearing Purple"—Gogol Bordello

Eating fish tacos on the beach after a long night of drinking in California.
"California Stars"—Wilco & BIlly Bragg

Leaving the Chicago city limits, ripping on a loud Harley Davidson headed north.
"You Are A Tourist"—Death Cab for Cutie

Landing back home at the airport after weeks of traveling, eating too much and drinking too much.
"Landed"—Ben Folds

Walking up to your place as the sun is coming up, thinking about the just-concluded evening out; your hands smelling like onions from the Maxwell Street Polish, mustard stains on your jeans, and one last lager belch dedicated to old friends and new pals.
"All My Friends"—LCD Soundsystem

Taking down that umpteenth bowl of poutine in Montreal without breaking a meat sweat.
"Working Man"—Rush

Writing recipes at the local coffee shop, mean-mugging the passersby like a thug who likes iced half decaf coconut milk lattes.
"Notorious Thugs"—The Notorious B.I.G.

Trying to drive through rush hour traffic to pick up the last few ingredients.
"Feel Good Hits of the Summer"—Queens of the Stone Age

Polishing off a bottle of Malort with a beautiful lady after almost getting blown up by neighborhood fireworks. The perfect moment, really.
"No One's Gonna Love You"—Band of Horses

Being hundreds of miles away from home and not being able to get her out of my mind.
"Sleepwalk"—Santo & Johnny

Drinking Maker's Mark on the rocks, alone in some dark wood-paneled dive bar with the lingering smell of cigarettes from years past.
"Your Love and His Blood"—Wayne Hancock

Grabbing some street food in Manhattan and walking across the Brooklyn Bridge on a breezy summer night.
"NYC"—Interpol

Driving back to Chicago after a long weekend of hot chicken, Malort and good beer in Nashville.
"Slowness"—Calexico

Waking up and getting ready for a long day of grilling and tattoos.
"14,000 Things To Feel Happy About"—Troubled Hubble

Having beers at Billy Goat Tavern on a late Saturday night with the die-hards, journalists, and drunks. Some are all three!
"Big City"—Operation Ivy

Winning a hot dog championship. Again.
"Little Green Bag"—George Baker Selection

Trying to figure out a recipe that seems to not be working as planned. The bastard.
"Long Division"—Fugazi

Driving around Rochester, NY contemplating life and taking down some leftover squirrel pot pie.
"Chasing Heather Crazy"—Guided By Voices

Watching a summertime concert in Coney Island with a footlong corn dog in one hand and a shitty beer in the other, people zipping by screaming on the Cyclone.
"Strange"—Built to Spill

Driving through the redwoods and almost driving off a cliff while spilling delicious coffee all over your lap.
"Kind/Brutal"—Heligoats

ACKNOWLEDGMENTS

John Carruthers

It's really amazing to have had another project like this with a group of incredibly talented cooks and wonderful, kind people. None of that happens without my beautiful, supportive wife Emily, who is a hell of a cook herself and the best person I've ever known. Thank you for teaching me to slow down, take a breath, and worry less. Also, for teaching me about Cuban food—I still have 23 years of eating to catch up on, but I'm trying my best.

Putting together a ManBQue book, or an event, or just our regular MEATings, takes a lot of time and effort from people who we aren't paying. It astounds me every month how many guys and girls want to help out, spread the meat/beer/rock n' roll gospel, and be part of what we're doing. Luke Gelman never stops asking me when we can work through a new recipe in the kitchen together, and his results are always incredible. Adam Palmer might be the nicest person on the planet, and might be the only person I've never heard complain about . . . well, anything. Naturally, we'll try our best to crush his spirit with asinine requests. Dave Koob is always ready to help, and is also the human answer to the question "What if you just made pizzas nonstop for an hour on the grill? How many would that be?" Jason Gilmore, despite being a more qualified cook than any of us, is always happy to work on our latest poorly-conceived scheme and make it sixty percent more delicious. Tom Brooks gave us his sharpening skills, and even managed to turn my dull finger-shredder blades into efficient German cutting tools again. Carlos Salgado helped

us with some huge catering jobs, and turning out 190 plates of German game dishes in a bowling alley remains maybe the highlight of my entire cooking life.

It's not just them, either. Anyone who comes to our event, tells their friends about ManBQue, invites us into their bar or restaurant, and spreads our pork-flavored message is just as responsible for this happening a second time. I'm truly grateful to every single person. It's bizarre when you get to shill your meat book or event on the same channels you grew up watching. It's nice to have media friends around town, and we can't imagine better ones than James Van Osdol, Marcus Leshock, Corey McPherrin, Matt Knutson, Elliot Bambrough, Val Warner, Ryan Chiaverini, Ji Suk Yi, and Andrew Huff.

A lot of professionals also let me into their kitchens to learn things for this book, and I had even more fun than I imagined possible. Jennifer Monti and James Gottwald, Gus Paschalis, and Joe Plonka are all great, generous restaurateurs, and I hope I'll be hitting up their places for decades to come.

Once again, shooting the recipes for this book meant putting on a miniature meat summer camp with Josh McDonnell, Clayton Hauck, Dave Rentauskas (*NEW GUY DAVE!*), Brad Danner, Liz Klafeta, and Collen Durkin. We cooked a lot of food, ate a lot of meat, and generally shit-talked each other until we suddenly had this gorgeous series of shots on our hands. We are as surprised as anyone that our food could come out looking like this, which I hope gives you an idea of the

talent that Clayton and the group brought to the project. Every night, when we finished shooting, we sat down for beers and some lovably horrid local liquor to relax and enjoy how bizarre it is that we're lucky enough to do this. Big thanks as well to Kain Knowles and Red Gate Brewing for hosting another phenomenal shoot party. Sorry if your house still smells like meat (not sorry).

Speaking of, thank you to Jeppson's Malort, who is not a sponsor of ours or at all affiliated with us, for producing a liquor so distinctive and foul that making out-of-towner first-timers try it has become as grand a civic tradition as catching a ballgame at Wrigley, standing under the Bean, or hostile toward petition-gatherers.

Thanks to Zachary Leibman from Running Press for supervising this circus and to Doe Coover for kicking it off in the first place. You are both consummate professionals who probably deserve better-behaved clients.

Mom and Dad, thanks again for putting up with the world's pickiest eater for the first 18 years. I'm making up for lost time. Maggie, Sarah, and Sam, I hope two out of the three of you will continue eating meat. And if not, we'll always have beer. To the Coodes, Brandts, Carruthers, Sabos, Orizondos, and everyone else I may be too forgetful to mention—everything decent about me came from you. Everything else you can blame on the schools or video games.

To my old friends—Steve and Meghan Settles, Trey and Melanie Pick, Sarah Guderyahn, and Steve Robertson—thanks for sticking around. You're all great.

John and Jesse, I'm so glad we've managed to keep this going for this long. Here's to another barbecue, another beer, and the two best cooks I've ever worked beside.

John Scholl

First thank you to my wife, Alana, and two kids, Sophie and Holden, for without your support and expert sampling skills I wouldn't have been able to write this book. Funny thing about testing recipes with your children is that they're brutally honest. Either it's awesome or it sucks. Sophie's favorite dish was the Bridgeport breaded steak, and Holden loved everything that had meat. Meaning he loved most everything in this book because it's a ManBQue book for god's sake.

While I'm the first one of the family to get a cookbook published, I'm not the first to write one. My mom curates a family cookbook that expands every year. Thank you to my mom who instilled in me that the kitchen was the heart of the house. Through good times and hard, we always sat down to eat dinner (or as she calls it "supper") at 5:30 each night. To my siblings, Kelly, Jay, Heather, and Cinnamon who livened up the conversations around the table. It's been far too long since we've all had a meal together.

The Otto family (Pat, Mary, Ryan, Ben, Jason) who welcomed me into their home and taught me that hard work and creating something with your hands results in great pride. From working on engines, sanding car body panels, to morel mushroom hunting, the experiences have made me what I am today. I am forever grateful.

We have this wonderful photographer who shoots most of our MEATings. It was after an event one night when she told me that she was going to quit her corporate grind job and become a nanny. It just happened that my wife and I were about to become parents. Since 2011, Aubrey

Boonstra has been a part of my family, all because of ManBQue.

Abe Taha, one of my favorite bosses, who showed me that fresh ingredients and quality always wins. Plus, he trained me how to make damn good pizzas.

My college professor, Catherine Mintler, who served as a writing mentor throughout my time at school and is now someone who I can always bounce ideas off of although our conversations are more beer-focused than writing-focused these days.

We received great recipes from members and friends around the world. I'd like to personally thank Patrick McBride, Jason Gilmore, Daniel Sisto, Adam Hotzapfel, Joe Rake, Matt Khunen, Dave Hanley, Brandon Frohne, and Matt Danko for working with us to develop some amazing recipes. Huge thanks to Kevin Lilly and David Dahl from Lo Rez Brewing for their contributions, but also for helping me become a better brewer.

To the ManBQue members, this thing we started on Jesse's rooftop in 2006 would not be what it is without you. Keep bringing the unconventional recipes and rare beers to the MEATings.

Finally, to John and Jesse who invited me to be part of this book, crazy how life led us together for this. To that: ManBQue!

Jesse Valenciana

My family, Alicia, Erika, Adrian, Daniela, Grandma Ana, & Gus, you have been the best support system I could ever ask for. Thank you for always believing in me and my crazy ideas. Keep being the amazing human beings that you are. I love you more than I could ever put into words. Gus, I wish you could read because you're the best and cutest dog ever.

To all of my friends and family that I thanked in the first book; thank you again for letting me be a part of your lives, you make me who I am and I will continue kicking ass because of you. Special thanks to: Mark Fajardo, you're a goddamn American hero and I'm proud to call you my friend. Samantha Hermansen, I love the hell out of you. Thank you for always being a goofball and laughing with me. Pete Pallasch, I miss you and I know you'll have some obscure music for me to listen to when we meet again. Sarah Parkington, you and your loud-ass laugh are my favorite super fans. Ben Clauss, thank you for always being down to cook with me, always there to lend a helping hand, and for finally being my friend on Facebook—it only took 10 years. Aubrey Boonstra, you're the best, thank you for giving the world a look inside ManBQue. Doug Sohn, thank you for being a food mentor, friend, and the best pizza chef in Chicago. Chase Weikel and Megan Klempa, thank you for all of the Vans love. (Can we make some ManBQue shoes?) Chris Otepka, Steve Mitchell, Erin Burks, Tom Wojcik, Jon Reens, Spencer Walling, Magoo, Kevin Kane, Jason Gilmore, you guys fuckin rule! Ricky Valenciana, thank you and your family for all the love.

Thank you to all of these great families: Valenciana, Rezendez, Slonina, Linus, Wetherell, Rubeo, Boucher, Janowski, Scholl, Gelman, Cuevas, Alvarez, Millers, Romero, Wagner, Waggoner, and Hefferan.

Thank you Doe Coover & Zac Leibman. I questioned your sanity when wanting to deal with us for the first book, now I'm just going with it and not asking questions.

INDEX

Index | 327